Encyclopedia of the Animal Kingdom

Encyclopedia
of the
Animal
Kingdom

Consultant Editor
Robert Burton

This edition produced exclusively for
WHSMITH

Acknowledgements

The publishers would like to thank the following for allowing permission to reproduce their photographs:

John Buckley 101; John A. Burton 15, 19, 21, 34, 114, 156; Robert Burton 39, 59 (top), 108, 121 (top), 211, 216 (bottom); Andrew Clarke 235 (top); Bruce Coleman: Bruce Coleman Ltd 184, Eric Crichton 86, M. P. L. Fogden 106, John M. Burley 107, Owen Newman 188-9, Jen & Des Bartlett 178, 187, G. Ziesler 195, 216 (top), Lee Lyon 199, Stephen J. Krasemann 204, Jeffc Foote 205, M. Timothy O'Keefe 38, Kim Taylor 37, G. D. Plage 200-1; Frances Dipper 79, 82; Format Publishing Services 35 (bottom), 73; Keith Hiscock 41 (top); Peter Loughran 44, 110, 111, 112, 151; Gosse Mitchell 22-3; Nature Conservancy Council 45, 49, 59 (bottom), 81 (top), 127; Ben Osborne 120, 206-7; R. F. Porter 138, 146, 148 (top), 150, 166, 174-5, 177; Prince and Pearson 12-13, 60 (bottom), 137, 139 (top), 141 (top), 147, 152, 153, 163, 226, 235 (bottom); Chris Prior 48; Keith Probert 28; Hugh Savile 126; Michael Tweedie 7, 25, 53, 56-7, 58, 60 (top), 64, 71, 74, 75, 76.

Produced for the publishers by Patrick Hawkey & company Ltd.

This edition published exclusively for WH Smith

Published by
The Hamlyn Publishing Group Limited
London - New York - Sydney - Toronto
Astronaut House, Feltham, Middlesex, England

Copyright © text The Hamlyn Publishing Group Limited 1982
Copyright © illustrations except those listed above
Agenzia fotografica E. Dulevant 1982
ISBN 0 600 37892 6

Printed by Graficoop, Bologna, Italy

Contents

Introduction

Life began on Earth at least 3000 million years ago, but the first animals, as far as we know, appeared only 700 million years ago. During the almost unbelievably long interval between that time and the present, countless animal species have come into being and have disappeared again. Sometimes entire animal groups, like the dinosaurs, have become extinct for reasons we can only guess at. Only within our lifetime, however, has the wholesale extinction of animal ·species and populations become a distinct possibility. Now, after hundreds of millions of years of animal existence, one species – man – has come to so dominate the world that the character of its surface is being changed. The expansion of our species, both in numbers and technological capability, is threatening to destroy within a short time what has taken so many million years of slow evolution to construct. The hope for all animal life in the future is, more than ever, in the hands of man.

This encyclopedia covers the entire range of animal life, from smallest to largest, simplest to most advanced, and commonplace to exotic. The relationships of animals to each other, and their basic form and attributes, are described, together with some of the notable ways in which animals have developed varied, and often amazing, lifestyles to cope with different situations.

To set the scene, a summary is given of the evolution of animals to show that many kinds have arisen and that they are related to one another. Then the major habitats of the world are described. An animal's survival depends on its ability to cope with the particular features of its environment, and this results in each environment being populated by a unique set of animals. Conserva-

tion is an important part of any modern book about the animal kingdom, because without active attempts to save animals and the environments in which they live, there will be fewer animals to enrich the world.

There are today approximately one and a half million species of animals which have been described and studied by naturalists, although there may be as many as three to five million all told. Although each species is unique, many will never be seen by anyone except specialists, so the emphasis in this book is on those animals which may be commonly encountered, either in real life or through various forms of media, or which are particularly interesting.

How animals are named

When naturalists started to study animals they found it necessary to arrange or classify the bewildering array of creatures into orderly groups, and to give them names. The scheme for classifying and naming both animals and plants which came into universal use was devised by a Swedish naturalist Carl von Linné, often known as Linnaeus. His scheme was designed to show the relationship of each species to all other species.

The basic unit of classification of plants and animals is the species. This is a group in which individuals look and behave alike. They breed with each other but not with other types of animal, thus species stay separate and relatively unchanging. It is usually obvious to see what is a species, but sometimes there are only tiny differences which seem to be insignificant until it is realized that they distinguish two groups of living things which lead entirely separate lives.

Each species is given a two-part scientific name based on either Latin

or Ancient Greek, which were the international languages of scholars. The name for that animal, which is always written in italics, never changes (except by international agreement), and thus confusion is avoided when people in different countries talk about the same animal. For example, zoologists of all nationalities know that *Panthera leo* is the lion. Closely related species are grouped into a genus (plural genera) and the lion is in the genus *Panthera*. The tiger (*Panthera tigris*), the leopard (*Panthera pardus*) and the jaguar (*Panthera onca*) are closely related to the lion and belong to the same genus. The second part of the name – in the case of the lion *leo* – is the species name. The European wild cat (*Felis sylvestris*) and the lynx (*Lynx lynx*) are less closely related and have their own genera, but all belong to the cat family Felidae.

The families of animals are the next major grouping after genera. The cats (Felidae), the bears (Ursidae), the weasels, otters and badgers (Mustelidae), hyaenas (Hyaenidae), and dogs, foxes and wolves (Canidae) are families of

flesh-eating animals. They in turn are grouped together in the order Carnivora (which means flesh-eaters). Other orders include the bats (Chiroptera), whales (Cetacea), and rats and mice (Rodentia). These belong to the class Mammalia. Other classes include the birds (Aves), reptiles (Reptilia) and the fishes (Pisces). They, too, are divided into orders, families, genera and species.

The major division of the Animal Kingdom is the phylum. The mammals, birds, reptiles, amphibians, fishes and some little-known groups of animals belong to the phylum Chordata, because they all have a backbone or some other kind of stiffening rod in the body. The remaining phyla are often lumped together as the invertebrates or 'animals without backbones'. In fact, these animals without backbones form by far the largest portion of the Animal Kingdom. Worms, jellyfishes, insects, spiders, crabs and sponges are all examples of invertebrates; there are about as many species of insect alone as there are all other animals (with or without backbones) put together.

Everyone recognizes a butterfly and knows that it is a kind of insect, but how do insects differ from other animals, and what distinguishes a butterfly from a moth? All the animals in the Animal Kingdom are arranged in groups, based on their physical appearance. Four wings and six legs make this butterfly an insect; the shape of the wings and antennae show that it is not a moth.

How animals evolved

One important feature that the classification of species into different groups demonstrates is that all animals are related to each other, however distantly, and that they are descended from common ancestors. There was an ancestral carnivore, an ancestral mammal, an ancestral vertebrate and, ultimately the first ancestral animal. During the millions of years in which animals lived on Earth, there has been a process of gradual change resulting in new species being formed. This is called evolution, and it gives an explanation as to why there is such a wide variety of animals alive today.

The million and a half species living today represent only about one per cent of all the animal species that have ever lived, however. The majority have become extinct in past ages, but many have left their remains buried in the rocks as fossils to leave a record of how evolution progressed.

The fossil record

The story told by the fossils left in the rocks shows that the evolution of animals had not proceeded far until about 600 million years ago in the Cambrian period when a warming of the climate, probably combined with an increase in oxygen for breathing and lime for building skeletons, favoured the evolution of more active animals. One of the freak chances of fossilization has left a fine selection of specimens to show what was living in the seas at this time.

During this period the great groups of invertebrate phyla came into being. There were not only representatives of modern animals, like sponges, jellyfishes, corals, worms and crustaceans, but also forms which have since become extinct. There were animals such as trilobites – many-legged creatures rather like woodlice, which ranged from 3mm to 70cm long; and later there appeared sea scorpions, huge scorpion-like animals armed with pincers, and reaching lengths of 2m (6½ft); there were also brachiopods or lamp-shells; and ammonites which were related to squids and octopuses but lived in coiled shells.

How our own phylum, the Chordata, arose is still something of a mystery. The first chordates had no bones, only a stiffening rod for support, and no fossils have been found. Presumably they looked rather like the chordates that are still alive today. Even the first vertebrates, animals with backbones, are missing from the fossil record and the oldest fish fossils come from the Ordovician, around 500 million years ago.

In the Devonian period, from 395 to 345 million years ago, the fishes became the ruling form of life in the seas – a position that they still hold today. During the Devonian, the four main groups of fishes had already been formed. These were the cartilaginous and bony fishes, whose descendants are still living, and the extinct ostracoderms and placoderms. Many of these ancient fishes looked extremely odd when compared with modern species. The ostracoderms lived on the seabed where they sucked in mud and debris through their small mouths. Some had bodies armoured with bone plates and, unlike all other vertebrates, they had no jaws. The only modern representatives of these jawless fishes are the blood-sucking lampreys and hagfishes. The placoderms were predatory fishes with bony armour on the front part of the body. They had jaws, but no teeth, and used the jagged edges of the jaws to grab and crush their prey. *Dinichthys* was a fearsome hunter measuring 9m (29½ft) long, but the antiarchs were slow-moving mud-eaters whose front fins were also armoured.

Left: Fossil ammonites are very common. These animals were related to squids and octopuses, but their fleshy tentacles were not preserved in the rocks and only the shells remain. In some species these measure 1 m (3¼ft) across. Studying the fossils has shown how ammonites evolved over the course of millions of years.

Below: The trilobites, which resemble woodlice, have no close living relatives. All of the 10000 known species lived in the sea, mostly on the muddy bottom, but a few swam in midwater. Some species could roll up in a ball like a hedgehog.

The greatest degree of fish evolution has been in the bony fishes, to which most modern species belong. One evolutionary 'branch' led to a most significant event in the Earth's history. The lobe-finned fishes, as their name suggests, bore their fins on fleshy lobes which could support some of the fishes' weight as they lay on the bottom. One such lobe-finned fish is the coelacanth which was discovered alive in 1938, having been presumed extinct for 65 million years. The lungfishes are another group of lobe-finned fishes. Lungs were also a feature of the lobe-fins and they could come to the surface and gulp air if the swampy water became short of oxygen.

During the Devonian period most fishes lived in fresh water but, since it was a time of seasonal droughts, there was an advantage in being able to breathe air and struggle over the mud from one pool to the next. Thus, these fishes were already preparing for a life on land, a course of action which would lead to the evolution of the amphibians. They also came on land to avoid the attacks of larger animals and take advantage of alternative food supplies, such as the

Right: Fossils of coelacanths showed that they flourished in the sea until about 65 million years ago. Then the absence of fossils made it look as if they had become extinct, but a live coelacanth was caught in 1938 and others have been caught since.

Opposite: The reptiles were the first backboned animals to live entirely on land. They evolved from the amphibians which still have to return to water to breed. Reptiles lay eggs with waterproof shells and their skins are also waterproof, so they can live in dry places.

new land plants. The joint-legged arthropods followed the amphibians onto the land in the Carboniferous period, and gave rise to the land-dwelling insects, spiders, scorpions and their relatives.

The amphibians still spent much of their lives in water which was, and still is, essential for their breeding. Total independence of water was finally mastered by the reptiles, which during the Carboniferous period (345-280 million years ago), developed eggs with waterproof shells. They also improved their skeletons and muscles so they could move more efficiently, their skins became more waterproof and their heart and lungs also became more effective. So, while the amphibians dwindled into insignificance, the reptiles inherited the world during the Permian (280-225 million years ago) and ruled it until the end of the Cretaceous (135-65 million years ago).

Although many of the dinosaurs are familiar to most people, they were only a part of the immense diversity of reptiles which ruled the Earth for 100 million years. Other types included the turtles and tortoises, snakes and lizards, crocodiles and alligators, and the tuatara of New Zealand, all of which are still living today. Many now-extinct groups – the mesosaurs, cotylosaurs, ichthyosaurs, plesiosaurs, pterosaurs, thecodonts, and so on – also flourished. The most dominant reptiles, known as the archosaurs or ruling reptiles, included the dinosaurs and the pterosaurs,

and have two living descendants: the crocodiles and the birds. The name dinosaur means 'terrible lizard', and the 'terrible lizards' were divided into two groups, the Ornithischia and Saurischia, which were not closely related. Not all dinosaurs were giants, however – *Compsognathus* was the size of a chicken – but they included the largest land animals ever to have lived. *Brachiosaurus* weighed 51 tonnes and measured 24m (79ft) from snout to tail, and *Diplodocus* measured 27m (88½ft).

Some dinosaurs like *Brachiosaurus*, *Diplodocus*, *Apatosaurus* (once called *Brontosaurus*), *Stegasaurus* with bony plates on its back, and *Triceratops* with three horns and a bony frill on its head, were plant-eaters and moved on all fours. Other plant-eaters, like the 'duckbilled' dinosaurs and *Iguanodon*, were bipedal, as were the carnivores. *Allosaurus* and *Tyrannosaurus* were fierce predators; the latter was the largest land carnivore. It stood 6m (20ft) high. Its front legs were tiny and useless for seizing prey but its hind feet bore slashing claws.

The ancient reptiles conquered the sea as well as the land. As well as crocodiles and turtles, the sea was inhabited by the long-necked plesiosaurs and the short-necked pliosaurs, which swam with paddle-like flippers, and dolphin-like ichthyosaurs which had tail-flukes for propulsion. The plesiosaurs and pliosaurs probably came ashore to lay their eggs, like modern turtles, but ichthyosaurs stayed at sea and gave birth to live young.

In the air, the pterosaurs developed wings which, to judge from fossil imprints, were leathery and stretched from a greatly elongated fourth finger to the hind legs. Some pterosaurs were sparrow-sized, but one giant has an estimated wingspan of 15·5m (51ft). Pterosaurs were not powerful fliers but had light bodies and glided well.

There are many theories as to why the dinosaurs and other reptiles became extinct at the end of the Cretaceous period. These include disease, increased solar radiation, climatic change and an asteroid colliding with the Earth, but no clear explanation has emerged. Nevertheless, their departure left the way clear for the mammals and birds, which were already in existence, to inherit the Earth.

Our knowledge of the evolution of birds would be very poor if it were not for the discovery of *Archaeopteryx*. By exceptional good chance, this fossil shows perfect impressions of feathers and is, therefore, the remains of a bird. If no more than the bones had been preserved, the fossil would have been labelled as a dinosaur because it is so similar to a dinosaur skeleton. *Archaeopteryx* had a long tail and teeth, like a reptile, its wings bore claws and it had weak breast muscles. It probably flapped and glided from tree to tree but could not take off from the ground.

The mammals evolved from reptiles in the Triassic period, before the giant reptiles appeared. These early mammals were small, shrew-like animals which probably came out at night to avoid predatory reptiles. Their bodies were covered by fur, and they were warm-blooded. From about sixty million years ago, there was a rapid evolution of mammals, resulting in the development of many species. Many were of great size and had strange arrays of horns and tusks. Although there are only two very similar elephant species living today, their ancestors were very diverse. *Deinotherium* had tusks coming from the lower jaw and curving backwards. *Baluchitherium* was the largest land mammal ever to have lived; it looked like a giraffe, and stood 5m (16½ft) high.

One of the last mammals on the scene was man. New finds of fossils are continually being found to alter the view of our early evolution, but the first human-like ancestor to be discovered is *Ramapithecus* who lived fourteen million years ago. It had teeth more like a man than a chimpanzee. About three million years ago, *Australopithecus*, the 'ape-man', walked upright but still had a small brain, although he was a hunter and used sticks and stones to kill prey. Neanderthal men of 150 000 years ago were the first race of our species, *Homo sapiens*, but true modern men have existed only for the last 40 000 years.

Habitats

All species of animal are limited by geographical boundaries, and the area that they occupy within these is called their range. However, a species is not evenly distributed throughout its range, as it is further restricted by its preference for a particular type of habitat. A habitat can be thought of as an environment with certain associations of plants common to it. The overall nature of the habitat is usually dictated by prevailing physical conditions. An ecosystem is a habitat together with all its associated animals, forming a relatively self-contained unit.

Ecologists have broadly defined the main habitats throughout the world, and these can be classified as the polar ice caps, tundra, forests, grasslands (steppes and prairies), deserts, wetlands, and freshwater and marine habitats – including islands. Today, there are also areas of the world that have been radically altered by man providing new habitats, such as cities and areas of intensive farming.

These are broad classifications, useful in teaching geography, but too general to be of much help in the natural history field of conservation. Conservationists have therefore created detailed classifications such as that used by Britain's Nature Conservancy Council. The major divisions used are: coastlands; woodlands; lowland grasslands; heaths and scrub; open water; peatlands; upland grasslands and heaths; artificial ecosystems. These are then subdivided. In the case of woodlands they were divided into the following: oakwood; mixed deciduous woodland; beechwood; ashwood; pinewood; birchwood; alderwood; other types. Then all the categories were sub-divided regionally. If this degree of detail is necessary to begin to understand the complexity of the ecosystems found in Britain, on a

world scale it is even more difficult (since there is so much more variety). In this book there is only room to briefly discuss some of the major habitats, for in truth they could each warrant books to themselves.

Ice caps

On the true ice caps of the poles and on the tops of snow-capped mountains little life exists. Therefore there is no ecosystem in the normal sense of the word. However, around the edge of the glaciers and snowfields a wide variety of wildlife has adapted to these harsh conditions. In the Antarctic, for example, emperor penguins (*Aptenodytes forsteri*) breed far inland, protected from predators by the very bleakness of the environment.

The first plants to become established are lichens, which are able to grow on rocks which are warmed above freezing point for a few weeks of the year. Then gradually, in addition to lichens, mosses and grasses are able to colonize where the summers become warmer and the winters shorten as one travels away from the poles. Interestingly, many of the insects living in the extreme north are very dark – possibly an adaptation to enable them to absorb the maximum amount of heat from the short summer's sun. Many of the other animals are white, for camouflage – the polar bear (*Thalarctos maritimus*), the varying hare (*Lepus timidus*), the ptarmigan (*Lagopus mutus*), and the arctic fox (*Alopex lagopus*), for instance.

Tundra

The habitat adjacent to the polar regions is the tundra zone. It is treeless and characterized by the low-growing vegetation and very limited number of species. The tundra is a simple ecosystem and for that reason is relatively unstable. Con-

sequently many of the animal species found in this habitat are subject to wide fluctuations. The populations of ptarmigan, lemmings and voles are cyclical, and as they build up so, too, do the numbers of predators such as snowy owls (*Nyctea scandica*) and short-eared owls (*Asio flammeus*).

Among the larger mammals of the tundra, the reindeer or caribou (*Rangifer tarundus*), is found in both the Old and New Worlds, and so is the glutton or wolverine (*Gulo gulo*).

The timberline, often so clearly visible on mountains is not just caused by an increase in altitude, but is a result of decreasing temperature. Consequently the altitude of the tree-line and the beginning of tundra-like mountain vegetation, varies with latitude as well as altitude. In the tropics the tree-line may be 4200m (14 000ft) high, whereas in the European Alps it is only 2000m (6 000ft), and in southern Alaska it may be as low as 330m (1000ft) above sea level.

The waters around the Antarctic ice cap are extremely rich in food. Penguins, like these gentoos, are adapted to spend nearly half their life in the icy water, protected by waterproof feathers and a layer of fat under their skin as they feed on the teeming plankton.

Taiga and northern forests

Below the tundra, taiga gradually takes over. It is characterized by dwarf forms of trees such as willow, birch and juniper, with conifers and others becoming dominant and full sized in the northern forests. The northern coniferous forests are a rich and varied habitat, far removed from the sterile monocultures of spruce, planted for commercial purposes. Voles, lemmings and other small mammals are prey for several species of owl, and mammal predators such as stoats.

Temperate forests

At one time most of the temperate lands were wooded. Temperate forests are of two main types: deciduous and coniferous. The former provides the greatest diversity of habitat and Europe was once dominated by deciduous and mixed forests. Consequently the fauna of much of Europe is characteristic of woodlands. Today, most of the fauna is still found in woodland, and woodland edge habitats such as hedgerows and parklands. Even the larger mammals of Europe, such as deer and boar, were primarily woodland spec-

Trees in temperate regions need to be able to survive through hot and cold seasons. In winter, water is not extracted easily from the cold ground. Therefore deciduous trees lose their leaves to reduce water loss, which allows light to penetrate to the ground so that undergrowth can colonize deciduous woodland. Evergreen trees, found in cooler regions, adopt a different strategy; their shiny needle-sharp leaves retain moisture all the year round. There is little undergrowth on the dark floor of an evergreen forest. Animals living in deciduous temperate forests must be able to adapt to the changing conditions.

Specialization and microhabitats

Some species require extremely specialized habitats. The giant panda (*Ailuropoda melanoleuca*) is perhaps the most spectacular example. It is a highly specialized feeder, almost exclusively eating bamboo, and consequently it is confined to bamboo forests in southwestern China. But, for some species, their habitat requirements are even more specialized. Parasites are often adapted to living on a single host species and this, therefore, is their habitat.

Each habitat is composed of numerous such microhabitats, with the species adapted to exploiting one or more aspects of this habitat. In some cases a single plant can form an almost complete ecosystem. For instance, in the tropical forests, bromeliads, which have hollow centres which accumulate rain water, have algae growing in them, and in addition to aquatic insects breeding in the water, highly specialized species of frogs live and even spawn in these miniature 'ponds'.

ies, adapted to dense forest interspersed with glades and clearings.

Similarly bird species such as tits and woodpeckers, adapted to nesting in holes, are characteristic of mature woodlands. With the destruction of the woodlands for farming, other species such as the skylark (*Alauda arvensis*), more adapted to open, more steppe-like agricultural habitats, were able to spread.

One of the most important aspects of forest cover is its part in water regulation. Forests, particularly in mountain habitats, often act as vast 'sponges', soaking up seasonal rain and slowly releasing it into the rivers. Once the forest cover is removed, the rain runs off the hillsides taking with it the topsoil and, in a matter of a few years, the hillsides can be reduced to barren rock. Additionally, the rapid run-off results in flooding downstream, and also causes the rivers to dry up as soon as the rains stop. Many of the craggy mountains of Europe are the result of devastation of this kind centuries ago. The forests of the temperate Northern Hemisphere are strongholds for species such as woodpeckers, lynx, martens and many species of small birds and bats.

Tropical forests

Like the temperate regions, larger areas of tropical and subtropical lowlands were once forested. They stretched from Florida to Brazil, and across Africa, India, through southeast Asia to Queensland in Australia. In fact, there is enormous variation in the woodlands and forests of the tropical and subtropical regions, supporting a huge number of animal species. The tropical moist forests can be grouped, broadly, into two types: those receiving an extremely high annual rainfall – the true rain forests of the Amazon and Zaire River basins; and the deciduous moist forests such as on the coast of Kenya near Mombassa.

Tropical rainforest, in its pristine condition, is the opposite extreme, in almost every way, to the Arctic tundra. Whereas the Arctic tundra is subjected to violent extremes of temperature and other climatic factors, tropical rainforest has a climate remarkable for its regularity and consistency. Tropical rainforest is an extremely complex habitat, with a huge number of plant and animal species living in very specialized niches, with each species having relatively stable populations, often at

Tropical rainforests are, in a way, relics from a much earlier geological age when the whole Earth was warmer and wetter than it is now. Today, the existence of these forests depends on the trees, which keep the moisture captive. If they were cut down, rains would wash the soil away and leave a desert. Loss of the world's tropical forests might even change the pattern of weather over the whole globe.

low densities. A few of the common species to be found are African sunbirds and South American hummingbirds which feed on nectar, parrots and eagles which live in the canopy layers, sloths which browse on leaves, and peccaries which root around the forest floor. Okapis (which were not discovered until this century) browse in the forests of central Africa; gibbons live in the canopy of the forests of southeast Asia, where tigers roam the undergrowth. Each species lives at its own particular level. Although it is popularly known as 'jungle', many typical 'jungle' animals – such as lions – inhabit the more open bush country. Despite its stability, once disturbed, the balance of a tropical forest can be easily upset. If the trees are cleared, the sponge effect of the vegetation is lost and water runs off causing erosion, washing away the top soil. Sunlight scorches the Earth's surface, once protected by lofty trees with a canopy 50m (165ft) or more above the forest floor. In fact, some tree species only germinate at temperatures of 23-26°C (73-79°F), but when the tree cover is removed the temperature soars to over 40°C (100°F). Because of its stability and the specialization of the species in the ecosystem of the rainforests a small disruption could easily have wide-ranging and disastrous chain reaction effects. For instance, the fig trees of Central America are extremely important sources of food for many animals, and many have a single insect species adapted to pollinating them. If anything should eliminate the pollinator at any stage of its life-cycle the results would be disastrous, not only for the tree but for a host of animals dependent upon it.

The classic 'tropical rainforest' is dominated by woody vegetation over 50m (165ft) tall and has a closed canopy, which prevents much light reaching the forest floor. The vegetation is mostly evergreen and often festooned with epiphytes and climbers such as ferns, mosses, orchids, bromeliads, lianas and vines. By growing on the branches of trees, or climbing, the plants can move out of the gloomy forest floor and reach sunlight which may be 50m (165ft) above. High above, various butterflies, monkeys and birds such as tanagers live without ever descending to ground level.

The tropical evergreen forests contain the greatest diversities of both plant and animal life per unit area, than any other part of the world. It is estimated that possibly two-fifths to a half of the total number of species on the Earth occur in these habitats. Yet still we know little about these forests. Even in the present century large mammals previously unknown to science have been discovered in the forests; for instance the okapi and giant forest hog. Every major expedition to the unexplored tropical forests brings back unknown species of frogs, bats and hundreds of plants and insects. In fact, there are not enough scientists available to describe all the unknown species estimated to live in the forests, before the end of the century.

The richness of the vegetation of tropical forests is staggering. For instance, southeast Asia has only 2·5 million km (1·5 million square miles) left, and yet it is estimated to have some 25 000 species of flowering plants. The Malay Peninsula which is half the size of Britain, has nearly 8000 flowering plants compared with around 1500 in Britain! In the Amazonian forests a single hectare (2·4 acres) of forest may contain 100 species of tree. It is this incredible richness of vegetation which gives rise to a bewildering diversity of animal life.

The birds of the tropical forests are often paralleled in the Old and New Worlds. For instance, the Old World equivalent of the humming-birds are the sunbirds. Both groups are adapted to nectar feeding and are often brilliantly coloured. The toucans of South America have their African equivalents in the hornbills; the jacanas parallel the Old World bee-eaters.

The primates are particularly diverse in the tropical forests, with the greatest diversity of all occurring in Amazonia. Bats, which are the most numerous mammal group, are also species rich in the tropical forests. In Africa and Madagascar a wide range of chamaeleons are found. The rainforests are also famous for their huge array of splendid coloured frogs and toads.

A few tropical forests, such as those of Costa Rica, have been studied in some detail and it is apparent that they consist of many similar ecosystems, each based on a separate group of plants. These ecosystems, although separate, may overlap with

Man-made habitats

Increasingly, the landscapes of the world are dominated by man-made or man-modified habitats. In some countries, such as the highly developed countries of western Europe, it is extremely doubtful if there are any habitats in which the influence of man cannot be detected. Even such apparently natural looking areas as the Brecklands and Broads of East Anglia where stone-curlews nest and where bitterns can be heard booming, result entirely from man's action. Few of the forests of New England are the original primeval forests, nor are the deserts of the Middle East of nature's making – they all are the result of man's activities over the many centuries he has been modifying the ecosystem.

Many types of wildlife are remarkably resilient, and as man devastates natural ecosystems, there is a tendency for a limited number of species to adapt even to this destruction. In the most extreme man-made habitat, the city, a number of species have not only adapted to this artificial habitat, but flourished; pigeons, sparrows, and starlings are found almost worldwide, wherever human dwellings are found. Many of the species are those adapted originally to cliff habitats (such as martins and swallows) or scavenging detritus feeders (such as kites and cockroaches). Others were forest-edge species which have adapted to parks and gardens.

From the view of wildlife many of the man-made habitats are very similar to those naturally occurring. Gravel pits and reservoirs are similar to glacial lakes; mines are similar to caves; sewage farms similar to estuaries, and so on. Although reservoirs can be stocked with fishes which will attract birds, bats will roost in mines, and snipe will feed on sewage farms, the major difference is that the man-made habitat always lacks the diversity and complexity of its natural equivalent. Ecosystems based on man-modified ecosystems are simple, and as such unstable, and the populations of animals living in them are liable to fluctuate much more widely than those in the naturally occurring wild equivalent ecosystem.

There are an enormous number of man-made agricultural habitats ranging from monocultures of fast growing conifers to species-rich alpine meadows; from rolling plains of wheat to terraced vineyards; from intensively cultivated mixed smallholdings to vast copra plantations; from rice paddies to estates managed for game.

Some man-made habitats can be species-rich, and some, such as traditional meadows, are of considerable wildlife value. Many of the meadows of Europe contain relics of habitats once widespread, but modern agriculture is increasingly ploughing up ancient meadows, or 'improving' them by seeding with grasses, spraying with selective herbicides and dressing with artificial fertilizers. The meadows of lush grasses interspersed with fritillaries, orchids, meadowsweet and many more species are valuable habits which need to be preserved, for once destroyed they will never be replaced.

While in the developed world there is a tendency for farming to become more and more mechanized, using more and more artificial chemicals, with less and less room for wildlife, in the less-developed countries agriculture not only often tolerates wildlife but often actively utilizes it. For instance, rice paddies are an ideal habitat for a wide range of fishes, molluscs and frogs, and in many parts of southeast Asia, while rice is growing, fishes are introduced into the paddies to be harvested later. The fishes play a vital function in controlling invertebrate pests of the rice, as well as mosquitos and other insects. In India cobras and other snakes are often protected for their value as rodent predators. In this way they help to keep pests down.

Even the monoculture spruce forests of Europe could provide a habitat for animals such as bats. However, despite the often abundant food supply – often insects which are pests – the bats lack roosting sites, since plantations lack natural holes in the trees. Consequently by placing artificial roosting boxes for bats – and nesting boxes for birds such as tits – they can be encouraged to colonize the habitat.

Farmers often plant small amounts of cover especially to provide a nesting habitat for partridges which, although they can adapt to the open landscape for feeding, need cover for nesting. This cover also provides a habitat for mice, shrews, slow-worms, lizards and other small animals which soon colonize the new source of food and shelter.

Opposite: A butterfly living on the Solomon Islands. Island faunas are often quite unique, having developed in isolation from larger landmasses.

Conservation

Wildlife conservation is often mistakenly considered to mean preservation, in the way that one preserves a building in order to keep intact features of a byegone age. Conservation today, while including an element of preservation, is often a very dynamic activity, frequently demanding as much management of the landscape and its animals as a farmer does with his fields and livestock.

In certain senses, both the concept and practice of conservation have been established for centuries. For instance, in fifteenth century England, an Act of Parliament gave the Mayor of London responsibility for the 'Conservation of the water and river of the Thames'. There are also isolated examples of wildlife conservation scattered throughout history. In ancient Africa, Asia, Europe and elsewhere, rulers have, from time to time, established wildlife reserves or passed various forms of protective laws. But none of these can really be said to form a tradition which has led to wildlife conservation as we know it today.

Modern conservation has its origins in two quite distinct and often opposing fields. The first started with the game laws. These laws are ancient as, from prehistoric times, ruling classes have protected species and areas so that they might hunt the animals for food or, increasingly, for sport. The second origin was the bird protection movements which began towards the end of the last century. There was a fashion at this time for birds' plumage in the millinery trade and this caused the death of hundreds of thousands of birds of paradise, hummingbirds, pheasants, egrets and many others, providing the impetus in Britain and North America for a protection movement. Their early success in bringing to the attention of the public the appall-ing slaughter of these birds was to pave the way for legislation protecting birds and other wildlife. This was a new direction, as previously laws had been established to preserve animals solely for hunting. In Britain, the Royal Society for the Protection of Birds started out as one of these 'Plumage Groups' and now has a membership approaching half a million. It is active today, not only in protecting birds and their habitats, but also in encouraging a greater awareness of the role of conservation in the countryside.

The modern conservation movement is basically an amalgam of these protectionist and hunting lobbies, both of which generally accept the need for continued exploitation of wildlife by people living in traditional life-styles. It is also generally recognized that, of all the problems confronting wildlife, the most important overall threat is the loss of habitat. Some of the conservation measures described in this section can help individual species, but for the vast majority under threat, the large-scale protection of undisturbed tracts of land and the rational use of man-managed landscapes is the only long-term solution.

Calculations of the numbers of species threatened with extinction are fraught with difficulties, but it has been estimated that as the rate of destruction of the tropical forests accelerates towards the end of this century, a million species could disappear. If one includes plants, this works out at around 100 species per day.

The United States once had around a million square kilometres of prairie – now there are less than 16 000 square km (10 000 square miles); the rest has been ploughed, degraded or otherwise altered. Prairies are not particularly rich in species – though they did support an enor-

Protozoans

Examination of just a few drops of pond water under a microscope reveals a bewildering array of tiny animals that creep, whirl and corkscrew across the field of view. Some of these creatures consist of a large number of cells, often with a recognizable head complete with tiny brain and sense organs, and a trunk with reproductive, digestive and excretory organs – while others consist of just a single cell. The former belong to a number of different phyla, but the latter belong to just one phylum – the Protozoa. Protozoa are found wherever there is moisture: in the sea, in fresh water, in the soil, and both in and on the bodies of other animals and plants. In adverse conditions, such as drought, many of them survive by covering themselves within a protective layer called a cyst, coming 'alive' again, often years later, when favourable conditions return. The worldwide distribution of protozoans can be explained by the wind, and other agencies such as birds' feet, which transport the encysted forms to new habitats.

The Protozoa are divided into four classes.

Flagellates (class Flagellata)

The flagellates are considered by many zoologists to be the most primitive Protozoa, having affinities with both the Plant and Animal Kingdoms. They move by means of long whiplash-like structures called flagella. Some species possess chlorophyll and make their food by photosynthesis. The green scum that often forms on ponds is due to blooms of photosynthetic flagellates such as *Euglena viridis* and the colonial form *Volvox*. Despite their relatively simple structure, the individuals in a *Volvox* colony can beat their flagella for co-ordinated movement.

Sarcodinians (class Sarcodina)

The sarcodinians exhibit amoeboid movement. Finger-like projections of the body called pseudopodia are thrust forward and the rest of the animal flows into them, so that it creeps forward. Amoebas feed by flowing around and engulfing smaller organisms. They reproduce by splitting in two. Amoebas look like shapeless lumps of jelly, but their internal structure is very intricate and each species has its own characteristic shape. Amoebas are found everywhere, including inside the bodies of other animals. One species causes dysentery.

The foraminiferans are symmetrical amoebas possessing a chalky shell, or in the case of the heliozoans and radiolarians a delicate internal skeleton of silica. The skeletons of these animals are often preserved as fossils which have built up over millions of years to create rock and chalk formations.

Sporozoans (class Sporozoa)

The Sporozoa, or spore formers, are all parasites (although not all parasitic protozoans belong to this class) living, depending on the species, within the bodies of many different invertebrates and vertebrates. Malaria is caused by the sporozoan *Plasmodium*.

Ciliates (class Ciliata)

The ciliates are covered by a pile of short hairs – cilia – that are arranged in rows and beat in sequence. As the recovery stroke of each cilium is not in the same plane as the beat, this imparts a twist, thus producing the characteristic corkscrew motion. A very few ciliates are parasitic, but many live harmlessly in the intestine of vertebrate animals.

Small but deadly

Parasitic protozoans are responsible for a number of debilitating diseases in man. In some, the life-cycle is simple. For example, amoebic dysentery occurs in insanitary circumstances and the infection is spread directly from one person to another by cysts that are passed out with the faeces and later swallowed. Others, such as sleeping sickness and malaria, have a complicated life-cycle involving a second host. Malaria is caused by the protozoan *Plasmodium* and the infective stage (called a sporozoite) lives in the salivary glands of the female *Anopheles* mosquito. When she bites, she also injects saliva and several hundred sporozoites enter the bloodstream. The sporozoites quickly make their way to the liver where they undergo a period of asexual multiplication. After about twelve days the proto-

zoans, now called merozoites, are released back into the bloodstream where each enters a red blood corpuscle. Here it grows and undergoes a further multiplication. Eventually the corpuscle bursts and releases fresh merozoites to attack other corpuscles. Each time the merozoites, together with their waste products, are released the victim suffers an attack of fever. In due course, the sexual phase takes over and the merozoites develop into the male and female stages. They are sucked up when another mosquito bites, and fertilization takes place in the mosquito's intestine. New generations of protozoans develop in the mosquito's body before moving to the salivary glands to complete the cycle ready to be injected into a new host when the mosquito next takes a meal.

Volvox is a colonial flagellate large enough to see with the naked eye. Each fluid-filled colony grows to about 2mm in diameter. Although it appears to roll along in the water, there is, in fact, a front end and a back end. The sex cells, which give rise to new colonies inside the parent colony, are always at the back.

Sponges

The largest Protozoa are only a few millimetres long. They are unable to grow much larger because of the limitations inherent in a single cell having to perform all the bodily functions. These limitations are overcome by multicellular animals which have a body made of a number of small cells. Each cell then performs only a limited number of functions and is dependant upon the activities of the others. Increasing specialization leads to the development of tissues – layers of similar cells – which in the higher groups lead to the development of organs.

Sponges are the most primitive form of multicellular animals. All sponges spend their lives attached to one place. Nearly all are marine (only one family lives in fresh water) and they usually inhabit shallow water, though some are found more than 4·8 km (3 miles) down. The simplest sponges are shaped like a vase whose surface is peppered with many tiny pores that lead to a large internal cavity with an opening at the top. It is the large number of pores that give this phylum its name – Porifera means 'pore-bearers'.

Sponges have two layers of tissue – an outer skin and an inner surface lined with special cells called collar cells. The collar cells are equipped with whip-like flagella which beat to draw water through the pores and into the body cavity where bacteria and other microscopic particles are strained out and digested. Between the two layers of cells there is a jelly like material which contains wandering amoeboid cells called amoebocytes. The amoebocytes are general-purpose cells which can change into any type of cell as required. They secrete the spicules that make up the sponge skeleton, give rise to sperms and eggs, and transport food and waste material to and from the other cells. The skeleton may be made of calcareous or siliceous spicules, or fibres of spongin – a horny, elastic substance akin to silk and horn. The common bath sponge is made of spongin. The type and shape of the spicules are important guides used by zoologists in the classification of the Porifera.

Sponges usually go unrecognized as shapeless red, orange or yellow masses on the seashore, like the crumb o'bread sponge (*Halichondria panicea*) which looks like mouldy bread when dried out. More spectacular kinds live below the shore level. The most beautiful sponge, at least in skeleton form, is the Venus flower basket (*Euplectella aspergillum*) of the Philippines.

The great majority of sponges live in the sea. Of a total of around 4500 species, only about 150 are found in fresh water. All prefer clear waters. In still, deep or sheltered positions, sponges may grow into elegant shapes, but in rough or disturbed water they tend to form shapeless lumps or crusty growths.

Coelenterates

The coelenterates, which include the hydra, jellyfishes, sea anemones and corals have, like the sponges, a two-layered body structure. The body is shaped like a sack with a large mouth surrounded by tentacles. The tentacles seize passing animals and cram them into the mouth. Digestion takes place inside the 'sack' and the remains are ejected through the mouth. The tentacles are armed with stinging cells called nematocysts. They fire a hollow thread like a harpoon into the body of the prey and poison is injected to kill or paralyze. The stinging cells of the sea wasp (*Chironex fleckeri*) of the Indo-Pacific region are more deadly than the most venomous snake. They produce a neurotoxin that can kill a man within thirty seconds, although three to ten minutes is more usual. Two jellyfishes feed on organisms instead of catching prey. Members of the genus *Rhizostoma* suck a current of water through thousands of tiny mouths and trap food on strings of mucus. Members of the genus *Cassiopeia* feed in a similar way while lying on their backs on the seabed.

Some animals make use of stinging cells for their own ends. Certain octopuses anoint themselves with strips of coelenterate skin to provide a protective 'suit', and some sea slugs of the family Aeolidiidae manage to feed on sea anemones without setting off the nematocysts; these are then stored on the sea slugs' backs where they can be used for defence.

All coelenterates exist in one or other of two forms: the polyp or the medusa. A sea anemone is a typical polyp, cylindrical in shape, attached at the base and with mouth and tentacles at the other end. The medusa is a jellyfish form, and consists of a bell-shaped body with a convex

Hydra is a naked freshwater coelenterate common in ponds, lakes and slow-moving streams. Green-coloured hydras contain green algae within their tissues; the algae use carbon dioxide produced by the hydra to make sugars, which may help to nourish the hydra. The chief food of *Hydra* is small crustaceans, which it catches with its tentacles.

upper surface; from its concave under surface a mouth and tentacles hang down. Some coelenterates begin life as a polyp and at a later stage bud off medusa forms. The coelenterates are divided into three classes.

Sea-firs (class Hydrozoa)

The Hydrozoa, which includes the hydra-like animals, usually have both polyp and medusa phases in their life-cycle but the common hydra of freshwater ponds and ditches has only the polyp form. This group also includes the floating colonial forms such as the Portuguese man o' war (*Physalia physalis*) and the by-the-wind-sailor (*Velella velella*). Each 'animal' is a community of individuals attached to a gas-filled sac. The community includes polyps with long trailing tentacles whose stinging cells have venom as strong as a cobra's. Portuguese men o' war live in warm seas, but are sometimes blown to the coasts of temperate Europe and America where they are wrecked on the shore.

Jellyfishes (class Scyphozoa)

In the Scyphozoa, the cup animals that include the true jellyfishes, it is the medusoid stage that is the dominant form.

Jellyfishes swim by contracting the umbrella-shaped body, but they are at the mercy of sea currents. Most species are carnivorous, and catch animals with their tentacles, but some feed on tiny planktonic organisms. The tentacles are armed with stinging cells, and tropical species can be very dangerous. *Chrysaora* has 20m (65½ft) tentacles, but the largest is *Cyanea* of the Arctic, which measures 2m (6½ft) across the body.

Sea anemones and corals (class Anthozoa)

The Anthozoa, also known as flower animals, exist only as polyps. They include the sea anemones and the corals. Although sea anemones seem to remain rooted to the spot, some can move by creeping over the rocks, and members of the genus *Edwardsia* burrow in sand and mud. Species of *Stomphia* leave their rock and swim away when touched by a starfish or predatory sea slug. *Calliactis parasitica* travels by fixing itself to a whelk shell which is the home of a hermit crab.

The corals have a calcareous exterior skeleton and are responsible for building the atolls, fringing and barrier reefs which provide a home for thousands of different animals. A coral animal is like a tiny sea anemone sitting in a chalky cup. Although small in itself millions of coral animals make up coral reefs. The Great Barrier Reef runs for 2000 km (1260 miles) down the coast of Australia. Reef-building corals need to live in warm, clear water; sediment kills them. They also need shallow water because they contain algae which need sunlight for photosynthesis.

Opposite: Jellyfishes are well-named: even the firmest ones contain 94 per cent water. Jellyfishes immobilize the small creatures they feed on with a combination of poison and sticky tentacles.

Below: The jewel anemone is found on temperate shores. Only about 1 cm in diameter, it often lives in large groups.

Bottom: Reef corals grow in many different ways, depending on their preferred position and depth. Deeper corals, and those in sheltered, still water tend to form branches, while corals in exposed positions are usually compact.

Worms

Opposite: Feather or fan worms keep most of their body inside a parchment tube fixed to the seabed. They extend their feathery tentacles to catch small particles of food and absorb oxygen, but quickly retract these delicate organs into the tube when disturbed.

The first attempts by naturalists to classify the Animal Kingdom linked animals that were superficially similar but in fact were not closely related. Thus, the sea anemones were originally thought to be plants, the whales were believed to be fishes, the bats were classed as birds, and all the long, thin worm-like creatures were lumped together in the now obsolete phylum Vermes – the worms. Modern classification now recognizes the differences which exist, and groups the worms as follows: the flatworms (phylum Platyhelminthes); the ribbon worms (phylum Nemertina); the rotifers (phylum Rotifera); the round or thread worms (phylum Nematoda); the sea mats or moss animals (phylum Bryozoa); and the true or segmented worms (phylum Annelida).

Flatworms (phylum Platyhelminthes)

The platyhelminthes are the most primitive worms and their ancestors occupy a key position on the evolutionary tree that leads to the higher animals. The flatworm body is bilaterally symmetrical and made up of three layers of cells (compared with the sponges and coelenterates which are radially symmetrical and only two-layered). Flatworms are the most primitive group to possess an excretory system, a musculature on the lines of that found in higher animals, and a centralized nervous system complete with tiny brain. The gut, however, remains a simple blind-ending sac. There are three classes of flatworms.

Planarians (class Turbellaria)

The free-living flatworms or planarians differ from the other classes in having a body covered in cilia, which they use for creeping over the ground on a lubricating layer of mucus. The mucus also prevents the worm from drying-up and deters predators. In addition they may have a distinct head complete with eyes and other sense organs. Planarians have been widely used in behavioural experiments and, because of their regenerative powers, in the investigation of grafting. Planarians are common on seashores and in fresh water. They are carnivorous but if starved they survive for years by digesting parts of their own bodies. Tropical rain forests are the home of land-dwelling planarians which live on the damp ground and grow to 60cm (2ft.).

Flukes (class Trematoda)

The flukes are almost exclusively parasitic flatworms and most species are equipped with one, or two, suckers for hanging on to their hosts. Generally speaking those forms living on the outside of a host have a simple life-cycle involving just one vertebrate host. Most live on fishes, but one unusual species, *Oculotrema*, is found under the eyelids of the hippopotamus.

The flukes which live inside their hosts have a complex life-cycle involving two or more hosts. *Fasciola hepatica*, the common liver fluke, causes 'liver-rot' in sheep and cattle, and spends part of its life in water snails. For this reason farmers traditionally kept sheep off low-lying, riverside pastures.

Schistosomiasis – a particularly prevalent disease of man affecting hundreds of millions of people annually in South America, Africa and the Far East – is caused by flukes that live in the blood vessels. Eggs are passed out of the host with the faeces. Each egg hatches into a larva which burrows into a freshwater snail. Here it multiplies enormously into millions of further larvae. When these are liberated into the water they search out and actively penetrate the skin of man and usually make their way to the abdominal veins. The disease is not often fatal but causes a pronounced lethargy.

Tapeworms (class Cestoda)

Tapeworms are flatworms which usually live in the intestine of vertebrates. There, bathed in the host's digesting food, a digestive system is superfluous for the tapeworm, and in all cases has been lost. Instead, food is absorbed through the skin.

Most tapeworms are ribbon-like, as the name suggests, to provide a large surface area for absorption. The broad tapeworm of man (*Diphyllobothrium latum*), may attain a length of 18m (60ft) and live for thirty years. The body of a mature worm is made up of a head, complete with hooks and suckers for attachment, and a short neck from which bud a long string of segments.

Ribbon worms (phylum Nemertina)

Although basically similar to the free-living flatworms, ribbon worms differ in having a through-gut – mouth at one end and anus at the other – and a rudimentary blood stream. Both ribbon worms and flatworms have a solid body whereas all higher members of the Animal Kingdom have an internal body cavity.

Rotifers (phylum Rotifera)

The wheel animalcules or rotifers are among the commonest freshwater animals. Although they are roughly the same size as the single-celled protozoans they consist of about a thousand cells. They typically bear a crown of cilia, from which they get their name, which are used both for swimming and capturing food. They are present in great numbers in pond water and damp moss. Rotifers are past masters at surviving adverse conditions, and thrive in short-lived pools in the Antarctic summer. Some species can survive freezing or dehydration for long periods, coming 'alive' again when favourable conditions return. They are also one of the groups that reproduce parthenogenetically – the egg develops without fertilization into a new and identical individual.

Roundworms (phylum Nematoda)

The nematodes or roundworms are all very similar, having a long, slender unsegmented body which is covered by a tough skin. Parasitic nematodes are particularly important because of the damage they do to crops, domestic animals and man. Eelworms are parasites of plants, and cause enormous havoc among crops. The stem and bulb eelworm (*Ditylenchus dipsaci*) attacks such plants as rye, oats, clover, lucerne, onions, strawberries and tulips. Eelworms

are difficult to control because they can lie dormant for years and then spring to life again.

Roundworms also cause diseases such as pork trichina and elephantiasis.

Segmented worms (phylum Annelida)

The segmented worms, the annelids, are characterized by having a body divided up into a number of similar segments that appear as rings along the length of the body. The phylum is divided into three classes.

Bristle worms (class Polychaeta)

The polychaetes are usually equipped with a pair of flattened, fleshy lobe-like paddles projecting from each body segment which are used for swimming, burrowing and creating a feeding current. The class may be split into two groups – the errant polychaetes and the sedentary polychaetes. The errant polychaetes are free-living forms that burrow in the sand and mud, and also includes those tube dwellers that leave their tubes to hunt for food. The sedentary polychaetes are tube dwellers

that rarely, if ever, leave their tubes. Instead, their tentacles take food from the surrounding water.

The ragworms (genus *Nereis*) live on the sea shore and shallow seas around the world, where they can be found under stones or in U-shaped burrows in mud and sand. They come out to feed on tiny particles or to hunt small animals. One species, *Nereis fucata*, lives in the same shell as a hermit crab, coming out to share the crab's meals, and then retreating back inside for safety.

Palolo worms (genus *Eunice*) of coral reefs in the southern Pacific live in burrows or in crevices. The rear portion of the worm alters drastically as the reproductive organs develop. The limbs become more paddle-like and, eventually, that portion snaps off and swims away. The front portion stays behind and regrows the lost part. The free-swimming portions rise to the surface where eggs and sperms are shed. So that the chances of fertilization are increased, all the worms come to the surface at once. This happens in October or November, at dawn on the two days in which the moon is in its last quarter.

43

Earthworms are hermaphrodite. They lie head-to-tail to mate, each passing sperm to the other. The sperm is stored in special cavities in the worm's body until needed for fertilizing its eggs. When the eggs are ready, the worm secretes a girdle of thick slime and protein, into which the eggs and sperm are shed, and where fertilization takes place. Finally, the worm wriggles free of the girdle, leaving the eggs cocooned within it.

The sedentary polychaetes rarely, if ever, leave their tubes. Only the head is poked out of the tube. The fan worms, such as the peacock worm (*Sabella pavonina*), live in tubes of silt or sand bound together with mucus. A fan of delicate tentacles catch fine particles. The slightest shadow or vibration sends the fan back into the tube for safety. The lugworm (genus *Arenicola*) lives in a U-shaped tube in muddy sand through which it draws water by beating its limbs. The oxygenated water is used for respiration and it also brings in pieces of seaweed which are eaten. The inlet of the tube is marked by a slight depression in the sand while coiled 'cast' accumulates at the outlet.

Earthworms (class Oligochaeta)

The oligochaetes have far fewer bristles on their bodies than the polychaetes. To suit their burrowing habits the head is reduced and usually lacks eyes. Most species are scavengers and eat dead vegetable material. The common earthworm (*Lumbricus terrestris*) ingests vast quantities of soil and humus. Australia is the home of the giant earthworm. These monstrous creatures may grow to a length of 3·3m (11ft).

Leeches (class Hirudinea)

Leeches have a sucker at each end of the body. The smaller sucker at the head end is armed with teeth. Most leeches are parasitic and suck the blood of their victims, but some are carnivorous and eat small animals. The blood suckers inject an anticoagulant into the wound so that even after the worm has released itself the victim may continue to lose blood. In the past, the medicinal leech (*Hirudo medicinalis*) was used by surgeons to let the blood of their patients as it was falsely supposed that many afflictions could be cured in this way. Nowadays the medicinal leech is collected for its anticoagulant saliva which is used for research into the clotting mechanism of blood. As a result the medicinal leech has become very rare.

Molluscs

Molluscs are the second largest phylum in the Animal Kingdom, after the Arthropoda. They are one of the most successful invertebrate groups, with more than 100 000 living species. They have long been important to man, both as a source of food and for their shells, which have been used for a variety of purposes.

Molluscs have managed to exploit almost every type of habitat and life-style, and they are found on land, in the sea and in fresh water. About half of the known species are marine.

The body of a mollusc consists of a head, a muscular foot and a 'visceral mass' which contains the digestive and other organs. A sheet of skin covering the body and called the mantle secretes the chalky protective shell which is found in most species. Beneath the mantle is the mantle cavity. The mantle cavity houses the gills, when present, the anus and the opening of the excretory and reproductive organs. One structure unique in molluscs is the radula, or tongue. It consists of a band of tissue bearing a large number of teeth which vary in different species according to the type of food eaten.

Molluscs have no internal skeleton but instead the shell forms an exoskeleton. Shells come in an infinite variety of colours, patterns, shapes and textures which usually reflect the life-style of the animals. They are made of a material called conchiolin which is impregnated with calcium carbonate, and covered with a protein-like layer. Many shells have an inner layer of nacre or mother-of-pearl which is formed from tiny blocks of crystalline calcium carbonate arranged in layers, giving the shell interior its characteristic lustre. A few species such as the chambered nautilus (*Nautilus pompilius*) and the pearl oysters of the genus *Pinctada* consist almost entirely of nacre. The main function of the shell is protection. In marine species it provides protection from wave action; in terrestrial and seashore species it prevents drying out since the shell is almost impermeable to water; and in all molluscs it is the main defence against predators.

Some species such as the abalones and limpets have shells which can be clamped tightly to wave-swept rocks to avoid desiccation when the tide is

A group of periwinkles, dog whelks and limpets lying in a rocky crevice. These molluscs are commonly found on rocky shores at low tide, where their thick shells protect them from drying out. The limpet is particularly well adapted to this life, and grinds a depression in the rock that fits its shell perfectly.

out or to avoid being removed by predators. Others have streamlined shells for burrowing, particularly bivalves such as the razorshells. When alarmed a razorshell can plunge deep into the sand, by as much as a metre (3¼ft). Perhaps the strangest shells of all are the carrier shells of the genus *Xenophora* of the Indo-Pacific region and the Mediterranean. Not content with the natural form of their own shells, they attach stones, bits of coral and other empty shells to the outer surface. It has been suggested that this curious behaviour may camouflage or strengthen the shell. There are seven classes of molluscs.

Monoplacophorans (class Monoplacophora)

The Monoplacophora are the most primitive living molluscs of which only ten species are known, all belonging to the single genus *Neopilina*. They have small, conical, limpet-like shells and the anatomy of the body is partly segmented, suggesting that this group may represent the link between molluscs and annelids (worms like the earthworm). They live at very great depths and probably feed on organic matter in the bottom mud.

Chitons (class Polyplacophora)

The chitons (sometimes known as coat-of-mail shells) are accurately described as the armadillos of the sea. Their shells consist of eight overlapping plates which cover rather flattened bodies and they range in size from 1-33cm (½-13in) long. They are found throughout the world, mainly in shallow and intertidal waters where they feed on encrusting algae. Most species are nocturnal and live clinging to rocks with their large muscular foot, clamping themselves firmly to the rock surface if disturbed. If detached they roll themselves up like woodlice. One species, *Nuttalina californica* of southern California, lives in deep depressions which it makes by gradually wearing away the rock. Instead of wandering in search of food it eats fragments of seaweed washed into its hole.

Slugs and snails (class Gastropoda)

The largest and most diverse class of molluscs is the Gastropoda, of which there are between 65 000 and 75 000 species. They include marine and freshwater species and are the only class of molluscs which have members living on land. There are three subclasses.

Prosobranchs (subclass Prosobranchia)

Prosobranch gastropods are generally marine and possess gills, robust shells and an operculum with which they can close the opening of the shell. They include many of the species with the most attractive shells. The simplest forms include the limpets and abalones which clamp themselves to rocks like chitons. They are usually browsers and play an important role in controlling intertidal growth of seaweeds and other encrusting organisms. Limpets even have a radula which is adapted for rasping at limestone in order to feed on algae which bore into rock.

Most marine prosobranchs, however, are carnivores. Whelks feed on dead fishes and invertebrates, as well as decaying vegetable matter, and will also pry open bivalves such as oysters by wedging the valves open with the edge of their shells to obtain the flesh inside. One of the bonnet shells, *Cypraecassis testiculus*, eats sea urchins, carefully removing the spines before eating the inside. The dogwhelks bore holes through the shells of living molluscs using special teeth and then suck the tissues out. The conches of tropical seas have massive shells and pole themselves over the seabed using a modified operculum. Instead of being used as a trapdoor to close the shell, the conch's operculum looks like an outsize fingernail and is jammed into the sand while the muscular foot heaves the animal forwards. Conch shells have been used worldwide as trumpets. All that is needed is to knock off the apex of the shell. The cowries played an even more important role in primitive cultures. They were used as currency around parts of the Indian Ocean and in Africa. Although most cowries are found in the tropics a few live in temperate regions.

The cones have a long proboscis from which they eject a minute 'harpoon' into their prey, which includes small fishes, worms and other molluscs. The prey is then injected with a poison and swallowed: the poison is so venomous that it can kill a man.

46

Many of the marine prosobranchs, such as the mitres, olive shells and volutes are burrowers, and have developed siphons or tubes extending from the mantle and sometimes the shell as well, which act as snorkels. This enables them to burrow under the surface of the sand or mud whilst still continuing to suck a water current containing oxygen and food into their bodies. Quite the opposite of the borrowing species, the violet shell, *Janthina janthina*, is pelagic and floats on the ocean surface under a raft of bubbles secreted by the foot.

Opisthobranchs (subclass Opisthobranchia)

The opisthobranchs are entirely marine and occur mainly in tropical and sub-tropical waters. They include many of the most beautiful molluscs, flamboyantly coloured red, yellow, orange, blue, green, and often matching their seaweed backgrounds. The bubble snails have a very thin, almost translucent shell; sea hares have a very reduced shell; and sea slugs have no shell. The gills are often in the form of feathery plumes on their backs and many species also have fleshy extensions of

the digestive system on their backs as well. Most of them are herbivores but many are 'grazing carnivores' which might seem a contradiction in terms until one realizes that they feed on fixed animals such as corals, sea anemones and sponges.

One sea slug, *Calma*, feeds entirely on fish eggs. Its mouth is shaped like a half-globe and fits exactly over the eggs of small gobies and blennies. The sea slug sucks an egg into its mouth, carefully slits a hole with its radula teeth and then drains the contents. It feeds only once a year when the fishes are laying their eggs.

Many opisthobranchs use poison as a means of protection since they do not have shells for this purpose. Their bright colours may serve as warning signals to potential predators.

Pulmonates (subclass Pulmonata)

In the pulmonates the mantle cavity has been converted into a lung. The more primitive pulmonates are found in fresh water and occasionally intertidally. They include the common pond snails of the genera

Sea slugs are often flamboyantly coloured. They have practically no enemies, and their brightly coloured gills are probably a way of signalling their inedibility as they creep along, browsing on corals, sponges and bryozoans.

A green tree snail browsing on a leaf. Molluscs have made themselves at home in a wide variety of habitats, from the ocean depths to high mountains.

Lymnea and *Planorbis*, which can stay submerged for up to two hours.

The more advanced pulmonates include all the terrestrial species such as land snails and slugs. The large foot is covered in cilia, and glides over a secretion of mucus – this is one of the reasons why the pulmonates have been able to colonize the land. They prefer humid environments but are very well able to survive drying out.

Many species have developed special ways to avoid desiccation. Those which live in extremely dry places such as among rocks, dunes and deserts may be active only at night or after rainfall. Tropical tree snails, such as the bright green Manus tree snail (*Papustyla pulcherrima*) from Papua New Guinea and the little agate shells, *Achatinella*, from Hawaii, rest during the day sealed to the branches of trees or to the underside of leaves and only come out at night. Under particularly adverse conditions snails may go into a kind of hibernation, lasting for months or even years.

Most pulmonates are herbivores and, as well as the radula, they often have jaws to enable them to tear off pieces of vegetation. A few land snails and slugs are carnivorous and feed on earthworms and other land snails.

Bivalves (class Bivalvia)

The Bivalvia are the second largest class of molluscs and comprise about 7 500 species, including the mussels, clams, oysters, cockles and scallops. Their shells or valves are in two hinged parts which are held tightly together by a pair of powerful muscles. They range in size from the tiny freshwater peashell cockles of the genus *Sphaeridium*, only 0·2mm in length, to the giant clam (*Tridacna gigas*) of the tropics which reaches up to 1 metre (3¼ft) in length and can weigh over 200kg (440lb).

No bivalves live on land and the majority live a sedentary existence on or in the seabed. Burrowing species have a large, flattened foot which, through a combination of muscle action and blood pressure, digs through the sand or mud. Bivalves have a pair of large gills which are generally used for feeding as well as respiration. These are shaped like leaves or curtains and are covered with cilia which beat continuously to draw in a current, and plankton is trapped by mucus on the gills and carried by the cilia to the mouth.

Burrowing species include razorshells and cockles as well as a number of freshwater clams and mussels. They have siphons reaching to the surface of the mud or sand and are well protected from predators.

Others attach themselves in different ways to the seabed. Mussels are attached to rocks and hard surfaces by structures called 'byssus' threads which are secreted by a gland in the foot. Mangrove oysters are similarly attached to mangrove roots, and winged oysters to sea fans and corals.

Some bivalves are quite mobile. The scallop swims by opening and closing its shell so forcefully that it moves under a form of jet propulsion. It also has a row of tiny eyes around the mantle edge so it can detect danger and can make a rapid escape from predators.

One group of bivalves has adopted a boring way of life, living beneath the surface of hard materials such as wood or rock. As soon as the larvae settle they start excavating using the shell valves, which often have serrated edges, as drills. The ship worms (family Teredinidae) have long cylindrical bodies and bore into timber using the excavated sawdust as food.

Tusk shells (class Scaphopoda)

The Scaphopoda or elephant tusk shells are burrowers. They have a distinctive curved tapering shell (like an uncoiled snail shell) which gives rise to their common name. The narrower end of the shell projects out of the sand and a constant current of water flows through the body bringing in tiny shelled protozoans which are used as food. The mouth of the elephant tusk shell is surrounded by hundreds of long fleshy filaments ending in sticky pads which pick up the protozoans and pass them to the mouth, where the radula teeth are used to crack open the shells.

Aplacophorans (class Aplacophora)

Aplacophorans live in all the world's oceans, and could easily be mistaken for worms. They have no shells, and in some cases no foot either. The worm-like body has spicules of calcium carbonate in the cuticle covering it, and they live in burrows or among coral and algae.

Squids, cuttlefishes and octopuses (class Cephalopoda)

The Cephalopoda is the third largest class of molluscs and includes the squids, cuttlefishes and octopuses. They are the most highly developed molluscs and include some of the most intelligent, if also rapacious, invertebrates in the world. The majority are quite large, and the giant squid of the genus *Architeuthis*, may reach a length of 18m (59ft). The shell is very reduced or even absent and complete shells are only found in fossils, such as the ammonites, and in the chambered nautilus (*Nautilus pompilius*). However, unlike gastropods, the chambered nautilus only lives in part of its shell, the rest being filled with gas and used as a buoyancy organ. It lives a floating life in the Pacific Ocean at a depth of about 100m (328ft) or more. The so-called shell of the paper nautilus (*Argonauta argo*) is secreted by the female's tentacles. It serves as a container for her eggs and she withdraws into it when alarmed. The much smaller male also lives in it as a lodger.

Unlike most molluscs which are fairly slow moving or even immobile, cephalopods are able to move very rapidly. In the squids and cuttlefishes the mantle cavity has become a pump that squirts water through a funnel in a form of jet propulsion. Squids reach the greatest swimming speeds of any aquatic invertebrates. There are even flying squids (members of the genus *Ommastrephes*) which can shoot out of the water and glide for some distance, sometimes reaching a speed of 25·5kph (16mph) through the air.

Cephalopods' mouths are surrounded by a ring of tentacles. (The tentacles are derived from the foot which is found in other molluscs.) Octopuses have eight tentacles, squids and cuttlefishes ten, and *Nautilus* has thirty-eight. All cephalopods are active predators and use their tentacles for locating and cap-

Opposite: Closely related to octopuses, squids have ten arms and a longer body. They are very abundant in cold seas, and have been found at great depths. The giant squid is known to attain an arm-span of 20m (65½ft).

Below: The peak of mollusc development is reached in the octopus, one of the most intelligent invertebrates in the world. It has no shell. Its eight-armed body is strong and muscular, supported internally by rods of cartilage. Despite their reputation, most octopuses are shy creatures, hiding in rocky crevices.

turing prey. The mouth has a strong beak for tearing pieces from the prey which the radula pushes into the mouth. Shrimps, crabs and fishes form the major part of the cephalopod diet.

The cephalopods have the largest brains of all invertebrates and they also have well-developed senses of touch and taste in the tentacles. The eyes closely resemble those of vertebrates. Well-developed senses are important to help locate their prey. Many cephalopods are capable of rapid colour change which is sometimes part of the courtship display. Some deep-sea forms are luminescent and a number of cephalopods have a characteristic defence mechanism. They produce a smokescreen by ejecting an inky substance, which is the source of the dark brown ink called sepia. The ink hangs as a cloud in the water, fooling the predator while the cephalopod escapes. However, smokescreens can be little help to the squids which are the main food of sperm whales, for it has been estimated that whales consume over 100 million tonnes of squid in a year.

Reproduction in molluscs

Marine species of molluscs generally shed their eggs and sperm into the sea at the same time, and fertilization takes place in the water. A planktonic larva hatches from the egg and floats in the ocean currents, often over huge distances. Oysters are known to have been dispersed over 1 300 km (780 miles) in this way. Once the larva settles in a suitable habitat it develops into an adult.

Some marine species, like the octopus, have internal fertilization. Octopuses go through an elaborate form of courtship in which the male changes colour and arouses the female by stroking her. Then he transfers a sperm 'packet' to the female on the tip of one of his arms. The eggs may be brooded underneath the female. Cowries also sit on their eggs to hatch them.

Internal fertilization is the rule for terrestrial and freshwater molluscs and the eggs are deposited in gelatinous masses or in well-protected egg cases. In many species the eggs hatch as small replicas of the adults. A number of land snails brood their eggs internally and give birth to their young.

The freshwater mussels have a highly unusual method of reproduction. The male sheds the sperm into the water and these are drawn into the female on the current which is continually passing over her gills. The gills are modified to form a brooding pouch and, after fertilization, the eggs are incubated and minute spined or hooked larvae hatch and are shed into the water in large numbers. The larvae then attach themselves to a fish, becoming parasites. The host fish provides food and protection and also helps to disperse the larvae which eventually drop off to develop into an adult.

The Pulmonates are hermaphrodite, which means that each individual has a complete set of male and female reproductive organs. Land snails such as the Roman snail (*Helix pomatia*) have a very elaborate courtship which ends with both snails fertilizing each other.

Molluscs are generally sexually mature by the time they are two or three years old. The majority have fairly short lives, but some of the freshwater pearl mussels may live for a hundred years.

Arthropods

The animals included in this phylum number over 800000 known species – eighty per cent of the entire Animal Kingdom – and they live in huge numbers in the sea, on land and in fresh water. The name is derived from the Greek words for 'joint' and 'foot' and refers to the jointed limbs possessed by almost all arthropods. The body is also jointed, and the segments of the limbs and body have the form of rings or tubes of more or less rigid material surrounding the muscles and internal organs. Some of the body segments bear pairs of appendages, usually limbs for walking or swimming. The various appendages on the head are adapted for feeding (the jaws and maxillae), and as sensory organs (the antennae). In the insects (but in no other arthropods) there may be wings. These are not developed from limbs but are outgrowths from the sides of the thorax.

The outer covering of the head, body and limbs is formed of a tough fibrous substance called chitin. This is often rendered hard and rigid, either by the combination of a protein with the chitin to form sclerotin (typical of insects), or by the deposition of calcium carbonate or chalk and calcium phosphate (seen in many crustaceans). This outer covering or shell, also known as an exoskeleton, serves the arthropod not only as a protective coat of armour but also as a skeleton. The muscles are attached to its inner surfaces.

The arthropods are subdivided into seven major classes.

Velvet worms (class Onychophora)

These are the most primitive arthropods and form a link with the annelid worms. They look rather like caterpillars with numerous short legs (from fourteen to forty-six pairs according to species) and a pair of long antennae. They feed on worms and small insects, especially termites, and in self-defence can discharge a sticky liquid from glands below the mouth. They breathe in the same way as insects, by means of internal tubes called tracheae, which have openings on the surface of the body. The South African species *Peripatopsis capensis* is one of the best studied. There are about seventy species altogether, all living either in the tropics or in temperate parts of the Southern Hemisphere.

King crabs (class Merostomata)

The so-called king crabs or horse-shoe crabs are 'living fossils', only four species having survived from early geological times. They are all marine and the best-known of them is *Limulus polyphemus*, found in shallow water on the more southern Atlantic coasts of North America. The others are found in the seas of the Far East. The body is covered with a hard shell or carapace and has a spike-like tail. All the species have five pairs of legs, the first four of which end in pincers or claws. The largest species, *Tachypleus tridentatus*, may be 75cm (2½ft) long. They feed on worms and other small animals.

Centipedes (class Chilopoda)

These are active predatory animals that have segmented bodies with one pair of legs on each segment. The number of pairs of legs ranges from 15 to over 170, the greatest number being found in the long slender earth centipedes (order Geophilomorpha), which burrow in the soil. The first pair of legs, situated just behind and under the head, is adapted to form poison claws; these, hollow and perforated at the tip and connected to venom glands, are used for seizing and killing prey and in self-defence. Most centipedes are small animals, but some species of *Scolopendra* are commonly 15–20cm (6–8in) long, while *S. gigantea* of South America reaches 30cm (1ft). The bite from the poison claws of these large centipedes is intensely painful, but rarely dangerous to human life.

The most familiar centipedes of temperate regions are species of the genus *Lithobius*, which have fifteen pairs of legs and are common under loose bark and stones and in the soil. The strangest are those of the family Scutigeridae, which have a fairly

short, stiff body and fifteen pairs of very long legs, and can run extremely fast.

Nearly all centipedes are active in darkness and live in humid surroundings because their bodies lose water quickly by evaporation. All of them lay eggs and the females of the big scolopendras, such as *Scolopendra morsitans*, brood and guard their eggs and young, defending them fiercely if molested. They feed by hunting insects, but the large tropical species are known to kill mice and lizards.

Millipedes (class Diplopoda)

Millipedes contrast greatly with centipedes in being slow-moving and in feeding on vegetable matter. Their legs are on average more numerous, one South African species, *Nema-*

The scorpion's sting is not generally used for catching prey, which is normally easily dealt with by the powerful 'pincers'; the sting is an organ of defence. Life is particularly hard in the desert, and small desert scorpions are more venomous and more aggressive than their larger forest-dwelling cousins.

tozonium elongatissimum, having 355 pairs. Most of the body segments are fused together in pairs, giving an appearance of two pairs of legs to each segment. The largest milli-pedes, of the genus *Spirostreptus*, live in the tropical rain forest, where some species reach 25cm (10in) in length.

Millipedes feed mainly on decayed vegetable matter, but a few bore into roots and tubers underground. They defend themselves by discharging a corrosive liquid from glands along the sides of the body. All of them live in humid surroundings and quickly die of dehydration if exposed to dry air. They lay eggs which in some cases are enclosed in 'nests' cemented with liquid excrement.

Arachnids (class Arachnida)

Spiders, scorpions, mites and ticks are the most familiar members of this class. Like the insects they dwell almost entirely on the land. They differ from insects, however, in having a body divided into two parts, a combined head and thorax (called the prosoma or cephalothorax) and an abdomen, and in possessing four pairs of legs (not three). The part of the prosoma corresponding to the head bears two pairs of appendages, the chelicerae and the pedipalps, which are used for catching and chewing up prey. There are no antennae. Most small arachnids breathe by means of tracheae, but scorpions and the larger spiders have 'book-lungs' which are pockets containing leaf-like plates through which the blood circulates.

Many arachnids, including scor-pions and spiders, perform a court-ship ritual before mating. This is probably a result of their predatory habits; each partner must be sure that the other is in a mood for mating rather than feeding.

Scorpions (order Scorpiones)

Scorpions are always large enough to be seen distinctly and cannot be mistaken for any other sort of animal. Their most striking features are their large claw-shaped pedipalps, and the division of the abdomen into two parts; the front part is as broad as the prosoma but the hind part is slender and looks like a tail. Both parts are segmented. At the end of the 'tail' is a thorn-like sting with a pair of poison glands at its base.

Scorpions are confined to warm climates, extending from the tropics into southern Europe and the southern United States. Some species inhabit tropical rain forests, while others are found in desert regions. All are secretive in their habits, burrowing into earth or sand or living under logs and stones. They feed by hunting insects and other small animals.

Their mating habits are remarkable, usually involving a courtship dance with the two sexes 'holding hands' with their pedipalps. The young are born alive and spend the first few days of their lives riding on their mother's back.

Scorpions readily use their stings in self defence. The effect of their venom on humans varies widely with the kind of scorpion. That of the huge tropical rain forest species is, curiously, never dangerous, though the sting they give is painful. On the other hand some of the small scorpions (*Buthus occitanicus*) of dry regions in North Africa, and species of *Centruroides* in southern North America) inject neurotoxins or nerve poisons which have serious effects and may be fatal.

Pseudoscorpions (order Pseudoscorpiones)

Pseudoscorpions or false scorpions are small arachnids, widespread in hot and temperate climates. They are so-called because they look just like tiny scorpions without a tail. Their pedipalps are enlarged, like those of scorpions, to form claws. Most of them are less than 4mm ($\frac{1}{10}$in) long. They are found in leaf litter and under bark, where they live by hunting small insects and mites. They have minute poison fangs on the 'fingers' of the claws.

Spiders (order Araneae)

Spiders are by far the most familiar of the arachnids and are found in all habitable parts of the World. The body is clearly divided into prosoma and abdomen. The chelicerae are developed as poison fangs and the pedipalps, usually called palps in spiders, are simple jointed appendages in the female and complex organs associated with mating in the male. All spiders are predatory, feeding mainly on insects. Most of them live on dry land, but some species skate on the surface film of fresh waters, and one, the water spider (*Argyroneta aquatica*) lives and makes its bubble-like silken nest under water.

The most remarkable attribute of spiders is their capacity for spinning silk. A spider stores its silk in glands in its abdomen as a sticky fluid which is drawn out of special organs called spinnerets under its hinder end. All spiders spin silk, which they use for a great variety of purposes.

The mating habits of spiders are unusual. The male first spins a minute platform of silk, discharges semen on to it and then takes it up with his palps, which are designed to work as tiny syringes. He then approaches the female, usually with great caution since she otherwise may eat him, and uses the palps to inject his semen into her genital orifice. Female spiders are usually bigger than males and in some genera the male is relatively tiny.

When an insect is trapped on the sticky spiral strands of its web, an orb spider runs along the clean radial threads to secure its prey. The victim is rapidly turned over and over, while the spider smothers it with silken strands, to be sucked dry at its leisure.

Above right: Web-weaving spiders have poor vision, which makes courtship something of an ordeal for the small male spider. He signals to the female by plucking a message on her web and, when she responds, he approaches to place two silk pads impregnated with sperm inside her genital opening. If he is lucky, he may retreat quickly enough to seek another mate.

Spiders range in size from just over a millimetre to the mouse-sized mygalomorphs of the tropics, often called bird-eating spiders or tarantulas.

Spider venom varies in potency and the largest species are not, in fact, the most dangerous. The redback or black widow spider (*Latrodectus mactans*), which lives in warm dry regions around the world, is quite small, but its bite causes severe symptoms. The Australian funnel-web spider (*Atrax robustus*) is probably the most dangerous species and has been the cause of many deaths.

Harvestmen (order Opiliones)

Harvestmen, known as daddy-long-legs in North America, resemble spiders, but the prosoma and abdomen are fused together to form a single round head-and-body. Most of them have extremely long slender legs which are so easily detached that many captured specimens are found to have less than the eight legs with which they started life.

The suborder Laniatores, mostly tropical, have large claws or pedipalps and often angular shaped bodies; in the suborder Palpatores of temperate regions the pedipalps are small and the body rounded. These include the common *Phalangium opilio* which is found right across the Northern Hemisphere. Harvestmen are all predatory and are almost as widespread as spiders.

Mites and ticks (order Acari)

Mites and ticks are small to minute arachnids found almost everywhere, often in great numbers. The ticks and some mites feed on the blood of vertebrate animals, often causing severe irritation. Some of the mites live in enormous numbers in the soil, hundreds or even thousands or millions of them to one acre. Many mites are pests of other species of animals or plants.

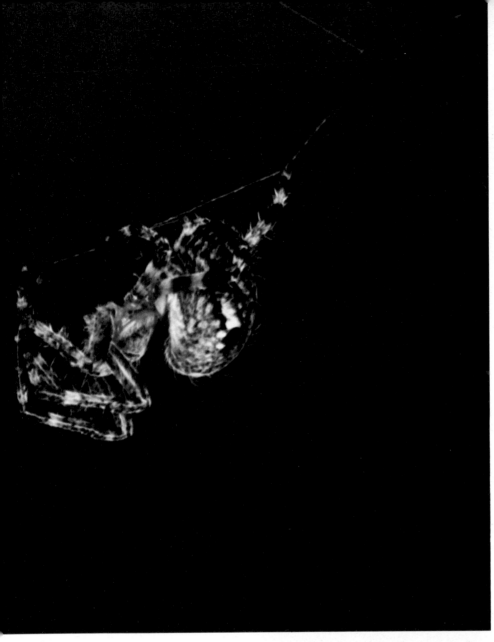

Right: Wolf spiders do not weave webs; they hunt by stalking their prey. The female spider carries her eggs with her in a large cocoon and, when the young spiders hatch, they ride on their mother's back for days or even weeks according to the species, until they are ready to disperse.

57

Mites, like this velvet mite, are extremely abundant arachnids, although their small size means that they are seldom seen.

Crustaceans (class Crustacea)

Crustaceans have been called, quite aptly, 'the insects of the sea'. They are mostly aquatic animals and the great majority are marine, and in this environment they have invaded every possible habitat and exploited almost every way of life. Like the rest of the phylum Arthropoda they have an outer covering which serves both as a suit of armour and as an external skeleton, and which must be shed at intervals as they grow. The covering consists basically of chitin but in most large crustaceans it is strengthened with carbonate and other salts of calcium to form a rigid shell.

Despite being a distinct group within the Arthropoda, the Crustacea have few features that readily identify them as crustaceans. The number of body segments and associated limbs and other appendages varies between species, and there is nothing in the way the body is divided into head, thorax and abdomen which is particularly characteristic. The only constant and unique feature is the possession of two pairs of antennae on the head.

Reproduction is normally sexual and the fertilized eggs are often retained by the female until they hatch, either contained in a brood pouch as in ostracods and water fleas, or attached to appendages as in crabs. The eggs usually hatch into a free-swimming larva called a nauplius. Following the nauplius the life-history involves changes of form, or metamorphoses, that vary with the type of crustacean.

There is a strong tendency for bottom- and shore-living forms, or those that are attached like barnacles, to have protracted larval stages that float in the plankton and in this way secure wide dispersal for the species. However, in some crabs inhabiting freshwater streams in the tropics (species of the family Potamonidae) the eggs are large and development proceeds inside them until they hatch, still attached to the female, into tiny crabs, and even these stay clinging to their mother for some time. Here, survival depends on not being washed downstream into the hostile environment of the sea, so the stages in the life-cycle involving small free-swimming larvae are suppressed.

The class Crustacea is divided into eight subclasses of which two include only a few small and rare species and are excluded here.

Branchiopods (subclass Branchiopoda)

These are mostly very small crustaceans, and almost all are inhabitants of fresh water. They have gills on their feet and one species, the water flea (*Daphnia pulex*) is familiar to all aquarium keepers as an excellent diet for small fishes.

Mussel shrimps (subclass Ostracoda)

The whole body of the animal is enclosed in a hinged shell like that of a bivalve mollusc. Nearly all ostracods are minute animals inhabiting both the sea and fresh waters in great numbers.

Copepods (subclass Copepoda)

Most of these are minute animals living in the marine plankton. Their importance lies in their enormous numbers and the great part they play in the food chain that is based on diatoms and other microscopic plants, on which the copepods feed. *Calanus finmarchicus* is a large species, about the size of a grain of rice, and has an elongate-oval body and very long antennae. It is abundant in the northern seas and is the principal food of the herring.

Fish lice (subclass Branchiura)

These are all external fish parasites. The body is round and flattened, and bears a pair of sucking discs with which the animal clings to its host. They are active, moving about on the fish's body, and they feed by sucking blood.

Cirripedes or barnacles and their allies (subclass Cirripedia)

This subclass includes the barnacles of which two types are familiar, the sessile or acorn barnacles and the

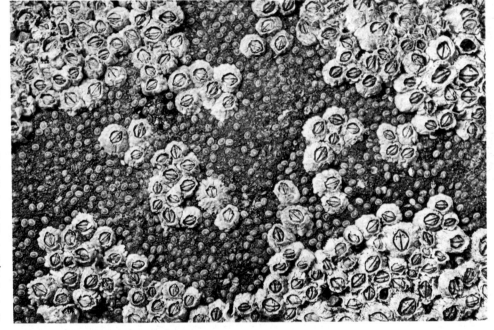

stalked barnacles. They are all marine, and pass their adult lives attached to rocks or some other suitable substratum. The animal is enclosed in a shell consisting of a number of plates. That of the acorn barnacle is conical, and that of the stalked barnacles symmetrical and flattened; the latter have a thick fleshy stalk. They feed by circulating water through the shell and extracting minute nutrient particles. Sessile barnacles such as *Chthamalus stellatus* are abundant on rocks on the shore. Others live attached to turtles or whales and can live nowhere else.

Above: Barnacles do not travel in search of food. They lie on their backs, enclosed in their shells, and kick their feathery feet out to breathe and sieve small edible particles from the water. When their shells are exposed to air, they draw in their feet and close the shell until the water returns.

The commonest stalked species is the goose barnacle (*Lepas anatifera*). It is worldwide in distribution and often lives attached to floating timber. Other cirripedes are parasites of crabs.

Crabs, lobsters, prawns and woodlice
(subclass Malacostraca)

Prawns, lobsters, crabs and the terrestrial woodlice are included in this subclass which contains almost three-quarters of all known species of crustaceans. It is divided into a number of orders, five of which are mentioned here.

The order Isopoda includes the woodlice or sowbugs, the only crustaceans that have successfully colonized the land, but there are many marine and some freshwater species as well. Most isopods have a body which is flattened from above, and woodlice are typical examples in this respect. These animals live entirely on land, but are confined to damp habitats such as under loose bark and in leaf litter. A marine isopod, the gribble (*Limnoria lignorum*), is notorious as a borer in submerged timber.

The order Amphipoda are small crustaceans, typically flattened from side to side. Sandhoppers are the most familiar of the amphipods, and they can be seen hopping about on sandy beaches anywhere in the world when the tide is out. *Talitrus saltator* is the commonest European species. The freshwater shrimp (*Gammarus pulex*) is found in shallow running streams.

The mantis shrimps of the order Stomatopoda are fairly large crustaceans found mostly in tropical waters. They are flattened from above and their front legs are formed like the handle and blade of a penknife in just the same way as those of

Below: Very few crustaceans live entirely on land. The woodlouse can, however, survive far from water, but it stays in cool, damp places, breathing by means of gills and feeding on rotting vegetable matter.

Right: On many tropical beaches, ghost crabs live in burrows away from the water, emerging at night to scavenge on the beach. Adult ghost crabs have practically no gills, although their young must start life in the sea.

Opposite: This brightly coloured barber-shop shrimp scavenges on coral reefs and wharves in the West Indies. When alarmed, it darts backwards into a crevice, trailing its long antennae and conspicuous pincers.

Crustaceans in the plankton

The plankton is the collective name given to the plants and animals (phytoplankton and zooplankton respectively) that drift in the waters of the sea, carried around by ocean currents rather than by their own swimming power. The zooplankton consists mostly of small animals living in the surface waters. The smallest of them subsist directly on the minute but exceedingly abundant diatoms which make up the bulk of the phytoplankton; the slightly larger ones prey on the smallest and so on, in a continuous progression.

A large proportion of the animal plankton consists of crustaceans, and the most numerous of these are the copepods. Species of the genus *Calanus* are typical copepods — bullet-shaped animals with a distinct

'tail', often forked at the tip, and with a pair of enormous antennae which are directed outwards on each side. Most of them are primary feeders on diatoms, but some of the larger species like *Calanus finmarchicus* prey on smaller copepods as well as on small larvae. These larval forms of larger crustaceans are the most abundant form of microplankton after the copepods; they are produced in huge numbers of which only a tiny proportion reach maturity. Those that do so may grow up in surroundings hundreds of kilometres away from their parents.

Among the adult Malacostraca the opossum shrimps (family Mysidae) include some species which live as members of the plankton. They average about 1 cm ($\frac{1}{2}$in) in length, and owe their name to the fact that they

carry their young in a pouch until they have completed their larval stages, and are miniature replicas of their parents. The largest planktonic crustaceans are the shrimps of the order Euphausiasia. These are most abundant in the cold waters of the north and south polar seas and form an important link in the oceanic food chain between the small and relatively large animals. They feed on smaller crustaceans and other animals and are themselves food for numerous fishes, seabirds including penguins, and are best known under the name of krill as the food of the great whales. The krill form densely packed swarms in the surface waters and this enables the whales to engulf them in huge masses; a large whale may consume 4 or 5 tonnes of krill in twenty-four hours.

Crabs keep their segmented abdomen curled under a wide, flat and strong carapace. Of their ten legs, two are specialized into large gripping claws and they can run (usually sideways) on the other eight. Sometimes the last two legs are flattened into oars for swimming.

a praying mantis, and they serve the same purpose – that of seizing prey. Mantis shrimps live in shallow water on coral reefs or burrow in sand or mud, and species of the genus *Squilla* are common on tropical coasts.

The order Euphausiacea are shrimplike crustaceans of the open sea, mostly 2–5cm ($\frac{3}{4}$–2in) long, and are best known under the name of 'krill' as the food of the great whales.

The order Decapoda or ten-footed crustaceans includes almost all the large and familiar members of the class, such as the crabs, lobsters, crayfishes and prawns. Largest of all is the giant spider crab (*Macrocheira kaempferi*) of the northern Pacific, 45cm (1½ft) across the body and spanning 3·6m (12ft) with its outstretched arms. The huge Tasmanian crab *Pseudocarcinus gigas* is not far behind, with a body width of

40cm (16in) and a weight of 13·5kg (30lb). A 20kg (44lb) lobster has been recorded from the coastal waters of Long Island, in the United States.

Crabs run on eight legs and have a pair in front of these modified as claws. Crabs and lobsters are most noticeable for the huge claws that are used for seizing and shredding prey, for protecting themselves and, in fiddler crabs (*Uca annulipes*) for waving to proclaim territory and in an attempt to attract females. Shrimps and prawns are other typical free-swimming decapods found throughout the World. Among the most unusual crabs are the hermit crabs which use the empty shells of gastropod molluscs as a protection for their soft, vulnerable hind bodies, and trundle about the seabed with their mobile homes.

Insects (class Insecta)

The insects are the most numerous and diverse class of the phylum Arthropoda. Although almost completely absent from the sea, they are present in greater numbers on the land than any other animals. In fact, there are more types of insect than *every other* kind of animal put together. They fall into three divisions: the Apterygota, Exopterygota and Endopterygota. The first group are all wingless, and have no evolutionary history of being winged. The Exopterygota and Endopterygota comprise the more advanced insects and are divided into orders, all of which have members that are winged or appear to have had winged ancestors. They are distinguished by the type of life-history they undergo. In the Exopterygota the changes from young to adult are gradual; in the Endopterygota there are distinct larval and pupal stages. Insects differ from other arthropods most clearly by having three pairs of legs; almost all the other groups or classes have more. The body of an insect is divided into three parts – head, thorax and abdomen – and, as already mentioned, many insects also have wings.

On the head of an insect there is a single pair of antennae (usually carrying organs of touch and smell), simple and compound eyes and a set of sideways-working mouthparts.

The legs and body are jointed and have an external covering which is usually more or less rigid and serves both as a protection for the body and as an external skeleton. The covering, known as the cuticle, has as its basis a tough fibrous substance called chitin, which forms the flexible part of the cuticle between the joints and on the bodies of grubs and caterpillars. In the parts that are stiffened or hardened, a protein combines with the chitin to form a horny substance called sclerotin. This is transparent when very thin, as in the wings, but thicker structures are brown or black. Whether it is made of chitin or sclerotin, an insect's cuticle is covered with a thin waterproof waxy layer. This not only keeps water out, but also prevents loss of body water by evaporation.

The possession of a 'suit of armour' has obvious advantages, but fails in one respect: it cannot change its size and form to allow the insect to grow. It must therefore be shed or moulted at intervals during growth to maturity. This process of moulting, called ecdysis, is almost always a hazardous one because it imposes a period of inactivity on the insect, and the hard covering is soft and vulnerable for a short time after ecdysis has taken place. Growth can proceed immediately after ecdysis because the new cuticle is wrinkled as well as soft and can therefore expand.

How insects breathe

Insects breathe by a system totally unlike our own. Instead of oxygen being dissolved in the blood in lungs and then carried around the body, air is conveyed to the tissues by fine tubes called tracheae, which branch repeatedly over and among the muscles and internal organs. The tubes communicate with the outside through openings on the sides of the body called spiracles. In the larger and more active insects such as bees, hoverflies and some beetles, parts of the tracheal tubes are dilated to form air sacs; pumping movements of the body performed by the insect force air in and out of the sacs by an action something like our own breathing. In small insects, and in the fine innermost tracheal tubes of larger ones, gaseous diffusion is the only means by which respiration takes place. Among the water insects many, such as the diving beetles and water boatman, come to the surface for air, but the aquatic larvae or nymphs of mayflies, dragonflies and some other insects extract oxygen from the water by means of filamentous or leaf-like gills.

Wings and flight

We know from the fossil record that insects learned to fly, in the evolutionary sense, long before any other animals. The earliest fossils of winged insects date from a period about 300 million years ago when most of the world's coal was formed. There were cockroaches at that time and dragonflies, some of which had a wingspan of over 60cm (2ft) and are the largest insects known to have existed.

Typically insects have two pairs of wings, which are not modified limbs, as are those of birds and bats, but outgrowths from the sides of the thorax. They are believed to have evolved from small lobes like those present on the silverfish (*Lepisma saccharina*), a wingless and primitive modern insect. The flies or Diptera are the only group of winged insects that never have more than a single pair of wings. The wing consists of two very thin and often transparent layers of sclerotin.

Insect flight is more like that of a helicopter than that of an aeroplane because lift, as well as propulsion, is provided by the movement of the wings rather than by the air flow resulting from forward movement. The difference is, of course, that the wings of insects oscillate with an up-and-down motion. The effect of this is to fan a stream of air downwards and backwards, propelling the insect forward and supporting it against the pull of gravity.

Large insects such as dragonflies and locusts beat their wings fairly slowly, at about twenty up-and-down strokes a second. In small insects the speed may be much greater. Bees and flies beat their wings about 200 times a second, and mosquitoes up to 600 times, while a minute midge called *Forcipomyia* attains the surprising frequency of 1000 wing-beats a second. The act-

ual speed of flight of insects is difficult to measure as they can seldom be observed flying over a determined distance. Bees and butterflies fly at 10-15 kph (6-9 mph) and the maximum speed of a large dragonfly has been estimated at 58 kph (35 mph). The big hawk moths, which fly at night and are almost impossible to observe, may well be the fastest insects of all.

The senses

Insects keep in touch with the world around them by the senses of smell, taste, sight and hearing very much as we do, but the organs concerned are very different from our own sense organs.

In most adult insects the sense of smell resides in the antennae. The receptors have the form of minute plates or pits on which scent molecules settle and are instantly perceived and identified. Insects can often be seen cleaning their antennae with their mouthparts or forelegs, presumably to remove dirt from the receptors. The sense of smell is used mainly to find food and by the more

The shy silverfish, often taken by surprise when the bathroom light is switched on, is a primitive insect which probably evolved about 300 million years ago. Silverfishes feed on a variety of organic debris, including dead skin and wallpaper paste, and can also digest cellulose.

active male insects to locate females.

In moths the females produce a substance called a pheromone, which is chemically unique to the species and is readily perceived by the male. The antennae of male moths are often elaborately branched or feather-like so that their sensitive surface is increased, and some of them can pick up the female scent from two kilometres (just over a mile) or more down-wind.

The sense of sight may or may not be well developed according to the insect's mode of life; many that live underground are blind. In the adults of those that live in the open there are usually two kinds of eyes, situated on the head. On the top there is a group of three ocelli or simple eyes, each of which consists of a single lens at the surface of the cuticle with light-sensitive cells below it. In caterpillars there are similar ocelli on the sides of the head. They can detect movement and light intensity but little more, and their function is obscure in insects that have compound eyes in addition to ocelli.

Two compound eyes, which are the visual organs of most adult insects, are situated one on each side of the insect's head. They are much more complicated. The whole eye has an external transparent layer divided up into hexagonal facets. Each facet is the outermost part of a structure called an ommatidium. Each ommatidium makes its own image and sends its own signal to the brain, so that the insect sees a 'mosaic' made up of many small images. The picture is not sharp but the compound eye is good at detecting movement. The efficiency of this type of eye depends on its size and the number of ommatidia, and dragonflies, which hunt their prey by sight on the wing, have the largest and most highly developed eyes of all insects.

In night-flying insects a black pigment which isolates each ommatidium optically may be absent, allowing light to 'leak' from one ommatidium to the next. When there is no pigment the insect cannot see images so clearly but has better night vision. The nocturnal moths have it both ways: in the dark their ommatidia permit the passage of light, but do not do so in bright light.

Some insects certainly have colour vision. This has been demonstrated by experiments with bees in which transparent saucers are placed on an

arrangement of coloured squares. One saucer contains a sugar solution, the rest water. When the bees have found and become accustomed to the saucer with sugar, and to the colour it is on, the saucers are rearranged and the bees then visit saucers containing water on squares of that colour, ignoring the one with sugar if it is placed on a square of a different colour.

The visual sense of most insects is insensitive to the colour red but extends beyond violet into the ultra-violet part of the spectrum, so that the insects see ultraviolet – a colour we cannot see at all. Photography reveals that many flowers have ultra-violet patterns; these are invisible to us but are readily seen by bees and butterflies and, in fact, act as guides to the nectar hidden in the flowers. As the insects collect the nectar, they pollinate the flowers.

Hearing is not a dominant sense in insects, but in some groups communication by sound takes place between the sexes. Both sound-producing and hearing organs are situated in various parts of the body.

Insect eyes have evolved in a very different way from our own. They are made up of many small facets, called ommatidia. Each ommatidium has a lens, and the picture seen by an insect is a mosaic of the images picked up by all its little lenses; it is probably not a very sharp picture, but dragonflies – whose huge bulging eyes contain about 20000 ommatidia – can see well enough to capture insects on the wing.

Insect ears and voices

Many insects, both young and adult, can detect loud noises through the impact of the sound waves on tiny bristles situated on various parts of their bodies. Caterpillars react to sounds by flinching or throwing up their heads, but they have no organs specially adapted for hearing.

True hearing is confined to the adults of a few groups of insects, and in most cases is associated with sound production and concerned with recognition and signalling between males and females. The group in which this faculty is best developed is the Orthoptera, the grasshoppers and crickets.

In the crickets the forewings overlap to form a cover over the abdomen and a tooth-bearing rib on one of the veins of the right wing is rubbed over a ridge on the left wing. Grasshoppers produce their music with a different set of instruments. On the inner side of the largest joint (the femur) of each hind leg there is a row of minute, evenly spaced pegs which are stroked against the prominent veins of the forewings.

Organs of hearing or 'ears' are developed in both sexes of the Orthoptera. They consist of small stretched membranes or tympana, and in grasshoppers they are at the base of the abdomen on each side.

Male cicadas also sing to their mates, but they do not use stridulation to produce their song. Instead they have, at the base of the abdomen, a pair of stiff membranes called tymbals, which are rapidly snapped in and out by powerful muscles.

Many night-flying moths have ears on their bodies, which they use, not for communication with others of their species, but to provide protection from hunting bats. Bats use ultrasonic echo-sounding to locate both their surroundings and the flying insects on which they feed. The moths' ears, sensitive only to ultrasonic sound, enable them to take evasive action when a bat approaches. Some tiger moths (family Arctiidae) even produce ultrasonic pulses of their own to confuse the bats. There can be little doubt that this capacity, and the ears of other kinds of moths, have been evolved as a protection against this particular type of predator.

Insect numbers

Besides existing in greater variety than any other sort of animals, insects occur in enormous individual numbers. The inhabitants of a single large colony of ants or termites may number several millions, and the nests themselves, in the case of some common species, must amount to millions if counted over large areas. An abnormal increase in numbers or 'population explosion' sometimes occurs among insects, such as the big grasshoppers known as locusts. A large swarm of the desert locust (*Schistocerca gregaria*) may cover a hundred square kilometres (thirty-nine square miles). The total weight of such a swarm has been estimated at 70 000 tonnes, the weight of each insect being 2-3 grams. The largest populations that can be accurately estimated are of insects living in the soil.

Reproduction and growth

Sexual reproduction is the rule among insects, and the male usually goes in search of the female, guided most often by his sense of smell, though sight and hearing play a part in some insects. This is especially so when mating is preceded by ritual courtship. Males of the grayling butterfly (*Hipparchia semele*) fly up to intercept passing females; if ready to mate the female descends with the male to the ground. He takes up a position facing her, opening and closing his wings; at the climax of courtship he takes her antennae between them so that she can perceive the aroma of special scent-scales on his forewings. Only after this ritual has been completed will the female consent to mating.

Actual mating usually takes the form of tail-to-tail coupling, but there are variations. In most cases a capsule of sperm, called a spermatophore, is passed by the male into the female.

Reproduction without mating and fertilization of the egg occurs in some insects and is known as parthenogenesis. In many kinds of stick-insects males are either unknown or so rare that they play no significant part in reproduction, and the unmated females lay fertile eggs. In most aphids parthenogenesis prevails during the summer and leads to rapid multiplication, but in the autumn individuals of both sexes appear and mate, so fertilized eggs are laid. A strange kind of parthenogenesis is characteristic of the order Hymenoptera, including ants, bees and wasps. The female stores a quantity of sperm after mating. When she lays an egg she can release one or a few spermatozoa so that the egg is fertilized; the result is a female, in the case of the social species a queen or a worker. She can also withhold sperm altogether; this results in a male, and males are produced in no other way.

Nearly all insects lay eggs, and they are usually placed in a situation where the hatchling larvae can immediately find food. Butterflies and moths stick their eggs on to the leaves and twigs of the plants which will correctly nourish their caterpillars. The *Scolytus* beetles, including the notorious elm bark beetle, enter the space between bark and wood in pairs, making a small hole in the bark. After mating in a chamber gnawed out by both the beetles, the female makes an open channel under the bark and lays eggs in a row on each side of it. When the larvae hatch they burrow outwards, making characteristic patterns in the bark and wood. In a few insects, including the common earwig (*Forficula auricularia*), the mother broods her eggs and for a short time guards the newly hatched young.

Live birth, or viviparity, is occasionally encountered. The summer broods of aphids are born alive, and the female tsetse fly (*Glossina morsitans*) of Africa gives birth to fully grown larvae, which have been nourished in her body from the blood on which she feeds. In the course of her life of six months she produces about twelve offspring. Most insects lay eggs by hundreds, some by thousands, and the long-lived queens of some ants and termites produce offspring which are numbered in millions.

Among the higher insects moulting never takes place after sexual maturity is reached and, with the one exception of the mayflies, ends with full development of the wings.

As explained earlier, the higher insects are divided into two large groups by reference to the changes in form, or metamorphoses, that they undergo as they grow to maturity. In the more primitive group, the Exopterygota, the hatchling resembles the adult, but has no wings. A grasshopper is a typical exopterygote insect. In the course of growing up it moults five to eight times; after the

first or second ecdysis the wings appear as little pads on each side of the thorax. With each successive moult these become bigger, and after the last moult the insect can fly and is sexually mature.

The growth of the more highly developed group, the Endopterygota, is quite a different matter. The hatchling caterpillar of a butterfly, for instance, bears no resemblance to its winged and active parents. It looks more like a tiny worm, and continues to have this aspect until it reaches full size. During this period of voracious eating and periodical ecdysis the growth of the insect, in terms of size, is completed. The caterpillar then pupates: it suspends itself with silk and an internal process called histolysis begins, in which almost all of its muscles, and those of its internal organs which cannot serve the perfect (adult) insect, are destroyed by wandering blood cells called phagocytes, which digest and liquefy them. From the substance so produced comes the energy and material for building up the body, appendages and wings of the butterfly. At the same time a hard external shell is grown, and is revealed when the caterpillar sheds its skin for the last time. This determines the outward appearance of the pupa or chrysalis, an object totally different from the caterpillar and from the butterfly which forms inside it. When the butterfly breaks the shell and emerges, its wings are at first like little crumpled bags, but by pumping liquid into them and then withdrawing it they are expanded to full size, and in an hour or two are dry and stiff enough for the insect to fly.

The pupae of almost all insects are incapable of active movement. They are very diverse in form but fall into two types. In the *obtect* pupa of the butterfly the legs and antennae are cemented down on to the shell; in *exarate* pupae, such as those of bees and beetles, the appendages are free so that the pupa looks rather more like the adult insect.

Social insects

These are familiar and conspicuous because of the way they live in organized communities. The social insects comprise the ants and some of the bees and wasps, all of them members of the order Hymenoptera, and the termites (order Isoptera), which look and behave rather like ants but are only very distantly related to them.

The definition of a social insect is a species in which the young receive food and care from individuals that are not their parents. These individuals are commonly known as workers, and in the ants and social bees are all females. In the termites the workers are of both sexes and may include specialized fighters known as soldiers. Bumblebees are social insects on a small and simple scale and provide a good introduction to the subject.

When a queen bumblebee wakes from her winter hibernation she flies about feeding on nectar from flowers and seeking an abandoned mouse hole in which to make her nest. Having found one, she constructs a cell of wax in it, fills it with honey and pollen and lays eggs on it. She mated with a male the previous year and her eggs are fertilized. When they hatch into larvae she replenishes the food as it is consumed and eventually a number of small female bumblebees appear. They fly out to collect food, some of which is brought back to the nest to feed the queen and the new larvae which are their younger sisters. The queen may do a bit more foraging, but her main business is to stay at home and lay more and more fertilized eggs from which more female workers are produced. These workers never mate and seldom lay eggs, and around midsummer there may be one or two hundred of them. Their job is to bring up as many of their sisters to maturity as possible, and many of them die in the course of their work. In the autumn the old queen lays eggs whose larvae are given special feeding and other treatment so that they grow large and produce queens; she also lays unfertilized eggs which result in males (drones). Queens and drones meet outside the nest and mate and the young queens go into hibernation. The old queen and the remaining workers die, and so do all the young males.

This is the pattern for most social bees and wasps in temperate regions. The honeybee and most ants differ in that the whole colony hibernates and renews activity in the spring. New colonies are established by young queens and males flying in swarms out of the nest, or, in the honeybee, single queens accompanied by workers. Bees build their nest and cells for the young and for storing honey out of wax; social wasps use paper made of wood pulp. Honeybee colonies, and those of some wasps, may contain thousands of workers. Most ants' nests consist of galleries and chambers in the soil and the young are not reared in separate cells. Ant workers are always wingless.

Termites, which are mainly tropical insects, are related to cockroaches, but have come in the course of evolution to lead an ant-like existence. They differ from ants in having a life history without larval and pupal stages; the young which hatch from the eggs are just tiny termites. They do not have the peculiar means of sex determination seen in the Hymenoptera; their workers are both male and female, and a 'king' and a 'queen' termite live together in the nest. Some termites feed on dead wood and are serious pests of structural timber. Others build huge nests of hardened earth, 5-6m (16-20ft) high and inhabited by millions of workers.

Feeding

The feeding of insects can be described conveniently under four headings. There are those that bite and chew solid food, and those that take up only liquids; and both these groups include herbivores and carnivores. Scavengers are feeders on organic material that is already dead and may be decomposed.

Locusts and caterpillars are good examples of insects that chew vegetable food, in both cases leaves and other herbage. It is bitten off by the mandibles, manipulated and packed into the mouth by the maxillae, then swallowed and digested. Insects with this mode of feeding often do serious damage to agricultural crops. The myriad insects of the soil – those that are not carnivores – subsist on vegetable matter in various stages of decay and to a great extent on the fungi that promote decay. The same is true of such feeders on dead wood

Insect parasites

There are many insects which are parasites in the ordinary sense of the term. Fleas and lice live and feed on the bodies of various animals and, provided they are not infected with disease, they do their host little harm. The larvae of some flies are internal parasites of cattle; they may injure the host to some extent, but it is in their own interest to keep it alive.

Insect parasites that afflict other insects are very numerous, and the parasite-host relationship is different. If your cabbages are attacked by the caterpillars of white butterflies, a search of nearby walls and fences in late summer may reveal pupae suspended by silk threads to pass the winter, and sometimes caterpillars preparing to pupate as well. Some of these, however, fail to turn into pupae; instead they remain on the fence and sooner or later a crowd of little grubs appear all round the caterpillar and themselves pupate in tiny yellow cocoons. They have eaten their way out of the caterpillar, leaving only its shrivelled skin, after passing their larval lives feeding and growing inside it. At an earlier stage in the caterpillar's life their mother, a tiny wasp called *Apanteles glomeratus*, laid her eggs in its body, and from that moment it was doomed never to

become a butterfly, living instead with an ever-growing horde of little wasp larvae feeding on its blood and fat and only attacking its vital organs and killing it at the last moment before it pupates. This type of parasite, which inevitably kills its host before either is mature, is often called a parasitoid.

Almost all species of butterflies and moths are afflicted by parasitoids, which are by far their most serious enemies. The mature insects – various ichneumon wasps and also bristly flies called tachinids – often turn up in collectors' breeding cages. Here they are generally unwelcome, but parasitoids are of great value in the biological control of insect pests. When a pest like the cabbage-white butterfly (*Pieris brassica*) is accidentally introduced to a country where it did not previously exist, it is usually without its normal parasitoid enemies. Cabbage-whites reached New Zealand in 1930 and multiplied disastrously. Another parasitoid of these butterflies, *Pteromalus puparum*, (also a small wasp), was taken to New Zealand and released and the butterflies were quickly reduced to the status of a minor nuisance. Numerous introductions of this kind have been made to control pests all over the world.

two encounters are enough to persuade them that burnet moths are better left alone. The moths' bright coloration serves to make them unmistakeable. In this way a few individuals are sacrificed for the benefit of the species. Examples of this sort of warning coloration are numerous among insects. The shield bugs (family Pentatomidae) are almost all evil-smelling and, no doubt, ill-tasting creatures, and many of them have startlingly bright colours.

The monarch butterfly (*Danaus plexippus*) is a native of northern and central America, and has a distinctive wing pattern of tawny brown, black and white. It belongs to a genus whose poisonous food-plants render the insects poisonous in all their stages. Experiments with aviary birds have shown that an inexperienced bird will attack and eat a monarch, and is then usually violently sick. The experience is unpleasant enough to dissuade it from ever attacking a monarch again. In the same region there exists another butterfly, the viceroy (*Limenitis archippus*), not related to the monarch but resembling it in size and coloration. Experiments with birds show that this species is palatable and wholesome, and they readily attack and eat viceroys. But a bird that has experienced the unpleasant effects of eating a monarch always refuses a viceroy. There can be no doubt that the edible species derives benefit in the wild from this resemblance. This is an example of the adaptation known as mimicry, and it is widespread among insects.

How insects are grouped
Apterygota
Only one group of apterygotes is abundant, the springtails or Collembola, which teem in the soil and leaf litter and can generally be seen hopping about when a log is turned over in a garden or in woodland. They are all very small and most of them can jump, using a forked appendage underneath the body. They are land-living arthropods with three pairs of legs, but apart from this they have little in common with true insects, and are sometimes put in a class of their own.

The little silverfish (*Lepisma saccharina*) of our kitchen cupboards represents another apterygote order, the Thysanura, which can be regarded as very primitive true insects. The silverfish seems to have become a purely domesticated insect, since it is not known to live in the wild.

Exopterygota
Mayflies
(order Ephemeroptera)
Mayflies pass their early stages in water, where they may live for two or three years, but the winged adults have very short lives. They are unique among insects in having one ecdysis or moult after the wings are developed.

Dragonflies and damselflies
(order Odonata)
These also live in water until they become adult, and are also considered to be primitive insects. Damselflies differ from dragonflies in being more slender, usually smaller and having the fore- and hind wings similar in shape; in dragonflies the hind wings are broader. They are predators, both in their aquatic early stages and as winged adults. Dragonflies possess powers of sight and of flight superior to those of most other insects.

Cockroaches (order Blattodea)
These are best known as domestic pests and they live in the wild mainly

in hot countries. All the species that infest houses in temperate climates are invaders from warmer regions. The common cockroach (*Blatta orientalis*) is found in human dwellings all over the world; the much larger American cockroach (*Periplaneta americana*) is almost as widely distributed. Both species probably originated in northern Africa, '*americana*' being a misnomer. Most species are completely omnivorous.

Mantises (order Mantodea)
Related to cockroaches, these were formerly included with them in the order Dictyoptera. Both groups have leathery forewings and lay their eggs in capsules. The mantises are inhabitants of warm climates and all species are predators. Their forelegs are adapted for grasping and mantises, well-camouflaged, wait for other insects to come within reach. The common European mantis (*Mantis religiosa*) is often kept in captivity and can be fed on flies and moths.

Termites (order Isoptera)
Termites are highly developed as social insects, somewhat resembling ants but related to cockroaches. Like ants, they live in large nests or

Above: Termites are primitive insects quite unrelated to ants, bees and wasps, although their social behaviour is highly developed. They live communally in large nests, like this one built of earth in Nigeria.

Opposite: Mole crickets feed underground on grubs and roots. They are relatives of grasshoppers, and have powerful front legs modified for digging. Most of the body and legs are covered with fine velvety 'fur'.

colonies in which most of the inhabitants are sterile workers, with one or more 'queens' laying eggs to maintain the population. Some kinds of termites feed on dead wood and are serious pests of structural timber. Some of the African and Australian Termitidae construct enormous above-ground nests of earth and sand. Those of the Australian *Nasutitermes triodiae* may be over 8 m (26 ft) high. The nests of the Australian compass termite (*Ornitermes meridionalis*) are flattened from side to side and the narrow ends always point north and south.

Stoneflies (order Plecoptera)
Members of this order are seldom seen far away from the water in which they pass their early stages. The adults are soft-bodied weakly flying insects. The young breathe by means of gills and may live for as long as four years before they leave the water.

Earwigs (order Dermaptera)
Earwigs are well known from a few common species. They have rather ineffective pincers at the hind end of the body, and the females guard the eggs and young with great devotion.

Stick-insects and leaf-insects (order Phasmida)
These are large, mainly tropical, insects noted for their remarkable camouflage among twigs and leaves. They can easily be kept in captivity in colder climates, the so-called laboratory stick-insect (*Carausius morosus*) being the usual species. It is easily fed on privet leaves and almost all individuals are females which lay fertile eggs without mating; males are extremely rare.

Grasshoppers and crickets (order Orthoptera)
These are a large, widely distributed order characterized by their ability to jump and to sing. The hind legs are usually enlarged for jumping, and their singing is performed by stridulation (the scraping of a hard ridge on one part of the body over a series of closely set pegs or teeth on another part). Some kinds of large grasshoppers may multiply to form huge destructive swarms and are known as locusts. The migratory locust (*Locusta migratoria*) and the desert locust (*Schistocerca gregaria*) of Africa and Asia are probably the most damaging species.

Lice (order Anoplura)
Lice are all small, wingless, blood-sucking parasites of mammals. Most of them are specific to a particular host, and one, *Pediculus humanus*, is confined to humans.

Bugs (order Hemiptera)
The name is confined by entomologists to this one order. The Hemiptera are very diverse, but piercing and sucking mouthparts are similarly developed in all of them. They are divided into two sub-orders: the Heteroptera (bed-bug, shield-bugs and water-boatmen); and the Homoptera (aphids and cicadas).

Above: Rhinoceros beetles derive their name from the huge head appendage found on the males. The reason for the head appendage is not known; many other beetles of the same family have similarly strange growths.

Opposite: Many hoverflies mimic wasps and bees as a form of protection. The majority are useful to the gardener and farmer as the adults live on plants, pollinating them in the process, and the larvae feed on aphids.

Most bugs live on the sap of plants but some are preadtors or parasites. They may or may not have wings. The aquatic water-skaters and water-boatmen are familiar members of the Heteroptera. Some of the Homoptera, particularly the aphids, are serious pests. The black bean-aphid (*Aphis fabae*) is known to every vegetable gardener, and *Myzus persicae* spreads virus diseases in a variety of field crops.

Endopterygota
Neuropterans
(order Neuroptera)
These insects have no comprehensive common name, but the delicate lacewings are familiar members of the order. All neuropterans have predatory larvae and those of the lacewings prey on aphids or greenfly.

Scorpion-flies
(order Mecoptera)
This is a small order, but some of them are common day-flying insects. They have dark-spotted wings and the males have up-turned tails, recalling the sting of a scorpion.

Caddis-flies
(order Trichoptera)
Caddis-flies are best known from their larvae which live in ponds and streams and build protective cases of sand grains or pieces of plant stems around themselves. The adult insects fly by night and are rather like moths, but their wings are covered with short fine hairs.

Butterflies and moths
(order Lepidoptera)
These are too well known to need description. Their wings are covered with minute coloured scales that determine the patterns on them. Most of them have a long proboscis that is used for taking nectar from flowers and is curled up like a watch-spring when not in use. The larvae are caterpillars and most of them feed on the leaves of plants. Exceptions to this rule include the larvae of the clothes moth (*Tineola bisselliella*), which feeds on woollen fabrics, and that of the goat moth (*Cossus cossus*) which eats wood and takes three years to complete its growth.

Flies (order Diptera)
Flies are a very distinct group in which only the front pair of wings is developed, the hind wings being represented by small club-shaped balancing organs called halteres.

central disc, unlike those of the starfishes. The tube feet are also without suckers. Brittlestars get their name from the way that the arms snap off. If this happens the lost arm is replaced. Brittlestars feed either by collecting tiny edible particles on their arms as they weave them about, or they can tear off pieces of seaweed or dead flesh.

Starfishes (class Asteroidea)

Starfishes are most easily recognized, since they have (usually) five well-developed legs radiating from the centre of the body. The tube feet are on the underside of the arms, and the mouth is also underneath, positioned in the centre of the body. Some starfishes are brightly coloured blue or scarlet.

They can detect food by smell and crawl towards it at a surprisingly fast rate. Some starfishes feed on minute particles but most prey on live animals, forcing open shellfishes, or chewing sponges. They can be a pest in commercial oyster and mussel beds. The crown of thorns starfish (*Acanthaster planci*) causes great damage to tropical coral reefs be-

cause it consumes the polyps which create the reef.

Like other echinoderms, starfishes lay millions of eggs which are usually shed into the sea where they are fertilized. The larva spends some time floating in the currents before settling and turning into an adult. Some polar species, however, lay a few, yolky eggs which they brood in the body and hatch as young starfishes.

Sea urchins (class Echinoidea)

The sea urchins, sand dollars and sea potatoes have globular or flat bodies enclosed by a shell of closely fitting plates, and covered by spines. They can be thought of as starfishes with their arms bent upwards and with the intervening spaces filled in. Some sea urchins, like the heart urchin (genus *Echinocardium*) burrow in sand and mud. The heart urchin lives in a burrow, keeping a vertical shaft open to supply water for breathing while it picks edible particles from the sand around it. Other sea urchins burrow into rock, using their spines to scrape the surface, and one Californian species

manages to bore holes in steel piers. Although the spines are useful in defence, they are quite mobile and, together with the tube feet, enable sea-urchins to climb up rocks and jetties.

Sea cucumbers (class Holothuroidea)

The sea cucumbers – together with the sea gherkins – are elongated, sausage-like echinoderms. The tube feet around the mouth have become sticky tentacles. The pedicellaria and spines are either lost, or are reduced to small ossicles embedded in the skin that give a rough leathery feel. When attacked holothurians can discharge their entire stomach together with its contents to help them escape. The stomach and intestine are regenerated later. An alternative defence is to squirt sticky threads. Sea cucumbers make a home for several animals which live inside their mouths. Some shellfishes live inside sea cucumbers and others ride on their backs. Pearlfishes, slender-bodied almost transparent fishes, regularly live inside the bodies of sea cucumbers, sea stars or sea urchins, emerging at night to feed.

Above: The spiny sunstar feeds on other starfishes in northern waters. It may have up to fifteen arms.

Right: Sea urchins are well protected within a spiny shell called the test. It is not really on the outside of the animal, but is covered with a thin layer of living tissue, and the spines can be moved, and are used for getting around. Some sea urchins are considered a delicacy, either raw or cooked, particularly when the shell is full of ripe eggs.

Opposite: This Mediterranean starfish grows to 25cm (10in) in diameter. It has thick, long arms; other species may be more delicate and may have much shorter arms.

to the Mississippi river, migrates downstream into the larger rivers and lakes to feed, and thus spends all its life in fresh water.

Hagfishes are all marine animals. There are about thirty species known, with several previously unknown species having been found in deep water in the last twenty years. As a group, they are worldwide in distribution.

The eyes of hagfishes are minute and covered by skin, and they have fleshy barbels around the slit-like mouth. They have sets of sharply pointed teeth within their mouths which are moved outwards when they feed. Much of their food appears to be composed of dead animals found on the seabed, and they are frequently captured in traps baited with strong-smelling fish, although their food also consists of shrimps and marine worms. The Atlantic hagfish (*Myxine glutinosa*), is well known as a pest attacking fishes caught on the hooks of longlines. The hagfish attacks the captured fish using its sharp teeth to bore into its prey, usually entering through the tender gill region. Once within its prey it feeds on the body organs and then the flesh.

The exceptionally slimy skin of the hagfish is probably a means of lubricating the passage of the hagfish's body into the hole bored in its prey, but it may also be a means of keeping competing scavengers like whelks and certain crustaceans away. The slime is produced by a line of special pores running along the underside of the body. This slime can be produced in great abundance: a healthy hagfish placed in a bucket of water will turn the water into a sticky mass only a little thinner than wallpaper paste within two hours.

Sharks and rays (class Chondrichthyes)

The sharks and rays – of which there are about 625 living species – are primitive representatives of the superclass Gnathostomata – the animals with jaws (to distinguish them from the lampreys which have no jaws). This superclass comprises two major groups: animals with fins – fishes excluding the lampreys and hagfishes; and animals with limbs – the amphibians, reptiles, birds and mammals. So the sharks are the living representatives of the evolutionarily most primitive of the jawed

animals. Sharks belong to the class Chondrichthyes – the cartilaginous fishes.

Sharks are mostly long-bodied animals with well-developed fins, and five to seven gill slits on each side of the head. Their bodies are covered with rather small scales, which are like fine teeth and are rough to the touch. Their skeletons are composed of cartilage, although some parts of it are reinforced with a chalky substance giving it the superficial appearance of bone. They have numerous rows of teeth in their jaws, which are regularly replaced by new teeth formed on the inner surface as the outer teeth wear and are shed.

The sharks are some of the most exciting of living fishes and they include the largest of all fishes, the whale shark (*Rhincodon typus*), which grows to 18m (60ft) in length and to a weight of 20 tonnes. The whale shark is a surface-living shark of tropical oceans, but the second largest shark lives in the temperate waters of the world. The basking shark (*Cetorhinus maximus*) is common in the North Atlantic off both the North American and European coasts. It also occurs in the Southern Hemisphere – but less is known of its

Above: The dusky shark shows the characteristic torpedo-shaped body of the hunter. Members of this family, the requiem sharks, bear live young, as do a number of other sharks.

Opposite: Fishes are supreme rulers of the sea. Many species have changed little, if at all, over millions of years.

Man-eating sharks
Several kinds of shark are known to attack man, and possibly the most dangerous is the great white shark (*Carcharodon carcharias*), a worldwide inhabitant of tropical and warm-temperate seas. It grows to a length of at least 6·4m (21ft), and has massive triangular, serrated-edged teeth. At this size, and with these teeth, it can shear through an arm or leg with ease. Most attacks have been on swimmers or surfboarders, and occasionally small boats have been attacked. The tiger shark (*Galeocerdo cuvier*), hammerhead sharks and several requiem sharks, like the bull shark (*Carcharhinus leucas*), are also man-eaters. Attacks on humans are virtually unknown in temperate seas; the water has to be warm for these sharks to be aggressive.

occurrence there. Both giants of the shark world are harmless feeders on plankton – the minute crustaceans, shellfish larvae, and eggs and larvae of young fishes, that float near the surface of the sea – and they have special filtering mechanisms in their throats to capture this food.

All sharks are predators on other animals. Many eat fishes and squids, but a few, like the smooth hounds, and the leopard shark (*Triakis semi-fasciata*) of the Pacific coast of North America, have flattened teeth in their jaws. These teeth are well adapted to crushing the hard shells of crabs, and even some molluscs, on which these sharks feed.

Male sharks all have structures called claspers on the inner sides of their pelvic fins which are used to convey sperm to the female's cloaca when breeding. Fertilization of the female's eggs is thus internal, and many sharks give birth to fully formed young. In a few species, for instance the blue shark (*Prionace glauca*), the developing embryo's yolk-sac forms a placenta which is in contact with the mother's uterine wall, the pup being nourished in this

way. Most live-bearing sharks are ovoviviparous, however, which means the young develop inside the mother without any physiological connection with her, and are nourished by the yolk of the egg. Other shark lay eggs in protective cases, among them the small dogfishes, and catsharks.

Rays and skates have many of the features of sharks, among them the cartilaginous skeleton, numerous and constantly replaced teeth in the jaws, and in most the rough skin formed from numerous tooth-like scales. However, they almost all have five gill openings which are placed on the underside of the head, and their pectoral fins are greatly enlarged and attached to the front of the head. They are all flattened from top to bottom. As a result most rays and skates appear roughly diamond shaped, and swim by movements of the pectoral fins, not by flexing the body from side to side as other fishes do. Their flattened bodies and most of their other distinctive features are a result of taking to a life on the seabed. Most skates and many rays are entirely bottom-living, their dor-

Thornback rays are found around European coasts, from the Black Sea to the Baltic. Fairly small members of the skate family, their main defence consists of a row of sharp spines along the midline of the back and tail – painful for a swimmer treading on one as it lies unseen on the seabed.

sal coloration matching the seabed, and their diets comprising mainly bottom-living animals.

Other bottom-living rays include the torpedos or electric rays, a fascinating group of about thirty-five species, some of which are blind, and some with either minute eyes as in *Narke impennis* of the Bay of Bengal, or with eyes covered with thick skin, like the two species of New Zealand *Typhlonarke*. All these have powerful electric organs in the head region. The Atlantic torpedo (*Torpedo nobiliana*) which grows to 1·8m (6ft) in length can produce up to 200 volts, and if handled can give a severe electric shock.

The stingrays, like the Indo-Pacific stingray (*Dasyatis brevicaudata*), grow even larger, to 4·3m (14ft) in length and to a weight of 340kg (750lb). It occurs on the Australian coast and in the Pacific islands. It has a very long tail, with one, sometimes two, barbed dagger-like spines on the back of the tail about one-third of the way down. Its habit is to lie partly buried in sand, and in shallow water it presents a serious threat to bathers should they step on it, for it brings its tail up over its back and stabs upwards with its venomous spine.

By contrast to the bottom-living stingrays, their relatives the eagle rays and manta rays are more often seen in mid-water or near the surface 'flying' through the water by beating their long pectoral fins with bird-like grace. The eagle rays also have venom spines in their tails. They have broad flattened teeth, for they feed on hard-shelled crustaceans and molluscs, and can become a pest on clam and oyster beds. Mantas, which are the giants among rays – attaining a width of 6·7m (22ft) and a weight of at least 1360kg (3000lb) – feed on small schooling fishes and plankton.

Bony fishes (class Osteichthyes)

The great majority of fishes belong to the second major class of fishes, the class Osteichthyes or bony fishes. They all have skeletons which are at least partly composed of true bone. The body shape varies enormously, as might be expected when one considers that there are some 18 000 species swimming in the lakes, rivers and oceans of the world.

The bony fishes are divided into several major groups. Among the

smaller groups are the lungfishes (subclass Dipneusti) of South America, Australia and Africa, all distinguished by having a sac-like structure known as a swim bladder which is used as an air-breathing organ. They live in water which with seasonal droughts becomes deficient in oxygen, or may even dry up completely, and their ability to breathe air permits survival in these conditions.

An even smaller group, in terms of number of species are the tassel-fins (subclass Crossopterygii) of which there is only one living representative, the coelacanth (*Latimeria chalumnae*). This species, like the lungfishes, has many features in common with fossil fishes which lived in the Devonian and Cretaceous periods (between 300 and 100 million years ago), and they could all be regarded as 'living fossils'. One of the more striking features of the coelacanth is that most of the fins are set on short, stubby limbs, while the tail fin is broad and has a distinct central lobe. The most remarkable point about the coelacanth is that although its relatives were well

The longnose gar of the southern United States lives in fresh water. Gars differ from typical fishes in a number of ways. Their vertebrae have ball-and-socket joints, their tail skeleton curves upwards like that of a sturgeon, and they have heavy diamond-shaped scales that do not overlap like typical fish scales.

Sea perches, or snappers, swim in shoals around coral reefs. Blue-striped snappers swim in particularly dense shoals during the day, deriving protection from this habit. At night, they disperse to feed on crustaceans.

known as fossils, the capture of a living specimen off South Africa in 1938 proved that in fact all the tassel-fins were not extinct. Since then about 100 more coelacanths have been caught.

Further small groups of fishes (belonging to the subclass Brachi-opterygii) which show many primitive features are the birchirs and the reedfish (*Calamoichthys calabaricus*), of which there are eleven species, all living in fresh water in Africa. They are rather slender, eel-like fishes with thick, shiny scales and a series of spines on the back with short rays

attached to them – they look a little like miniature flag staffs with flags flying.

The sturgeons belong to yet another subclass (Actinopterygii) the ray-finned fishes, of which there are around twenty-five living types widely distributed in the Northern Hemisphere, with most species living in eastern Europe and North America. They are fascinating animals one of which, the beluga (*Huso huso*), grows to 4·8m (16ft) in length and a weight of 1½ tonnes. As they all breed in fresh water they should be regarded as the largest freshwater fishes. Many of them are migratory, moving from river spawning grounds to the sea to feed.

Many of the more primitive bony fishes are the living representatives of fish groups which thrived hundreds of millions of years ago. The living species still show features which can also be distinguished in the fossilized remains. Some of the features of fossil fishes include a spiral section of the intestine (a feature also of sharks, skates, and rays), and heavy, shiny hard scales (ganoid scales). Although the coelacanth is the best-known 'living fossil' fish, if live bichirs, lungfishes, or sturgeons were suddenly discovered having hitherto been unknown, they would deserve to be called 'living fossils' also.

In contrast to all these small groups of fishes with primitive features the group known as the teleosts contains approximately 18 000 species, and more are recognized every year. They include the cods (family Gadidae), salmons (family Salmonidae), herrings (family Clupeidae), and the tunas (family Scombridae), which form some of the major food-fishes of the world. They also include the remarkably shaped box fishes (family Ostraciontidae), seahorses and pipefishes (family Syngnathidae), and the frogfishes (family Antennariidae), which as their name suggests look more like frogs than fishes.

Teleosts lead far more complex lives than their more primitive relatives. Their brains are larger and more developed. They make noises, and can hear, many can see in colour, many swim in shoals or schools, and many show interesting patterns of behaviour in courtship, mimicry, and in caring for their eggs and young. If there is such an animal as a thinking fish, it is bound to be a teleost.

How fishes swim

With so many marvellous adaptations of body form it is not surprising that there are numerous ways of getting around in the fish world. The basic method of swimming is by moving the tail-end of the body from side to side, so that the tail fin can exert pressure on the water, which results in driving the fish's body forwards.

The power for these tail movements comes from masses of muscle blocks, arranged in a 'W' shape,

running down each side of the body, and linking up with the vertebrae of the backbone. These muscle blocks are composed of thousands of shorter muscle fibres, each able to stretch and contract. A swimming fish therefore depends on the muscle blocks, all working in sequence, to pull its backbone first to one side then the other. This results in the regular gentle flexing of the tail which pushes the fish through the water. Close examination of the muscle blocks shows that along the middle of the side the muscle is dark in colour – this is known as the red muscle and

Seahorses swim in an upright position, which makes the pursuit of food difficult. Instead of chasing their prey, seahorses suck in small passing plankton with a powerful suction jet. Another unusual habit is the way in which the male seahorse incubates eggs in a special brood pouch under his tail.

its composition is such that it provides the steady swimming power; the vast mass of white muscle beneath it is 'sprinting' muscle – used mainly when the fish needs to swim fast. Fishes like mackerel, which are constantly swimming, have larger layers of red muscle than fishes like the pike (*Esox lucius*) which lie still for most of their lives but need to dash quickly to catch their prey.

While the strong swimmers have well-developed tail fins, others get about using other methods. Eels, for example, have very small tail fins, but they have very long, thin bodies. They therefore swim by making side-to-side curves of the body, so that they literally wriggle through the water. But the basic mechanism is the same as they, too, have muscle blocks each attached to its own vertebra.

Another means of swimming is seen in the skates, which usually lie inactive in the seabed partially buried in sand. However, when they need to swim they create a wave motion in their large pectoral fins which thrusts them through the water in a slow but nevertheless effective manner. The development of pectoral fins is taken further in the eagle rays and mantas, which live nearer the sea's surface than the skates, beat their pectoral fins up and down and progress by a bird-like 'flight' through the water.

Wave motion of the body or fins provides many other fishes with their motive power. Sea horses and pipefishes (which have relatively rigid bodies) swim in a slow and rather stately fashion by undulation of their dorsal fins. Oceanic trigger fishes, beat their dorsal and anal fins from side to side both at the same time, and achieve surprising mobility in doing so.

Of course, some fishes have no need to expend much energy swimming as they live in places where for much of their lives they need only move gently. Wrasses (family Labridae) live among seaweed or coral and can move by merely working their pectoral fins, which are situated at the sides of their body. Box fishes (family Ostraciontidae) which are protected by their heavy box-like armour, swim by paddling their dorsal, anal and tail fins from side to side.

Of the fins the dorsal fin (one or more are placed on the back) and the anal fin (one or two are placed beneath the tail) are employed as keels to keep the body upright while swimming. Both the pectoral fins (behind the head) and the pelvic fins (on the underside in front of the vent) act as keels also, but their main function is to help the fish make upwards or downwards movements. In the sharks, where the pectoral fins are usually held outstretched, they serve to provide an automatic hydrofoil to the front end of the fish, thus countering the downward tilt resulting from the high upper lobe of the tail fin.

Scales

Most fishes have scales; indeed in many they are a particularly noticeable feature. In the tarpon (*Tarpon atlanticus*) the scales are huge, each one in a large fish being the size of a saucer – but then the tarpon is a big fish growing to 2·4m (8ft) in length. Large size in a fish does not necessarily mean that its scales will be big, however. The Atlantic halibut (*Hippoglossus hippoglossus*), which also grows to a maximum length of 2·4m (8ft) has quite small scales, and nearly 200 rows of scales from head to tail.

There are three main kinds of scales in fishes. Sharks have small skin teeth called dermal denticles, with an enamel-like covering over the basic dentine and a pulp cavity (much like the teeth of vertebrates). Each scale has a broad base which lies in the skin, so that the toothed end is free and backward pointing.

Ganoid scales have a different structure. The most obvious feature is that they are relatively large, very hard, shiny, and usually have a regular rhomboid shape. They are characteristic of several primitive fishes, among them the bichirs and the North American garpikes. They form a very hard, protective covering.

Those bony fishes which have scales – and that includes most of them – possess what are known as bony-ridge scales – so-called because the outer surface is covered with ridges alternating with valley-like dips. There are two basic types of bony-ridge scale: cycloid scales, which are usually thin and rather rounded, as in herring, salmon, and minnows; and ctenoid scales which are often thicker, more rectangular and have fine teeth at one end. The basses and the perch (*Perca fluviatilis*) are examples, and on these

Scales tell a fish's age

Bony-ridged scales increase in size as the fish grows, but the number of scales remains the same. So a fish will have the same number of scales when it is 45cm (1½ft) long as it had when it was 5cm (2in), they will just be larger. However, as there is more food available for the fish during spring and summer it grows faster then than it does in winter when food is scarce. This variation is shown in the scales; the ridges that form during winter are fewer and closer together than those that form when growth is fast. As a result, examination of a fish's scale under magnification can tell how many winters the fish has lived through, and in that way tell how old it is. Reading the age of fishes is an important fisheries management exercise, as from it can be established whether the fishes are growing well. Scale readings have shown that the roach (*Rutilus rutilus*) can grow to be thirteen years old and the chub (*Leuciscus cephalus*) can live until it is about twenty-five years.

fishes you can feel the roughness of the edge of the scales.

Scales form a tough outer coat to the body, which with one overlapping the other forms a double thickness of armour but nevertheless allows the body to be very flexible.

Senses

The world of fishes is a highly sensory one involving all the senses that we possess, as well as some which cannot be experienced by man.

Almost all fishes have two pairs of nostrils, usually seen as two small holes on the snout. Very often one pair opens at the end of a short tube,

and the other pair opens level with the skin in front of the eye. They are not used for breathing, but are purely a means of smelling the water. Some fishes depend on their sense of smell more than others, and many of the more sensitive species are nocturnal or twilight hunters. Two particularly well-known species are the freshwater eel, which finds much of its food in the dark, and the salmon (*Salmo salar*), which can detect the river of its origin while still migrating at sea. In both cases these fishes are detecting smells which only have a concentration of two or three molecules within the olfactory organ at any one time.

The pike is a stealthy hunter. It lurks, camouflaged among vegetation, watching for likely prey with its large forward-facing eyes. When it sees a suitable victim, it can dart out like an arrow to snatch it in a large mouth full of backward-pointing teeth. Pike can grow to a weight of over 20kg (44lb).

Fishes which do not rely heavily on their sense of smell for feeding or navigating often have well-developed eyes. The trout (*Salmo trutta*) is a good example, although it is also sensitive to smells. The lens in each eye is spherical, and can be moved within the eye to some extent to permit changes in focus. The trout has good forward vision, and can also see movements and light and shade at the sides. Thus, the trout is well equipped to see and take a midge settled on the surface of the steam, but is at the same time watching for the movement of a predator attacking from the side. Study of the structure of the retina at the back of the eye shows that many fishes have the necessary equipment to see in colour. It would indeed be rather surprising if such colourful animals as coral reef fishes were unable to see in colour, as one of the functions of bright coloration is to be able to recognize and be seen by fishes of the same species.

The degree to which fishes can hear is difficult to establish without elaborate experiments. However, by using a special microphone under water it can be shown that many fishes make a variety of sounds, and the sea is far from the 'silent world' it was once labelled. The ability to make sounds is confined to bony fishes – although sharks and rays make involuntary sounds while eating – and there is no point in making sounds unless other related fishes can hear them. The drums (family Sciaenidae), which live near the bottom in many tropical seas and river mouths, are so called for the noises they produce.

The sense of taste in all fishes is highly developed. The small taste cells, which in man are confined to the mouth, are in fishes scattered around the mouth, lips, barbels, and even on some fins. Gurnards or sea-robins (family Triglidae) have taste cells on the extended finger-like rays of the pectoral fin which they use to probe the seabed for buried food (these fishes are also great sound producers). Many cod fishes (family Gadidae) have chin barbels which are also well equipped with taste cells, and some of the rocklings have as many as five sensitive barbels around their mouths.

Closely linked with the sense of taste is the lateral line system, a line of small openings down the side of the fish, but continuing over the head and jaws in many species. The small openings are merely pores leading from a canal under the skin, and along this canal there are sensitive cells which detect changes in the pressure of water surrounding the fish. This gives a fish an early warning of an oncoming predator, and also helps it avoid obstacles in the dark.

Habitats

Fresh water

Fishes that live in fresh water have to overcome problems that rarely affect marine fishes. Rivers and lakes are far more likely to suffer changes in temperature, level, and dissolved oxygen than marine habitats, and lakes may even dry up completely in drought conditions.

The stresses of life in fresh water result in numerous patterns of interesting behaviour and life history. Protection of eggs and young is well developed in freshwater fishes. This varies from the straightforward habit of live bearing, in which the female carries the eggs in her body while they develop and then gives birth to fully formed young fishes, to elaborate means of keeping the eggs in a favourable environment and giving them protection. One of the best-known groups of live-bearers are the members of the family Poeciliidae, of which numerous aquarium species are familiar, among them the guppy (*Poecilia reticulata*).

Killifishes are close relatives of the live-bearers but some of them have solved the problem of survival of the species in a hostile environment in a different way. Several lyretail species, found on the coastal plains of west Africa, live in marshy pools and ditches which dry up completely in the dry season. These lyretails, however, lay eggs which are buried in the bottom mud, and which will survive desiccation for weeks but hatch as soon as the rains return to refill their habitat with water.

Other fishes such as some tilapias (family Cichlidae) protect their eggs, and in some cases their young as well, by one of the parents taking them into its mouth. As well as providing physical protection from predators it results in the eggs being surrounded by water of good quality which the parents can select. Similar considerations produce the fascinating bubble-nests of the Siamese fighting

fish (*Betta splendens*). These fishes live in ponds, drainage channels, and the back-waters of sluggish rivers in Thailand, which often become low in oxygen. The male fighting fish makes a nest of bubbles with a rather sticky mucous secretion from his throat, and into this floating nest the female lays her eggs, and any that fall out are caught by the parents and spat back into the next. In this way the eggs, and in time the very young, are kept close to the well-oxygenated surface of the water. They are, of course, also easier to protect from any predators.

Adaptations to different foods are another feature of freshwater fishes, and this leads to many interesting behaviour patterns. Thus, the archer fish (*Toxotes jaculator*) which lives in the estuaries and lowland rivers of Southeast Asia and northern Australia, feeds on insects and their larvae, as well as spiders, which are found on overhanging vegetation. It catches these animals by knocking them into the water by spitting blobs of water at them from at least 1m (3¼ft) away. After a few ranging shots, targets 3m (10ft) away can be reached with considerable accuracy. It is a relatively small fish, only about 23cm (9in) in length, but it has large eyes, and obviously good forward vision.

Several vegetarian fishes are found in the Amazon basin in South America, among them *Triportheus elongatus* which grows to about 25cm (10in) and lives near the surface. Its teeth are strong, rather pointed with several cusps. About two-thirds of its food is composed of fleshy fruits from the forest trees, and it also eats quantities of flowers in season. Recent studies of the Amazon forests and the fishes that live in its rivers have shown that there is a large community of fishes dependent on the trees.

One interesting result of this study has been the discovery that several of the piranhas of the Amazon also eat large quantities of fruit. Even the piranha preta (*Serrasalmus rhombeus*) which grows to a length of 40cm (16in), and is often called the black piranha because of its dark colour, eats substantial amounts of fruit. Its triangular and razor-sharp teeth can shear through the husks of the fruits with no effort, but its major food is fishes which gather to eat the fruit falling from the trees. It eats a large

Above: These newly hatched salmon are called alevins. After a year of feeding in a fast-flowing mountain stream, they will be ready, at a length of about 10cm (4in), to travel downstream to the sea. They will stay for a year or more in the rich feeding-grounds of the North Atlantic, off the coast of Greenland, before returning to the river where they were spawned to start the cycle over again.

Left: Piranhas are related to minnows. Their fearsome reputation is well-earned, however. Although it would take a large shoal of piranhas to strip the flesh from a 50-kg (110-lb) capybara in less than a minute, they are all voracious feeders. There are four particularly dangerous species inhabiting South American rivers.

range of smaller fishes and will attack big fishes tangled in nets or caught on hooks – in fact, it can be a nuisance to local fishermen for this habit. Piranhas (there are about twenty different species in the Amazon) do occasionally attack other animals, especially if they are floundering in the water, perhaps unable to swim or injured, but it is quite exceptional for them to attack humans in the water.

In cooler zones the amount of food produced within or beside the rivers is much lower than in tropical forests and this is a factor in the migrations of many of the larger fishes from fresh water to the sea. In both Europe and North America several species of large fish migrate from spawning grounds in fresh water to feed in the sea. Several species of sturgeon and shads to this, as do most members of the salmon family. The Atlantic salmon (*Salmo salar*) migrates as a smolt at a length of around 25cm (10in) and returns in one, or several year's time, having at least quadrupled its length in the rich feeding grounds of the sea.

In tropical fresh waters a major problem may be shortage of oxygen in the water due to drought. It is not therefore surprising that numerous air-breathing fishes are found in fresh water. The African lungfish of the genus *Protopterus* is an example of a fish which has a pair of lungs, although it also has poorly developed gills. Even in favourable conditions it comes to the surface to gulp air, but when drought causes the water level to fall it retreats into a burrow in the mud, folds its tail over its snout, and secretes a mucous cocoon around itself. It can survive like this without water for up to five years.

Other air-breathing fishes include the bichirs, which live in swamps in Africa and have a lung; some African and Asian catfishes of the genus *Clarias* which have a special air chamber above the gills with branching structures which are used for breathing; and a number of catfishes and loaches which gulp air at the surface and can absorb the oxygen through the walls of the gut. Some

Long-distance swimmers

The salmon family are among the most important and exciting group of fishes. Only one species lives in the North Atlantic, the salmon (*Salmo salar*), which is found on both the European and North American coasts, but the North Pacific has seven species, five of them North American. All salmon species breed in fresh water, most migrating many kilometres upstream to their gravelly spawning beds. The coho salmon (*Oncorhynchus kisutch*) has been known to travel over 1600km (1000 miles) up the Yukon river to spawn. The adults range across the oceans feeding on fishes and crustaceans, and are captured in large numbers in surface nets. They navigate across the ocean by using the sun and stars, but once they come near their home river they find their way by an astonishingly acute sense of smell – they can even smell out the very stream in which they were hatched. All Pacific salmon die after spawning, and many Atlantic salmon also die, although some survive to breed two or three times.

species have turned the ability to breathe air into a positive advantage, and by breathing air can emerge from the water and move overland. The climbing perch (*Anabas testudineus*) of southeast Asia travels overland by pushing itself along by its tail while the spines in its pelvic fins and on its gill covers give it purchase, breathing all the while through an air chamber above its gills.

Temperate and cold shallow seas

The shallow seas of the temperate and near-polar regions contain many economically important fishes. To a great extent this is due to the configuration of the ocean bed, but other factors also have a bearing. Where the continental shelf (the shallow water surrounding the landmass of the continents) is wide, the great fisheries for near-bottom living fishes have developed.

The British Isles are sited on a particularly wide continental shelf which begins in Biscay and extends far to the west of Ireland and round almost to the Norwegian coast. South and north of the shelf deep water is to be found, lying only a short distance offshore. As a result the major fishing areas, developed long ago and still viable when properly managed, were the North Sea, the Irish Sea, and the seas to the south and west of the British islands. Here, huge schools of cod (*Gadus morhua*) overwinter, having moved down from breeding grounds off the Norwegian and Scottish coasts. Haddock (*Melanogrammus aeglefinus*) and coalfish or saithe (*Pollachius virens*) are common, and the fauna of the seabed is dominated by flatfishes, like the plaice (*Pleuronectes platessa*) and sole (*Solea solea*), as well as numerous species of skates. Smaller fishes find the seabed offers a hospitable environment, and some species

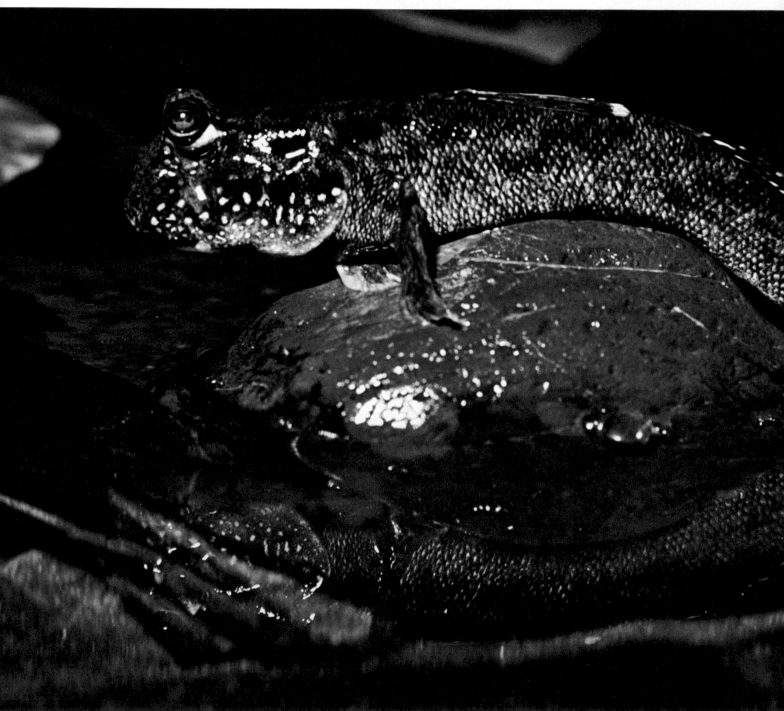

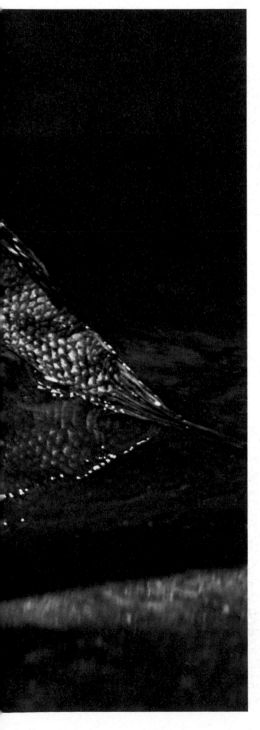

Mudskippers are tropical marine fishes that can stay out of water for long periods of time. They are often found in mangrove swamps, feeding on insects.

burrow into the sand – for instance sandeels and dragonets – whilst others are coloured like it – for instance several species of goby (family Gobiidae) and small flat-fishes like the scaldfish.

Similar wide continental shelves exist elsewhere: principally off the eastern coast of North America, and the Patagonian shelf off South America, off New Zealand, and off the coasts of China and Japan. All have proved to be productive fishing grounds (although some have only recently been exploited).

In temperate seas the fishes of the continental shelf are similar in most oceans throughout the World. Thus hake are found in the North Atlantic off Europe and North America, as well as in the South Atlantic off southern Africa and Argentina. They also occur in the North Pacific off North America as well as the South Pacific off Chile and New Zealand. Hake, however, live in rather deep water. Flatfishes of one kind or another are found in both Southern and Northern Hemispheres, as are the cod family (Gadidae), and the herring family (Clupeidae) members. Skates are also found in both hemispheres.

There are even similarities between the fishes of the Arctic shallow seas and the Antarctic, for sculpins (family Cottidae), a few cod family representatives like the blue whiting, eelpouts (family Zoarcidae), and skates can live in the subzero temperatures. The Antarctic fishes are, however, dominated by the so-called Antarctic cods (family Nototheniidae) of which there are about 50 species. Some of these show the most intricate adaptations to life in cold water and have a special antifreeze substance (glycoprotein) in their blood which lowers its freezing point – an essential precaution in such freezing seas. Virtually no fishes live on the polar shores, however.

The shore environment in temperate zones tends to be dominated by a few families of fishes which are resistant to the problems of extremes of temperature and desiccation. The total stock of true shore fishes is rather small, and the individuals are themselves generally small. The gobies (family Gobiidae), blennies (family Blenniidae), and clinids or klipfishes (family Clinidae) have proved particularly successful at living on the shore. Locally they may be joined by eelpouts (family

Zoarcidae) and butterfishes (family Pholidae). Most of these are slender fishes which insinuate themselves in the crevices in rocks, or burrow in the sand, but some shore dwellers, like the sea snails and clingfishes have developed powerful sucker discs with which they cling to rocks, but are saved from being swept away in the surf by the adhesion of their suckers.

Sandy shores and shallow water offer fewer habitats for fishes and those that thrive best are the fishes which can burrow into the sand, like the sandeels and flatfishes.

Tropical shallow seas

Fish life is at its most abundant on the coral reefs of tropical seas. These reefs are not evenly distributed throughout the tropics, as the coral requires special conditions in order to thrive – most particularly the warmth of the tropical sun, freedom from cold upwelling oceanic water from the deep sea, and water which is clear of sediment. These conditions are met most precisely in the shallow seas of the Indo-west Pacific and the Caribbean. Coral reefs are sparse in the Atlantic Ocean and along the Pacific coast of America.

The reefs are composed mainly of the calcareous skeletons of coral polyps, and the similar skeletons of

Venomous fishes

Several shallow water fishes have venom-laden spines which are capable of inflicting severe wounds. On European coasts the weever fishes of the genus *Trachinus* have sharp spines on the back fin and on their gill covers which have venom tissue in them. They bury themselves in sand, often in very shallow water, and can inflict severe pain by stinging, should an unwary bather stand on them. The stingrays also have venom tissue on the underside of their tail spines. They lie partly concealed in the sand, sometimes in shallow water, and if stood on raise their tails before making a sudden stab upwards with the spine. Stings from these rays are always intensely painful and can be fatal.

The sting of the tropical stonefish (*Synanceia verrucosa*), an inhabitant of coral reefs of the Indo-west Pacific can also be very serious. It has hollow spines in its dorsal fin which carry the venom into the wound made by the spine.

The little brown Mediterranean stonefish lurks among the boulders of breakwaters. It is very well camouflaged, and its spines can produce painful blood-poisoning if an unwary swimmer happens to step on them.

encrusting algae, and present a hard, irregular mass with numerous cracks and crevices; this is interspersed on the seabed with clean coral sand which provides an even contrast. The importance of a reef from the fishes' point of view is that it represents a three-dimensional living space. On its surface there is food. Within its crevices there are hiding spaces, or shelter for nest-making species, and the whole offers shelter to a mass of invertebrate animals, many of which are food for one fish species or another.

Fishes on coral reefs include a very large number of plant eaters and several groups of fish have become adapted to graze the green algae on the coral. Best-known are the surgeon-fishes, which have sharp-edged broad teeth, with numerous lobe-like cusps, perfectly adapted to scraping the fine algae off the coral. They also have an exceptionally long, coiled gut – a typical feature of any plant-eating animal. Surgeon-fishes get this name on account of the sharp scalpel-like blade on each side of the tail; when erected it points forwards, but mostly it is retracted under the skin.

Other fishes feed more on the small invertebrate animals which live in the coral. Thus, butterfly-fishes of the genus *Chaetodon* generally have long snouts, and all have very fine teeth in their jaws, which are well designed to pick out small crustaceans hiding in the coral, or even to nip off the tips of the coral's tentacles. The most extreme are the immensely long-snouted butterfly-fishes of the genus *Forcipiger*, the mouths of which almost amount to a pair of tweezers. Numerous other fishes such as many species of wrasse (family Labridae), damsel-fishes (family Pomacentridae), trigger-fishes (family Balistidae), blennies and gobies rely on the reef for food although their diets may comprise both algae from the reef and animals from within it.

Parrot-fishes (family Scaridae), some of the most brightly coloured of all the reef's inhabitants, are often responsible for the destruction of parts of it, for their food is the coral itself. With their strong, parrot beak jaws they break off pieces of coral which are crushed between their elaborate flattened throat teeth. These reduce even the rock-like coral to coarse powder so that the animal residue can be digested, the indigestible remains being voided to produce some of the clean white coral sand so greatly admired by travel brochure writers. Yet, this apparently unpromising food sustains large numbers of parrot-fishes, both individuals and species, some of them – like the 1·2m (4ft) long bump-head parrot-fish (*Bulbometopon muricatus*) – growing very large. Other parrot-fishes hide themselves at night in a crevice in the reef and go to sleep, lying in a sleeping-bag of mucus which they secrete. It is possible that this protects them from night-hunting moray eels, which also haunt the reef, and find their prey by scent.

Many of the brightly coloured fishes which swarm around the coral during the day simply hide at night, either taking shelter in crevices, or sleeping – as some wrasses certainly do. Their place is taken by other species, like the squirrel-fishes (family Holocentridae) and the cardinal-fishes (family Apogonidae) which emerge from their day-time caves and crevices to hunt around the reef. Many of these nocturnal fish are bright red – a colour which is as good as black in the poor light of a cave or at night – and have very large eyes. Another nocturnally active fish is *Photoblepharon palpebratus*, an 8cm (3in) Indo-west Pacific species which has a light organ under each eye. This light organ is filled with light-producing, symbiotic bacteria, which can only be 'switched off' by the fish extending a fold of jet black skin over the organ. *Photoblepharon palpebratus* is extremely abundant on some Red Sea reefs, which at night look like a busy city street with thousands of flashing lights.

Around the outskirts of the reef a distinctive fish fauna can be found. Red mullets (family Mullidae) haunt the coral sand probing for food with

Many smaller reef fishes feed only at night, but the triggerfish is active during the day. When danger threatens, it bolts headfirst into a rocky crevice and raises the backward-pointing spine on its back, thus anchoring itself in.

their long barbels, several species of shark hunt along the reef edge, and some catsharks (family Scyliorhinidae) lie close to the seabed. Jacks (family Carangidae) and some small tuna (family Scombridae) hunt in the open water for the sand smelts (family Atherinidae), halfbeaks (family Hemirhamphidae) and anchovy-like fishes (family Engraulidae) which frequent the water sheltered by the reef.

The wealth of life in warm shallow waters leads to fishes adopting highly specialized life-styles. The brightly coloured clown-fishes live in close association with the large sea anemones of the reef. They make them their home base, hiding within their tentacles – the venom of which would be death to most fishes – and they lay their eggs beside the base of the anemone. They survive because the fish's skin slime lacks the protein that causes the anemone to sting. Other fishes have evolved as accomplished mimics, some shrimp fishes and the clingfish *Diademichthys lineatus*, have bold lengthwise dark stripes and live head-down in the hat-pin sea urchin *Diadema savignyi*, concealed by their coloration and posture among the long spines of the urchin.

Life in the ocean

The open oceans offer the greatest living space in the world. More than two-thirds of the world's surface is covered by water and, as we have seen, the shallow waters occupy little more than the edges of the continents. Thus the ocean, from depths of over 200m (600ft) and with a mean depth of 4000m (12000ft) is an immense three-dimensional living space.

The surface of the ocean is the home of many of the giant fishes, and the tropical zones are richer than the temperate seas, as we might expect in fishes where the rate of life is closely associated with temperature. Typical of the near surface waters are the several species of tunnies, particularly the big-eye tuna (*Thunnus obesus*) and the yellow-fin tuna (*Thunnus albacares*). These huge

Above: The common moray eel lives along Mediterranean shores. It is rarely seen during the day, when it hides in a lair in the rocks. It is a powerful fish, growing up to 1·5m (5ft) long, and is known to attack octopus and squid and successfully bite off an arm. Related species of moray eels are found on tropical reefs and others live along Atlantic shores.

Opposite top: The pollack is a commercially important fish of the North Atlantic, related to the cod and whiting. It is sold as a salmon substitute, called saithe.

Opposite bottom: Contact with the spines of a turkeyfish, an inhabitant of Pacific coral reefs, can be very dangerous. This impressive fish will deliberately attack a swimmer with its venomous dorsal spines. Many other fishes of this region have similar defences to fend off attackers on the crowded reef.

fishes swim the world's oceans, their ranges circumscribed by the temperature of the surface and thus keeping to the tropics, although seasonal warming of the seas allows them to wander northwards and southwards into the edges of the temperate zones. The dolphin-fishes have much the same range and are, like the tunas, large near-surface predators on smaller fishes and squids.

Some sharks such as the mako (*Isurus oxyrinchus*), the blue shark (*Prionace glauca*), and the white-tip (*Carcharhinus longimanus*), share this habitat and food source, as do the billfishes such as the sailfish (*Istiophorus platypterus*) and the marlins, although the sharks are also known to attack these large neighbours from time to time. That these fishes are not simply aimlessly wandering through the oceans, but are making positive migrations to and from localized feeding or breeding areas is suggested by studies on the blue shark. It has for long been known that in the North Atlantic, sub-adult and a few adult female blue sharks occur in summer off the European coast, including the southwest of Britain.

Male sharks, however, are found seasonally in similar numbers on the coast of the United States of America. It has now been discovered that the 'European' blue sharks are migrating across the Atlantic and may in winter be near the Caribbean and off northern South America, while others have been captured near the Azores. These sharks in fact seem to be making an oceanic migration which takes them around in a great circle through the tropical Atlantic.

The uppermost surface of the sea offers sanctuary for a number of adult fishes, and many fishes have long-lasting larval stages which allows wide dispersal of the species. Some, like the Portuguese-man-of-war fish (*Nomeus gronovii*) a 15cm (6in) companion of the jellyfish-like siphonophore *Physalia physalis*, swims close to its surface-living host apparently immune to the stings of its trailing tentacles which would be death to most other fishes.

Many of the small fishes living near the ocean's surface share the same coloration, of dark blue-green back, silvery sides and silvery white belly. Conspicuous as this looks out of water it is excellent concealment in the sea, the blue back merging with the blue of the ocean to a predatory seabird above the fish, and the silvery belly merging with the reflecting mirror surface of the sea from beneath. This is the colouring adopted by sauries and the flying-fishes (family Exocoetidae), as well as many fishes which live near the surface in shallower seas, for example the herrings, mackerels and even some of the ocean giants like the blue shark, and the blue-fin tunny (*Thunnus thynnus*).

In the deeper waters of the ocean there is an array of fishes which are not well known, partly because many of them are large and active and thus escape all but accidental capture in fishing nets. Many of them we know as occasional visitors to shallow water, stranded wrecks, or perhaps as a result of having lost their bearings through disease, age, or other accident. These are the mesopelagic fishes, animals which live mostly at depths of 60-150m (200-500ft). They include the ocean sunfish (*Mola mola*), almost circular when seen from the side but with a narrow dorsal and anal fin pointing vertically and joined to the tail fin. It grows to a length of 4m (13ft) but, because of its shape, its weight is out of all propor-

tion to its length, being up to 1500kg (3300lb). This vast bulk is sustained mainly by a diet of jellyfishes and siphonophores, a diet notably deficient in calcium and, as one might expect, the skeleton of these giant fishes is paper thin and weighs no more than a kilogram or two.

Of similar shape is the opah or moon fish (*Lampris guttatus*), but it is smaller, attaining no more than 1·5m (5ft) in length. This is a brilliantly coloured fish with a deep blue back, silvery belly and crimson fins, the whole covered with distinct white spots. Despite its size and resemblance to the apparently lethargic sunfish it is an active hunter; its food consisting mainly of oceanic squids (many of them quite large) and midwater fishes. Paradoxically its nearest relatives are the long, slender ribbon-fish (*Regalecus glesne*) and the deal-fishes, which are almost ribbon-like, even if they exceed 3m (10ft) in length, as does the oarfish. They share this habitat with the lancetfish (*Alepisaurus ferox*) a 1·5m (5ft) long, huge-toothed predator, with a lean and muscular body shape. Its food contains virtually any smaller fish or invertebrate that it encounters; for example a single specimen caught off California contained forty-one fishes of five kinds, three squids of two kinds, and several other invertebrates. Occasionally biologists find hitherto undiscovered animals in the stomachs of these active predators.

Not all the inhabitants of the midwaters of the ocean are large, however. Indeed, many of them, like the numerous species of lantern fish (family Myctophidae) are small, and rarely grow longer than 15cm (6in). They are abundant in the open sea, and have rows of light organs on their heads and along the undersides of their bodies. They no doubt help schools keep together in the dark, and also help one species recognize another.

Similar light organs are found in many other fishes, for example the deep-bodied, large-eyed, gloomy-looking hatchet fishes have them, but these also have brilliant silvery sides and bellies. Possibly in addition to the advantage of light-organs just mentioned their conspicuously mirror-like scales help reflect other lights in the deep sea. Some stomatid fishes (family Stomiatidae) have large light organs below or in front of the eye and there is evidence that they use them as search lights, flash-

Flying-fishes

Perhaps the fishes most perfectly adapted for life at the sea's surface are the flying-fishes (family Exocoetidae). Torpedo-shaped, between 15-45cm (6-18in) in length, and with large eyes, their pectoral fins are enlarged to form a pair of large wings. The tail fin is deeply forked, with strong bones, and the lower lobe is longer than the upper. Their flight is achieved by powerful strokes of the tail fin which drive the fish to the surface at a speed of up to 32 kph (20 mph) at which point the pectoral fins are spread out and the fish takes to the air. It does not beat its 'wings', but merely extends them sideways to glide just above the waves, often following their profile, before plunging back into the water. However, sometimes it drops its tail into the water, beating it to attain further speed to continue its glide. The distance of these multiple glides may exceed several hundred metres. These 'flights' are made to escape predators.

(*Pelobates*) is often known as the garlic toad on account of its skin secretions.

Caecilians (order Apoda)

The 160 species of caecilians are among the least-known amphibians. They are worm-like burrowing species found in the warmer parts of South America, Africa, southern Asia, and on several tropical islands including those of the Philippines, the Malay Archipelago and the Seychelles. Unlike other amphibians, some species of caecilians have small scales embedded in their skin. They are totally limbless and do not even have a pelvic girdle. They are blind, at least in the adult stage, when the eye is usually covered with skin or bone. Another adaptation for their subterranean existence is a sensory tentacle between the eye and nostril. They probably feed on almost any small animals they encounter, but for most species their precise feeding habits remain unknown.

Although most caecilians are under 50cm (20in) in length, *Caecilia thompsoni* from South America grows to about 1·5m (5ft). Most caecilians retain the eggs in the body and give birth to young which look like miniature adults, but in a few species the young are aquatic, and some species are aquatic all their life.

Salamanders and newts (order Caudata)

The caudata are the tailed amphibians, and have much the same habits as the frogs and toads, but are often even more secretive, and may spend longer in the water. There are more than 300 species of salamanders and newts in the eight families making up the order Caudata. Their distribution is somewhat limited and they are mostly found in North and Central America, Europe and Asia, being absent from most of Africa, Australasia and with only a few species in South America. The terms newts and salamanders are used rather loosely; but generally newts are those species which enter the water for an elaborate courtship and mating, while salamanders at the most enter the water merely to deposit their eggs.

Above: Poisonous secretions for deterring predators are a feature of amphibians, but this has not always saved the arrow-poison frogs of South America. As their name suggests, they are caught to provide poison for the natives' arrows.

Opposite: The red salamander lives in cool, moist places in the eastern United States. It is one of many salamanders that entirely lack lungs, and breathe through the skin and the lining of the mouth.

The family Cryptobranchidae includes the largest living amphibians, the two species of giant salamanders of the genus *Andrias* of which one is found in the highlands of China, and the other in Japan. They grow to over 1·5m (5ft), and live in fast-flowing streams. Although now protected throughout most of their range, in the recent past they were exploited for human food, as well as for the pet and zoo trade. Although these species spend their entire life in water they are not neotenous (see below) and lose their gills when they mature. The hellbender (*Cryptobranchus alleganiensis*) is found in the mountain streams of the eastern United States. Although not as large as the Asiatic species, it grows to 75cm (2½ft) in length and it is known locally as the devil dog or the Alleghemy alligator.

The thirty species of the family Hynobiidae are thought to be among the more primitive of the living species of the Caudata; this is based on both their structure and also on their reproductive biology, which is thought to be like that of the ancestral amphibians. Unlike most other tailed amphibians fertilization of the eggs is external. The eggs are laid in water in paired sacs and are then fertilized by the males. Most species are found in, or close to, mountain streams and some species have reduced lungs or may even lack them altogether; the animals relying on breathing through their skin and mouth. The family is confined to Asia and several species have only been described in the last few decades including *Batrachuperus karlschmidti*, which is found in icy springs in Szechuan where it is known locally as the white dragon.

The three species of the family Sirenidae are neotenous, which means they never truly metamorphose but retain the larval gills throughout their life. Neoteny occurs in a number of amphibians and this character is often linked with the lack of body pigmentation known as albinism. The name siren is taken from the Greek dulcet-voiced temptresses of Odysseus – however, the amphibian sirens make only yelping noises when captured. Perhaps having any sort of voice is sufficiently remarkable in a salamander for zoologists to immortalize them as sirens! They live in the shallow, swampy waters of North America, and when these dry up they are able to form a cocoon in the mud in which to survive the drought.

Another important family of salamanders and newts is the family

Amorous newts
The courtships of the newts of the genus *Triturus* are among the most elaborate in amphibians, and the males of several species develop spectacular and elaborate breeding dress, with bright coloration and extensive fins on the back, tail and, in some species, feet. The crests of the male probably enable him to absorb more oxygen from the water during the activity of displaying. The display involves the male lashing and vibrating his tail before the passive female, before depositing a sperm-packet (spermatophore) which the female picks up by pressing her cloaca onto it. The female then lays her eggs singly, attaching them to vegetation or stones.

Once the breeding season is over, the males lose their nuptial crests and coloration, and both sexes normally leave the water and lead secretive lives on land. In a few localities neoteny occurs, and some populations of newts do not metamorphose, but no species of newts are exclusively neotenous. Generally the development of newt tadpoles is completed by the early summer or autumn, but at high altitudes and in northern areas the tadpoles may overwinter in water and complete their development the following year.

Proteidae. The olm (*Proteus anguinus*), is a translucent whitish species living in total darkness in Yugoslavian caves. It is completely neotenous with large feathery, salmon-pink gills, and almost useless limbs and eyes. The American species of the family are also neotenous and have large gills, and occur in eastern and central North America, where they are known as water dogs or mud puppies.

The forty species of the family Salamandridae are widespread in Europe, Asia and North America, with a few species extending slightly further afield.

The fire salamander (*Salamandra salamandra*) of Europe and north Africa is spectacularly marked, usually with yellow spots or stripes on a jet-black background, but the spots may merge to almost cover the animal, or may be almost entirely absent, and they may also be orange or reddish. The colouring is a warning, since they have numerous glands which secrete noxious irritants. The association with fire possibly arose because, living among damp wood, they would emerge from logs put on a fire.

The newts of North America are rough-skinned, with a rather different life-style to those of Europe. Some species, such as the eastern newt (*Notophthalmus viridescens*), leave the water after metamorphosis brightly coloured, and return to the water when adult, at which time they are more dingy coloured.

Some species of salamandrid such as the North American newts of the genus *Taricha*, and the spectacled salamander (*Salamandrina terdigita*) of Europe display threat postures when alarmed, while some, such as the golden-striped salamander (*Chioglossa lusitanica*) of Portugal can shed its tail like a lizard can. This species – in common with several North American species – is very agile, scampering among rocks, often in broad daylight. However, most salamandrids are nocturnal, and are most active after rain.

Some of the thirty species of North and Central American mole salamanders (family Ambystomatidae) are superficially similar to the fire salamander while others, such as the tiger salamander (*Ambystoma tigrinum*) are large, growing to 40cm (16in) in length. The best-known species is also one of the rarest, at least in the wild. It is the axolotl (*Ambystoma mexicanum*) which is confined to a few high-altitude lakes in Mexico where, due to pollution and drainage, it is endangered with extinction. However, since its discovery in the 18th Century it has been popular in aquaria, zoos and laboratories where it breeds freely. In fact it was first described as far back as 1789 but it was not until many years later that it was realized that the gilled larvae described as a separate species were one and the same. The axolotl is the best-known example of neoteny, in which the larval form is retained throughout life. Axolotls do occasionally lose

their gills and metamorphose into salamanders, but when this happens they do not normally survive for very long.

Some species of *Ambystoma* salamander are parthenogenetic, that is to say only females are known, which reproduce asexually. This phenomenon, which is being discovered in an ever-increasing number of amphibians and reptiles, is complex, but has important survival value for species which are periodically devastated.

Only two of the 190 or more lungless salamanders (family Plethodontidae) are found in Europe – the rest are confined to the New World. The exception is the genus *Hydromantes*; two of the five closely related species are found in Europe and the other three in the United States. They are all found in caves or rock clefts, and their distribution suggests that they are relics of a once much more widespread species. All the other lung-less salamanders are found in North, Central and South America, ranging in length from 3cm ($1\frac{1}{4}$in) to over 20cm (8in). Since they all lack lungs, breathing is done entirely through the skin and the mouth. But perhaps an even more remarkable feature is that it is the upper jaw which moves, the lower jaw remaining fixed. Like newts and salamanders of the family Salamandridae, many species of lung-less salamanders have elaborate courtship displays, and after the eggs have been laid the females may stay on guard until they hatch. Many species are surprisingly agile. Some, such as the arboreal salamander (*Aneides lugubris*) of southwestern North America, have been found nearly 20m (65ft) up a tree.

Frogs and toads (order Anura)

By far the greatest number of amphibians are anurans, tailless amphibians also sometimes known as the Salientia, and which are commonly known as frogs or toads.

The terms frog and toad are used for the two most abundant and widespread types in the Northern Hemisphere – frogs being the smooth, moist-skinned genus *Rana*, and toads the warty, dry-skinned genus *Bufo*. This terminology is really only adequate, however, in places such as Britain which has only three native species.

Above: A tree frog calls to warn off rivals and attract a mate. The floor of the mouth is inflated like a balloon and air is passed backwards and forwards across the vocal cords between the throat and the lungs. The 'balloon' acts as a resonator to amplify the sound.

Opposite: The newts are a form of salamander. During the breeding season the males, especially, become brightly coloured and develop a fin on the back and tail.

Anurans show considerable variation, both in their external form and in their behaviour. They range from the lithe, long-limbed tree frogs to the squat, warty burrowing toads; and from dingy camouflaged species, to the brilliantly coloured arrow-poison frogs. In addition to visual differences many species are highly vocal and, like birds, recognize members of their own species by their 'song'. Finally, the adaptations to their amphibious breeding cycle are amazingly diverse; even within a single family the various species have often developed a wide range of techniques for coping with the problems engendered by the need for an aquatic laval stage.

The mating of anurans is, with some exceptions, accomplished externally, and in the majority of cases in water. The exceptions are of course the more interesting and curious, but typically males and females meet in or near the breeding waters and the males clasp the females in an embrace known as amplexus. For this purpose the males often develop calosities, or nuptial pads, on their thumbs to help grip the slippery female. The amplexus can take a variety of positions, the most common being around the chest; other positions are just below the female's forearms or around the loins, and just above her hind legs. As the female lays her eggs, usually in a mass or in strings, the male sheds sperm over them, and on completion the eggs are abandoned. The gelatinous coating swells in the water, to form a protective coating, but otherwise they have to fend for themselves. Since the typical anuran will lay between 10 000 and 20 000 eggs, a

109

Newly hatched tadpoles of the European common frog start life as vegetarians, breathing by means of gills. As they grow and develop, they change to a diet of tiny animals, and the gills are replaced by lungs.

high rate of predation will not necessarily prevent one or two individuals surviving to maturity.

However, the variation on the typical breeding cycle, and the adaptations to extreme conditions, are considerable and are perhaps the most interesting feature of anurans, which apart from this, seem on the whole to do little more than hide away in damp places or feed on insects and other arthropods. Some carry the eggs and larvae in brood pouches; some build foam nests while others lay their eggs in pools of water inside plants high in the forest canopy.

Among the most curious of all amphibians are the sixteen species of the family Pipidae which are found in Africa and South America. One species, the African clawed toad or platanna (*Xenopus laevis*) has been used extensively as a laboratory animal. For a number of years it was in considerable demand for use in pregnancy tests, and although it has now been superseded in this field there is still a demand for it in biology classes and to a lesser extent in the pet trade. The platanna grows to about 15cm (6in) and is entirely

aquatic. Although it can move short distances overland in wet grass, it soon dries up on dry land. The platanna's South American relative, the Surinam toad (*Pipa pipa*), has a rather flattened squarish shape with a pointed snout and small eyes. It is the breeding behaviour which is so remarkable, however; the male in amplexus manoeuvres the female's extruded oviduct over her back and under his body. As each batch of about 60-100 eggs appears, the male gathers them up with his feet and places them on her back. After egg laying is completed the female remains still, and within a few hours the skin on her back swells and encloses each of the eggs in a large pocket. Inside this capsule the eggs hatch, and the tadpoles develop in safety, until one day the 'lid' of skin is pushed up and the miniature toad swims away, most of the young emerging together.

The primitive family Discoglossidae is the only family of amphibians which is predominantly European. They take their name from the disc-shaped tongue which, unlike the tongue of many other amphibians, cannot be protruded and so instead they grab their prey with their mouth. The family includes four species of fire-bellied toads of the genus *Bombina* which all have brilliantly coloured bellies – red, orange or yellow and black. The belly is exposed to predators as a warning that their skin secretions are noxious. When alarmed, fire-bellies often flip on to their back and reflex their bodies to expose these bright colours.

The Mexican burrowing toad (*Rhinophrynus dorsalis*) found in Central America from Costa Rica northwards to Texas is the only member of the family Rhinophrynidae. It possesses a 'spade' on the hind foot to assist it in burrowing into termite mounds, where it finds its principal food.

About seventy species of spadefoots (family Pelobatidae) are known, and are widely distributed throughout the Northern Hemisphere. They take their name from the horny protuberance found in the hind foot of some species, which enables them to burrow. Three spadefoots of the genus *Pelobates* are found in Europe, as well as the related parsley frog (*Pelodytes punctatus*) which is more slender but lacks the spade. In North America five species of spadefoots of the genus *Scaphiopus* occur; like the European species they have horny spades on the hind feet, since they often live in rather arid conditions, from which they are protected by their burrows.

The Leptodactylidae is among the largest families of anurans, and by 1970 around 650 species were recognized, and many more have been described since. Nearly half the species recognized belonged to a single genus, *Eleutherodactylus*, which is found exclusively in Central and South America (two species have also been introduced into Florida).

The Australasian genus *Crinia* is one in which new species are still being regularly described; the species are identified on the basis of the

A late stage in the development of a tadpole shows the 'double' life of an amphibian. The long tail is a reminder that it spends part of its life as an aquatic animal, but the legs show that it is becoming a land animal. The transformation will never be total, however, because the adult frog's skin must be kept moist and it has to return to water to breed.

calls they make, and the way in which they breed with each other. Many of the species have very localized ranges, and the entire pattern of their distribution suggests that they are a group in which new species are continuing to evolve.

Darwin's frog (*Rhinoderma darwinii*), which was discovered in Chile by Charles Darwin while voyaging around the world on the *Beagle* has one of the strangest of all breeding techniques. The females lay the eggs on moist ground where the males sit guard until they detect the movement of the tadpoles within the mass of jelly. At this point the male places the eggs inside his mouth. They are not swallowed, however, but are taken into the male's vocal sac, which is enlarged for the purpose. The larvae are retained there until they are fully developed, and hop out as miniature frogs.

The South African *Natalabatrachus bonebergi* lays its eggs encased in a stiff cake of jelly fixed to a leaf, twig or rock overhanging water, and after about six days the tadpoles wriggle free and drop into the water to continue their growth in the normal way. Another South African frog, *Anhydrophryne rattrayi*, lays only about twenty eggs in a jelly capsule in a chamber near the surface of the ground. The tadpoles develop within the nest, and after about four weeks emerge as froglets without ever going near water.

Other ranid frogs from South Africa, such as those of the genera *Arthroptella* and *Arthroleptis* have similar life-cycles. The eggs of *Hemisus marmoratus*, yet another South African species, are also laid in a mass of about 200 encased in a jelly capsule, in a cavity up to 20cm (8in) underground and anything up to 1m (3¼ft) from the water. The female stands guard over the eggs until they hatch, then she digs a tunnel down towards, and finally into, the water, and the tadpoles wriggle down behind her *en masse*, finally swimming off.

The two genera which form the family Atelopodidae are sometimes included in the closely related family Bufonidae, the true toads. They are widespread in Central and South America, and include some of the most stunning anurans. *Atelopus stelzeri* from Uruguay is jet-black with bright orange hands and feet, but even more remarkable than its appearance, is the fact that its tadpoles can hatch in a remarkably short time – twenty-four hours after they

Opposite: The goliath frog is the aptly-named giant of the frog world. It is a rare species found in the forests of west Africa. The largest specimen on record weighed 3·3kg (7lb) and had a head and body length of 81·5cm (2ft 8in).

Below: European common frogs mating. The smaller male grasps the female in a position called amplexus. He has to defend this position against other males until he can fertilize the spawn as it is being laid by the female.

are laid. This is presumed to be an adaptation to breeding in puddles and other temporary waters. *Atelopus zeteki* is a diurnal species, bright golden yellow with black spots, while other species have red or green spots on black. Like the arrow-poison frogs (family Dendrobatidae) to which they have more than a passing resemblance, the *Atelopus* frogs have poisonous secretions in their skins and their coloration is a warning to would-be predators.

The Bufonidae, or true toads, are a widespread family occurring almost worldwide but absent from Australasia and Madagascar, with some 300 species known. They include the common toads of Europe, North America and Africa. The common toad of Eurasia (*Bufo bufo*) is found from western Europe including Britain (but not Ireland) and North Africa eastwards through Asia to Japan. In some parts of their range they grow to 15cm (6in) in length (from snout to vent) but there is much variation in size, with the larger animals tending to come from the more southerly parts of their range; females, as is the case with

many toads, are often much larger than the males.

The tree frogs (family Hylidae) are among the most colourful and attractive species. In all, there are over 600 species of tree frog known – over 400 in the genus *Hyla* alone, and more are likely to be discovered. Most are diminutive, and some of the smallest are less than 5cm (2in) long, while one of the largest, *Hyla maxima* of South America, grows to over 11cm ($4\frac{1}{4}$in). Many tree frogs are bright green in colour, and most have suckers on the end of each toe, enabling them to grip seemingly perfectly smooth surfaces such as a sheet of glass. They are great jumpers; the North American cricket frog (*Acris crepitans*) – less than 1cm ($\frac{1}{2}$in) can leap thirty-six times its own length – equivalent to a man jumping over 65m (216ft).

The 250 species of the family Microhylidae are widespread and show considerable diversity in shape and form, and include some of the most specialized of all anurans, particularly in Africa and Asia. The rain frogs of the genus *Breviceps* are often to be seen gorging themselves on

Right: Like other tree frogs, the European tree frog is an expert climber. Each toe is equipped with a sticky disc to help grip vertical tree trunks. When an insect flies past, the tree frog leaps out to catch it and spreads its legs wide to seize a leaf or twig and effect a landing. Although they live in trees, tree frogs return to ponds to hibernate and breed.

Opposite: Every spring European common toads migrate to their breeding pools. They follow traditional routes and travel at night, the males leading and the females following, but with some males already on the backs of females.

Flying frogs

The family Rhacophoridae, takes its name from the most famous of its species the 'flying' frogs of the genus *Rhacophorus*. Some of these Asian species live high up in trees and possess webbed fingers as well as toes. In fact these frogs do not actually fly, but use their extensive membranes to help them extend their leaps into a downward glide, perhaps as long as 15m (49ft). The membranes are spread taut between splayed fingers and toes, and the body is stretched into a concave 'parachute' to gain maximum uplift.

termites which have emerged after rain until they are so distended as to be spherical and barely able to walk. When mating, the male glues himself to the female's back and then the pair, using their back legs, dig themselves into the ground, and with a revolving motion they rapidly disappear. About 50cm (20in) underground they hollow out a nest and about thirty eggs are laid which are guarded by the female, until they have developed into baby toads which hatch, and then dig their way out.

Another often brilliantly coloured group of frogs are the 380 species of the family Rhacophoridae which occur in Africa, Madagascar and southeast Asia. Over 140 species belong to a single tree frog-like genus *Hyperolius*, commonly known as the sedge frogs.

One of the smaller frog families, the five species of the Pseudidae are also among the strangest zoological curiosities. The paradoxical frog (*Pseudis paradoxus*) is named as such because of the enormous discrepancy between the size of the adult and its tadpoles. The latter grow to over 20cm (8in), and yet the adult is only about 7·5cm (3in). Not surprisingly the larvae of this and related species were often described as separate species to their parents!

Reptiles

The reptiles are a large and ancient group of animals, with some species still looking almost identical to their ancestors which roamed the Earth in the hey-day of the dinosaurs. Reptiles have developed the shelled egg. This is an evolutionary advancement over the amphibians and means that reptiles, along with the birds and mammals, are not dependent on returning to water for even part of their life-cycle.

The skin of reptiles is characterized by the presence of scales, which are thickenings of the outer layer of skin. It is dead tissue and, in the case of crocodiles and turtles and tortoises, it is constantly being rubbed off; but most snakes and lizards shed it at intervals either as a whole skin, or in large pieces. In most reptiles the structure and arrangement of the scales is usually very consistent and is the most important character used for classifying reptile species, although in recent years, as knowledge of the biology, ecology and behaviour of reptiles has improved, other criteria are being used to help classify them. Contrary to popular belief most reptiles are not slimy, though their shiny scales may give them a superficially slimy appearance; they are in fact usually very dry. Unlike most amphibians, reptiles are able to withstand dry hot climates, since their scaly skins help prevent them drying out. They have also been able to colonize the sea – whereas amphibians are only able to cope with slightly brackish water.

Reptiles are often referred to as being cold-blooded, and it is generally believed that they cannot control their body temperature, but remain at the ambient air temperature. In fact, this is far from true. Unlike mammals and birds, reptiles do not generate energy within their body, but gather energy from external sources, such as sunshine, or sun-warmed rocks. When reptiles are cold they bask, and when they are hot they retreat into shade or underground burrows. By darkening their skin colour, they can also increase the rate of heat absorption. By these and other means, many reptiles can keep their body temperatures within a few degrees of their preferred range for activity. The advantage of such a method of temperature control is that when the animal is not active, it is using hardly any energy – unlike most birds and mammals which use large amounts of energy merely maintaining their body temperatures.

Broadly, the reptiles are divided into four main orders.

The tuatara (order Rhyncocephalia)

The tuatara (*Sphenodon punctatus*) is the sole survivor of an ancient order, once numerous, but now a single species confined to a few offshore islands around New Zealand. The tuatara evolved directly from a line of reptiles which have remained virtually unchanged since the Jurassic period over 150 million years ago.

The most famous feature of the tuatara is its light-sensitive 'third eye', or pineal eye, its lack of any penis in the male, lack of external ear opening (although it can hear perfectly well) and teeth which are not set in sockets, but are mere serrations of the jaw, covered with enamel.

Lizards and snakes (order Squamata)
Lizards (suborder Sauria)

The lizards are the most numerous and the most adaptable of the living reptiles. The differences between lizards and other reptiles such as snakes are obvious in the extreme, but sometimes, particularly in the

case of the legless lizards, the differences are much less apparent. In fact the number or size of limbs and the number of toes of a lizard is often of surprisingly little importance when classifying them. Animals with robust limbs are often closely related to limbless species – a relationship only obvious after detailed anatomical examination, however.

Many lizards possess the ability to shed their tail – a characteristic known as autotomy. When the lizard is seized by its tail it fractures, and the attacker is left holding a violently writhing tail which continues to move for a considerable time after it has been severed. This distracts the attacker whilst the rest of the lizard escapes. After the tail has been shed, the lizard is able to grow a new, but never quite as good, tail.

Monitor lizards
(family Varanidae)

The giants among the lizards are the monitor lizards. The thirty or so species are found throughout the warmer parts of the Old World and Australasia, (they are known as goannas in the latter). The largest living lizard is the Komodo dragon (*Varanus komodoensis*), found in Indonesia on Komodo, Padar and Flores and a few other small islands, which grow to over 3m (10ft) in length and to a weight of over 50 kg (110 lb); it can occasionally grow to a length of 4m

Above: The agamas are a family of 300 species of lizards, which live in the warmer parts of the Old World, including southern Europe and Australia. Many are brightly coloured and can change colour according to their body temperature and emotional state.

Left: The basilisk is named after the mythical monster whose glance was fatal. The real basilisk is an iguanid lizard which makes itself look ferocious by erecting a crest on its head. It lives near water and, when frightened, jumps in and submerges or runs rapidly over the surface until it reaches the bank, or disappears underneath.

Opposite: Chamaeleons are well-known for their ability to change colour to match their surroundings, and for the way that they catch insects by flicking out a tongue which is almost as long as their body. The eyes are also remarkable because they move independently of one another.

(13ft). It is a voracious predator and occasionally attacks and kills humans – even tourists have been eaten. And yet it was not until 1910 that the first specimens were made known to science – rather surprising considering its size. Another species of monitor, *Varanus salvator*, which is widespread in southeast Asia, is only fractionally smaller and, like many of its relatives in India and other parts of Asia and Africa, has been important in the skin trade.

Agamas (family Agamidae)

Agamas are rather variable, both in habits and appearance. The largely terrestrial Australian agamas are often known as dragon lizards, and the males of some species have brightly coloured throats and bellies. Many of them, particularly those living in open, arid environments, are able to run on their hind legs — and are popularly referred to as 'bicycle lizards'. The most spectac-

ular of all these is the frilled lizard (*Chamydosaurus kingii*), which grows to about 60cm (2ft), and has an enormous ruff or frill of skin around the neck, which can be erected when the lizard is alarmed.

Iguanas (family Iguanidae)

In the New World the agamas are absent and are replaced by iguanas, some of which are quite large. The iguanid equivalent of the frilled lizard is the basilisk (*Basiliscus basiliscus*) of Central America – an equivalent in as much as it is able to run very fast on its hind legs, and is spectacular in appearance – the male having a large helmet-like crest on the head, and fins on the back and tail.

However, despite the fact that iguanas appear to displace the agamas geographically (the only part of Africa lacking agamas is Madagascar, where iguanas are found), in habits they are generally rather

119

different, with a large proportion of iguanas being tree-dwelling, and quite a few taking to water readily. In fact one of the largest species is marine.

Typical lizards
(family Lacertidae)
The typical lizards occur throughout much of Europe, Africa and Asia. All except one species lay eggs, the exception being the viviparous lizard (*Lacerta vivipara*), which is widespread in northern Europe, even reaching the Arctic Circle. By being live-bearing, it is able to take advantage of the heat absorbed by basking in the sun to incubate its eggs. The hatchlings are almost jet-black at birth – their dark coloration helps them to absorb heat, too.

Most lizards have very finely defined ecological niches – up to seven species have been found occurring in one locality in southwest Yugoslavia, all occupying slightly different niches. Those species living among rocks usually have the body flattened for crawling in crevices, while those living in bushes tend to have green markings on them.

In America the niche of the lacertid lizards is taken to a large extent by the family Teiidae – whiptails and racerunners – although two species of lacertid (*Lacerta viridis* and *Podarcis sicula*) have been introduced into the United States.

Chamaeleons
(family Chamaeleonidae)
The Chamaeleons are highly specialized arboreal (tree-dwelling) lizards. Most of the eighty-five species are found in Africa and Madagascar, although a few are found in southeast Asia, and the Indian Ocean islands, and one species is found in southern Europe. The ability of chamaeleons to change colour rapidly is particularly well-known, and they are also able to move their large bulging eyes independently of each other. They move relatively slowly, gripping twigs with their toes and with additional support from their prehensile tail. They stalk insects which are then caught on the top of the sticky tongue which can be shot out for more than the length of the body. Although most species lay eggs a few give birth to living young. Both the largest and the smallest chamaeleons come from Madagascar – *Chamaeleo oustatleti* grows to a length of nearly 70cm (28in), whilst *C. nasutus* is less than 10cm (4in) long.

Geckos (family Gekkonidae)
The geckos are another family which show adaptations from an arboreal life, though they exhibit considerably more diversity than the chamaeleons. The 650 species are found throughout the warmer parts of the world, and a typical gecko is a rather plump lizard with a large head and soft skin. Most species have a voice – the Tokay gecko (*Gekko gecko*) has a loud bark. They are often nocturnal, and many are spectacularly good climbers, and often have elaborate adhesive pads on the toes. These pads, which are covered with a network of miniature hairlike structures, enable the gecko to gain a purchase on apparently smooth walls and even ceilings, where they are often to be seen hunting insects.

Because of their adaptability to man-made environments, some species have been transported in cargo and are now found very widely; the Turkish gecko (*Hemidactylus turcicus*) has even crossed the Atlantic and is now widespread in Central and North America. Some species of gecko are brilliantly coloured: the genus *Phelsuma* from Madagascar and other islands in the Indian Ocean includes several bright leaf-green species. Others such as the leaf-tailed gecko (*Uroplatus fimbriatus*) of Madagascar have elaborate camouflage barely distinguishable from lichen-covered bark. A desert-living species, *Palmatogecko rangei*, from the sand-deserts of Namibia is web-footed, to enable it to run across loose sand.

Worm lizards
(family Amphisbaenidae)
A number of lizards have their limbs very much reduced or absent. It is

Opposite: Nearly 700 species of geckos are spread around the warm parts of the world. They are the only lizards with the ability to make sounds and the name 'gecko' imitates the calls of some species. Geckos often come into houses in search of insects. Rows of tiny bristles on their toes enable the geckos to climb walls and run upside-down across ceilings.

Right: The slow-worm is a legless lizard. All that remains of the limbs are some hip and shoulder bones. Loss or reduction of the limbs has occurred in several different groups of lizards. This one has lost its tail.

Above: The black-necked cobra is often known by the more descriptive name of spitting cobra. It defends itself against an enemy by taking aim visually and squirting venom into its eyes from a distance of up to 4m (13ft). The venom irritates the eyes, causing permanent blindness unless they are bathed promptly with water.

possible to find species of lizards possessing almost every stage of degeneration down to total loss of limbs. Perhaps the most un-lizard like species are the amphisbaenids, which are more like giant earthworms than any other creature. Even their scales are arranged in wormlike rings. Their Latin name means 'going both ways', and they are able to travel backwards and forwards, although not particularly well in either direction. They live almost entirely underground, where they feed mainly on earthworms and other invertebrates including ants and termites, but they are rarely seen and poorly studied.

Slow-worms and glass snakes (family Anguidae)
A better-known group of lizards, which includes some legless species is the Anguidae. The familiar slow-worm (*Anguis fragilis*) of Britain and Europe and the 1m (3¼ft) long glass snakes of America, Europe and Asia are examples of legless anguids.

Skinks (family Scincidae)
The skinks show wide variation in the development of their limbs among the 700 or so species, which are found all over the warmer parts of the world, but are particularly widespread and diverse in Australia. They range from the 50cm (20in) long, heavily built blue-tongued skinks to species which are less than 10cm (4in) long. Some have only hind limbs (for instance *Lerista humphriesi*); others are limbless (for instance *Anomalopus frontalis*); while many others are fully limbed and similar to true lizards. Those with reduced limbs may have one, two, three, four or five toes. The stump-tailed skinks and others which have fat tails, use them as a food store.

Snakes (suborder Serpentes)
Some 2700 species of snake are known, and they occur on all continents except Antarctica. Their most distinctive feature is their elongate shape, with the body lacking limbs. They also lack ear openings and eyelids. Although generally feared,

relatively few snakes are venomous, and provided proper treatment is received, fatalities are rare among snake-bite victims.

Movement

Having lost their limbs, snake locomotion is a highly specialized affair, and occurs in four basic ways. The first is the typical serpentine movement: the snake undulates in loops and curves, pressing against vegetation or irregularities in the ground, as waves pass down the body. They also use a concertina movement, in which the snake stretches forward using its scales to hold on to irregularities, hooking its body on branches or stones, then draws its body up after it; this method is often used in climbing. The method technically known as 'rectilinear' locomotion, and popularly (but erroneously) as walking on its ribs, is common in pythons and larger heavier-bodied snakes; the snake progresses in a straight line, with repeated ripples passing along the body in a caterpillar-like movement. The final, and certainly most spectacular form of movement, is side-winding. This is most commonly used by desert-living species such as vipers and rattlesnakes where, to help keep the body cool, only a part of the body comes into contact with the hot sand at any one time. In this method the snake lifts the front part of its body clear of the ground and places it down and forward in a new position, then draws the rest of the body after it, continuously repeating the action so that it appears to roll from track to track. It is particularly useful for moving rapidly over smooth, loose sand where there is little grip available for normal serpentine movement. Despite their apparent speed, it is doubtful if any snakes can exceed 6 or 7 kph (4 or 5 mph).

Feeding

All snakes feed on animal matter, though on rare occasions some species have been known to take fruit. Snakes are often largely opportunist feeders taking whatever suitable prey they can find, but they usually specialize to a greater or lesser degree; some specializing in birds, others mammals, some earthworms, slugs and so forth. Pit-vipers seek out their warm-bodied, largely mammalian prey using the heat-sensitive 'pits' which are located on either side of the head. Perhaps the most specialized of all are the egg-eating snakes (family Dasypeltinae). The throat vertebrae of the African egg-eating snake (*Dasypeltis scabra*) has sharp projections which crack the egg as it is pressed against it by muscular action while being swallowed. The contents are then drained and the crushed remains of the egg regurgitated. Most snakes swallow their prey alive, though some constrict it – not to crush the victim but to suffocate it.

Those species which have venom can attack prey larger than those which do not possess venom. Those with venom usually prey on mammals.

A considerable number of snakes are poisonous to some degree. The poisons involved are extremely complex and rather variable, with nerve poisons (neurotoxins) dominating in the cobras and sea snakes, and blood poisons (haematoxins) in the vipers and rattlesnakes. Venom is produced in a gland similar to the salivary glands of mammals. The back-fanged snakes (family Colubridae) are mostly harmless. However, one highly venomous species of colubrids is the boomslang (*Dispholidus typus*), which also has teeth nearer the front of its mouth modified for carrying venom.

In both the cobras and sea snakes the front teeth have been modified into hollow fangs down which the venom is forced by muscular action. If the fang is broken it is replaced by another growing behind. But it is in the vipers and rattlesnakes (family Viperidae) that the greatest modifications occur. The front fangs in many instances are so enlarged that they are folded back along the mandible and swing down as the mouth is opened.

The sea snakes are reputed to have the most deadly venom of all snakes, but are relatively harmless to man, since their heads are small, making it difficult to bite them; however, fatalities have occurred among fishermen extracting them from their nets. The largest venomous snake is the king cobra (*Ophiophagus hannah*) of India and southeast Asia, which can grow to 6m (20ft) in length.

A single king cobra may have sufficient venom to kill an elephant, but there has only been one verified case of human death from its bite. However, snake bites are still a major cause of death in some parts of the world. In India it is estimated that

6000-9000 people die from snake bites each year. Part of the reason for this large number is the fact that few victims seek correct medical attention. Nevertheless these deaths result in the continuing persecution of snakes, despite the fact that they have a valuable role to play in helping to reduce rodent populations.

Hatching the young

The king cobra or hamadryad (*Ophiophagus hannah*) is a species disappearing rapidly as its forest habitat disappears. The female scrapes together a heap of vegetation in which to lay her eggs, and the heat generated by it decomposing helps to incubate the eggs, and she then remains coiled around them. Pythons also coil themselves around their eggs, and their body temperature rises to help brood the eggs.

The commonest method of maintaining a high temperature – and increasing protection – for the incubating eggs is by viviparity – or more accurately ovo-viviparity – in which the eggs are retained in the body, and are therefore moved into the warmth of sunshine when the snake basks, and sheltered when the snake takes cover. Old wives' tales of snakes, such as adders, which ate their young when they were threatened were almost certainly based on observing a dead adder from which, when cut open, young adders wriggled away.

The boa constrictor lives in America from Mexico to Argentina and, although it grows to 4m (13ft), it is not dangerous to people. Boas are not venomous, but kill their prey by suffocation.

Defence mechanisms in snakes

Strangely, perhaps, for a group of animals often associated with attack and aggression, the defence mechanisms of snakes are of particular interest.

The usual first line of defence of most animals, including snakes, is to take flight, or remain motionless and hope to remain undetected. In order to help avoid detection some species of snake, such as the green mamba (*Dendroaspis angusticeps*) have very well-developed camouflage markings, often imitating dead leaves or live vegetation. They may also have disruptive patterns which serve to break up the outline of the animal, such as on the gabon viper (*Bitis gabonica*). If they fail to avoid detection, a common tactic is to suddenly display colours or markings which were previously concealed to startle the attacker. When snakes resort to this form of defence it is often accompanied by violent changes in shape. Some species inflate themselves, others raise themselves high off the ground. Cobras, for instance, rise up, inflating the neck into a hood, which exposes the 'spectacle' markings. Some snakes, for instance

the New World coral snakes have brightly coloured rings of red, black and yellow which warn other animals that they are highly venomous; some harmless snakes mimic these colours.

Another mechanism is for the tail to 'pretend' to be the head. This is common in burrowing species. Not only does the tail often look like the head, but often it is also moved in such a way as to further lead an aggressor into attacking that end of the snake, leaving the real head free for a counter-attack. The Malayan coral snake (*Maticora*) even 'strikes' with its tail, drawing attention to itself by its bright red underside.

Some snakes hiss when attacked, and rattlesnakes vibrate the ends of the tail as an auditory warning to intruders. Others roll themselves up into a tight ball with their head in the centre — the best known of these is the royal python (*Python regius*) of west Africa, often known as the ball python. The fishing snake (*Herpeton tentaculum*) goes rigid, like a piece of dead branch and stays stiff even if handled, and the Madagascan tree snake (*Mimophismah falensis*) which resembles a dead twig, also remains rigid and motionless. The

European grass snake (*Natrix natrix*) throws itself on its back in a series of contortions with its mouth open; simultaneously a foul-smelling fluid is ejected from the cloaca, and it feigns death. But by far the most spectacular feigning of death is that of the hog-nosed snakes from North America. After inflating the neck, striking and hissing, they then roll over and sham death; their mouth falls open and the tongue hangs out, convulsions run down the body ending with the tail twitching, and they lie limply. They will keep up the pretence, and can even be carried around by the tail in this manner.

A few venomous snakes have developed a defensive venom 'spitting' mechanism. By the time the normal venom of a snake has taken effect an aggressor could have killed the snake — consequently even highly venomous snakes make a considerable show of striking since the deterrent effect is much more important than the actual strike. The ringhals (*Hemachatus haemachatus*), black-necked cobras (*Naja nigricollis*) and several other species can spit venom into the eyes of an aggressor, allowing the snake to escape.

Boas and pythons (family Boidae)

The family Boidae includes the world's largest snakes. It is an ancient family with fossils up to sixty million years old; the extinct *Gigantophis* may have been 20m (66ft) long. Most boids have rudimentary pelvic girdles, and there are also often claw-like appendages on either side of the cloaca. The boas are found mainly in the Americas and the pythons in the Old World. The largest of the boas is the anaconda (*Eunectes murinus*) of tropical South America, which may grow to about 10m (33ft); the pythons of Africa may grow nearly as long, but are usually more slender. These large snakes all feed on animals up to the size of peccaries, pigs, antelopes, small deer and goats. Their large, attractively marked skins have led to a number of species of boas and pythons being exploited by the leather trade, causing concern for the survival of some species.

Boas give birth to living young, but pythons lay clusters of 20-100 or more eggs.

Just as myths abound about snake venom, so do they about the ability of pythons and other constrictors to crush their victims to a pulp. Although death is often very fast it is usually due to suffocation and heart failure.

Vipers (family Viperidae)

The family Viperidae is divided into two sub-families: the Viperinae, containing the Old World vipers; and the Crotalinae containing the rattlesnakes and pit-vipers of America and Asia. On each side of the head between the eye and the nostril, the pit-vipers and rattlesnakes have a heat-sensory pit – it is so sensitive that it can detect variations of less than 0·2°C. This organ is used to detect warmblooded prey in the dark. The 'rattle' of rattlesnakes is made up of hollow segments on the end of the tail; each time the skin is moulted another segment is added. Even some of the species lacking a rattle can make a noise – the crossed viper (*Trimeresurus alternatus*) from Brazil rustles the tip of its tail against vegetation. Although some vipers are highly venomous, such as the 3m (10ft) long bushmaster (*Lachesis muta*), the fer-de-lance (*Bothrops atrox*) and the cottonmouth (*Agkis-*

trodon controtrix), others are only relatively mildly venomous and rarely fatal to man. The European viper or adder (*Vipera berus*) is one of the more widespread species and, despite popular opinion, is rarely dangerous to man. Some of the forms of treatment – such as an incision of the bite – are probably more dangerous than the bite itself!

Colubrids (family Colubridae)

The family Colubridae is a large one, which many herpetologists divide into a number of families and subfamilies. Most colubrids are harmless, and only a few have venom that is dangerous to man, and none has specialized venom injecting fangs. They are mostly rather slender, active species and include the grass snake (*Natrix natrix*) of Europe, the garter snakes of the genus *Thamnophis* of North America, and the whipsnakes of the genus *Coluber* of Eurasia. Some of the most interesting species are the egg-eating snakes which feed entirely on bird's eggs. Others are specialist lizard or snake feeders, and the American king snakes of the genus *Lampropeltis* feed on poisonous snakes, including rattlesnakes to whose venom they are partly immune. The flying snakes of the genus *Chrysopelea* are able to flatten the body into a kind of elongated parachute and glide between trees in forests.

Cobras, kraits and sea snakes (family Elapidae)

The family Elapidae comprises two distinct groups: the subfamily Elapinae – the cobras and kraits; and the subfamily Hydrophiinae – the sea snakes. They are sufficiently different to often be considered as separate families. They are all venomous, some highly so, and have efficient mechanisms for delivering venom.

The cobras seen in snake charming acts from North Africa to India have usually been rendered harmless, and they rear up, not to the sound of music, but because this is the normal threat behaviour. In fact snakes are deaf, and are responding to the swaying movements of the charmer. The coral snakes of America come from the subfamily Elapinae, and in Africa the black mamba (*Dendroaspis polylepis*) and green mamba (*D. angusticeps*) are deadly, very large – over 4m (13ft) long – fast-moving snakes, but it is in Australia that the greatest variety of elapine snakes occur. The majority of Australian snakes belong to this group; they include the death adders of the genus *Acanthophis*, which are rather heavily bodied and appear to look super-ficially like vipers, and several which are similar to coral snakes.

Crocodilians (order Crocodilia)

This order includes the gharial, crocodiles, alligators and caimans. They live in marine, fresh waters and swamps in parts of Africa, Asia, Australia and America. They are closely related to the reptiles which roamed the Earth in the Mesozoic era, but are nevertheless well equipped to deal with life on Earth today. They all have large jaws armed with numerous teeth, and they lie in wait partly submerged in the water until a suitable animal comes to the water to drink. Then it is snatched into the water and drowned, to be eaten later. Fishes and other aquatic animals are also eaten.

Gharials (family Gavialidae)

The gharial (*Gavialis gangeticus*) is a fish-eating species once fairly widespread in the Indus, Ganges and Brahmaputra river systems of India. Their appearance is quite unlike that of any other crocodilian (other than the false gharial), since they have a very long narrow snout, with bulbous nostrils at the end with up to twenty-nine long, slender teeth in the upper jaw and up to twenty-six in the lower jaw. Although they grow quite large – up to 6m (20ft) in length – they are usually not much bigger than 3·5m (11½ft) in length.

Above: The American alligator has its main haunts in the Florida Everglades but its range extends from Texas to the Carolinas. The number of alligators have dropped disastrously through hunting and the collection of baby alligators as pets. In recent years, strict protection has assisted the species' recovery.

Opposite: A link with the distant past, the crocodiles are the closest living relatives of the ruling reptiles of prehistoric times. All crocodiles lead an amphibious way of life. The ears, eyes and nostrils are on the top of the head so they can function while the crocodile is almost submerged. The feet are webbed, but the main propulsion comes from the flattened tail.

Crocodiles
(family Crocodylidae)

Crocodiles are the largest living reptiles – which is also one of the reasons that they are so rare today. Man has long persecuted crocodiles since they are one of the few animals that will naturally prey on him, and in more recent years the large, thick, durable hide of crocodilians has become very valuable.

A male saltwater crocodile (*Crocodylus porosus*) – the largest species – of southeast Asia, can grow to over 6m (20ft) in length and the record is said to be over 10m (33ft), while the nile crocodile (*Crocodylus niloticus*) – the most widespread species in Africa – grows to a length of over 4m (13ft). Crocodiles build a lair dug out of the banks of the river they inhabit. They lie in this until the water has been warmed by the sun and it is time to hunt, at which time they slither into the water, often with just the back, eyes and nostrils above water.

Crocodiles can be distinguished from alligators by the fact that the teeth of a crocodile meet but do not overlap, whereas in an alligator they do. Also, the crocodile's fourth lower tooth is visible when its mouth is closed.

Alligators and caimans
(family Alligatoridae)

Members of this family are similar to the crocodiles, but they possess a shorter, broader head. Nor do they grow as large as crocodiles, although the black caiman (*Melanosuchus niger*) of South America grows to a length of 6m (20ft). North American alligators (*Alligator mississippiensis*), which occur in the southern states, grow to a length of 3m (10ft) normally.

Caimans differ from alligators in that they have bony plates on their bellies, instead of scales.

Tortoises, turtles and terrapins (order Chelonia)

Of all the reptiles the only ones which can claim any widespread popularity are the chelonians: the tortoises, turtles and terrapins.

The name turtle causes confusion. In American usage, the term turtle is used indiscriminately for all Chelonia, marine, freshwater or land dwelling; in British usage, turtle normally refers to marine, terrapin to freshwater and tortoise to land forms – but there are many exceptions.

The chelonians are an ancient order, with over 200 species, and have been on Earth for around 200 million years. The most obvious feature is the shell, which is divided into two sections: a carapace above and a plastron below. The shape and form of the shell is rather variable – sometimes it is flat and 'soft' (as in the genus *Trionyx*), while in others it is massive, domed and very hard (as in the genus *Geochelone*). The shell is made up of laminae (equivalent to the scales of snakes and lizards) which, as the animal grows, expand around and under it. In those species which hibernate, growth rings, like those of seasonally growing trees, can be seen. In many zoo and pet tortoises the shell is very knobbly, but this is the result of the animal having been fed too rich a diet and growing too fast. In some species, such as *Geochelone radiata*, the shell is very attractively marked and in the case of the hawksbill turtle (*Eretmochelys imbricata*) the individual laminae, or 'scutes' are of considerable value as 'tortoiseshell'.

Chelonians have horny jaws, rather like those of birds, and may be either herbivorous or carnivorous. Because they cannot expand their ribs to breathe, they must pump air in and out of their bodies; this they do by movements of the head and limbs.

Sea turtles come ashore to lay their eggs – usually at night when predators are fewer – but spend most of the time at sea swimming effortlessly with their large, flattened front legs. One of the most startling discoveries in recent years was of large populations of hibernating turtles. They were found in the Gulf of Mexico sleeping on the seabed.

Terrapins are found the world over, and some are very beautifully marked. The American alligator snapper (*Macrochelys temmincki*) lies on the bottom of a pond waggling its tongue. A fish, thinking the tongue is something to eat, closes in, only to be eaten itself by the snapper.

Land tortoises are found in the warmer regions of the world, and they are usually herbivorous.

Below: Members of the tortoise order which live in water have lighter, more streamlined shells than their land-dwelling relatives. This red-eared terrapin is a species living in North America.

Isolated giants

The land tortoises, in isolation on oceanic islands with no predators but man, have developed giant forms, often reaching 1·5m (5ft) in length. The Galápagos islands (which even take their name from the Spanish for tortoise) are the home of a giant tortoise (*Geochelone elephantopus*) which is represented by different races on each of the islands on which it occurs. Although the Mascarene and Seychelles tortoises are now extinct, the Aldabra tortoise still survives and is extremely abundant on the Aldabra Atoll. Apart from their slowness, tortoises are remarkable for their longevity and there are a number of famous long-lived tortoises. The record for longevity was one taken to Mauritius in 1766 which lived until 1918.

Birds

There are nearly 9000 species of birds throughout the world. They have colonized virtually every available habitat from equatorial rain forests to deserts, and from oceans to polar regions.

Body structure

The most distinctive features of birds are their feathers, their unparalleled powers of flight and the possession of a beak. Feathers are only found on birds. Their main functions are to provide support in the air and insulation of body heat. In many species they also aid camouflage and are used in display. Most birds have two basic types of feathers: the outer flight and contour feathers consisting of a central shaft which supports two converging webs (these webs have a remarkably intricate structure consisting of interlocking filaments); and the inner down feathers which are fluffy and provide an efficient warm insulating layer next to the body.

Fliers must reduce weight to a minimum so birds have developed an extremely light, robust skeleton. In addition, many bones are honeycombed with air spaces. In parts of the skeleton where strength is particularly needed, bones which were separate in the ancestors of birds have fused together. The most striking feature is the large breastbone with a keel which acts as an attachment for the powerful flight muscles. The wing skeleton of birds has evolved from the forelimbs of their predecessors and resembles a human arm in shape. A heavy jaw and teeth would be a great disadvantage to any creature attempting to fly. Modern birds have instead a lightweight construction of keratin, the beak.

The tail consists entirely of feathers and acts as a rudder in the air. The wing is an efficient aerofoil, providing lift for the bird in flight. It has a thickened leading edge and a tapered trailing edge. By adjusting the position of their wings birds have total control of their speed and altitude. The widely varying wing shapes of birds are adapted for different methods of flight. Swifts and falcons have slender swept-back wings to allow great speed and agility. Vultures and eagles have long broad wings to provide maximum lift, and effortless, sustained flight. Their deeply slotted wing tips smooth out turbulence. Albatrosses have long narrow wings which are the most efficient for long periods of fast gliding.

The feet of birds are highly diverse and are adapted for swimming, running, wading, perching and climbing. Swimmers' feet are usually webbed or lobed to provide maximum propulsion. Many ground dwellers especially game birds, have strong feet which are useful for scratching on the ground for food. Woodpeckers and other tree-climbing birds often have two toes facing forward and two facing backward to enable them to grip bark more easily. Birds of prey have powerful talons which are used to seize and kill prey.

Senses

The senses of sight and hearing are particularly important for birds although those of smell and taste are relatively weak in most species.

Hunters need keen vision to spot their victims and prey species also rely on sight to warn them of danger. Birds' hearing is much more acute than our own. They can detect details of song which are too rapid for our ears to distinguish. Birds rely on sound for communication. Their rhythmic songs and calls make them the best musicians in the Animal

Birds of the sea

Relatively few bird species have exploited the oceans and coastal waters which cover nearly three-quarters of the surface of the globe. The number is less than 300, only about three per cent of the total species found throughout the world. However, some of these species contain enormous populations of individuals. Often these large concentrations of seabirds are found in the more turbulent regions of the oceans where there are upwellings of nutrient-rich water. These nutrients provide food for the plankton which nourish the marine creatures which in turn are eaten by the birds. The cold Humboldt Current which flows off the coasts of Peru and Chile provides a feeding ground for immense numbers of birds in this way.

There are four main orders of seabirds, although other species such as some ducks, grebes, phalaropes and divers are more or less maritime in their habits. The four main orders are: the penguins (order Sphenisciformes); the albatrosses, shearwaters and petrels (order Procellariiformes); the pelicans, gannets, cormorants and their allies (order Pelecaniformes); and the sheathbills, skuas, gulls, terns and auks which form part of the order Charadriiformes.

Some, such as the albatrosses, are truly pelagic, only coming to land to nest, while others, like the cormorants, are usually found close to the shore throughout the year.

no keel on the breastbone for the attachment of flight muscles. With the loss of flight, the filaments of the feathers have lost the ability to interlock, as in most birds, giving them a hair-like quality. The ostrich, rheas, cassowaries, emu and kiwis are all ratites.

Cassowaries and emus (order Casuariiformes)

There are three species of cassowaries, all found in Australasia. They are powerful, heavily built birds standing as high as 1·8m (6ft). The legs are comparatively short and thick. A distinctive feature of the cassowaries is the large bony crest on the forehead. Together with their coarse hair-like plumage, the crest protects them from thorns and prickly vegetation, especially when running through the forest. Cassowaries are bad-tempered, wary birds which are seldom seen. They are thought to be monogamous, with both parents rearing the young. These number from three to eight and may remain with their parents for up to five months.

The emu (*Dromaius novaehollandiae*) is a huge bird, second only to the ostrich in size, standing up to 1·8m (6ft) in height. It is also a very fast runner and running birds have been estimated to reach speeds of 50km (30 miles) per hour.

It lives in the open grasslands of Australia where unfortunately it is very harmful to agriculture.

Ostriches (order Struthioniformes)

The ostrich (*Struthio camelus*) is the only living species within this order. It is also the largest living species of bird, a large male reaching 2·4m (8ft) in height. As it is flightless, the ostrich is adapted to a terrestrial way of life. An unusual feature is that it only possesses two toes on each foot. All other birds have three or four toes. The very long powerful legs enable it to run very swiftly when necessary and speeds of up to 64kph (38mph) have been estimated. A long neck allows it to view wide expanses of the open African savannahs where it lives. In general it is omnivorous but vegetable material probably forms the greater part of its diet.

In the breeding season each cock mates with a harem of hens. Eggs are

laid by several hens in the same nest, which is made by the cock. They may total between fifteen and thirty-five, but many fail to hatch. Although the egg is larger than those of all other birds, it is peculiarly small considering the size of the ostrich. When only a month old, the young can run as fast as their parents.

Rheas (order Rheiformes)

Rheas are similar in shape to the ostrich but stand at least a metre (3ft) shorter in height. There are two species, the greater rhea (*Rhea americana*) and the lesser rhea (*Pterocnernia pennata*). Both live in southern South America. Like the ostrich, rheas can also run as fast as a galloping horse.

At the onset of the breeding season males fight each other viciously to determine which birds are dominant. These males then acquire harems of six or more females each. All the members of a harem lay their eggs, up to sixty in total, in a single nest on the ground.

Kiwis (order Apterygiformes)

Although kiwis must be the most popular birds in New Zealand, few people have ever seen one in the wild. Their shy, nocturnal habits make them very difficult to observe. All three species are restricted to dense forests in New Zealand.

In appearance kiwis resemble small, hair-covered mammals. The body is rounded and tailless with short, thick legs and only rudimentary wings. They are unique among birds in having nostril openings near the bill tip. They forage at night on the forest floor, using their long sensitive bill as a probe as they search for earthworms and insects. Food is detected using their well-developed sense of smell.

Relative to the size of the bird, the kiwi's egg is the largest known.

Tinamous (order Tinamiformes)

There are about fifty species of tinamous which all live in Central and South America.

Tinamous are terrestrial birds, inhabiting open grasslands, scrub and forests. In appearance they resemble partridges. They have

plumb bodies, small heads and short rounded wings. As tinamous are weak fliers they often prefer to escape danger by hiding. Most species have attractive but plaintive flute-like whistling calls.

Unlike most birds the male tinamous incubate the eggs and care for the young instead of this duty being performed by the females. Up to twelve eggs are laid.

Penguins
(order Sphenisciformes)

The clownish demeanour and inquisitive nature of penguins is captivating. All eighteen species are found in the Southern Hemisphere and belong to the family Spheniscidae. They are the most efficient of bird swimmers, being supremely adapted for an aquatic life as they hunt for fishes to eat. They lost the power of flight long ago, and now their wings

are modified to form strong flippers. They propel themselves through the water like torpedoes, at times breaking the surface in the manner of porpoises. They range in size from the largest, the emperor penguin (*Aptenodytes forsteri*), standing 1·2m (4ft), to the smallest, the fairy penguin (*Eudyptyla minor*) standing just 30cm (1ft).

The breeding habits of the delightful Adelie penguin (*Pygoscelis adeliae*) have been well studied. In the spring they waddle across the broken ice floes to their traditional breeding colonies on the Antarctic ice sheet. Winter storms have frequently totally changed the appearance of the route; nevertheless they manage to find the same site and even sometimes the same mate as in the previous year. Like many of the other penguin species, they form vast rookeries, some containing many thousands of birds.

Opposite: 'Foul-gull' is the origin of the fulmar's name. Like its relatives, it defends itself while on the nest by spitting an evil-smelling oil at intruders. The oil comes from the fishes and other marine animals which fulmars eat.

Below: The wandering albatross has the longest wingspan of any bird, at 3·5m (11½ft). It glides around the Southern Ocean and returns to land only to breed. The incubation of the single egg and rearing of the chick takes so long that the wandering albatross can breed only every other year.

Albatrosses, shearwaters and petrels (order Procellariiformes)

Contrasting with the penguins, most of the Procellariiformes are experts in the air. A characteristic of the birds in this order is the 'tube nose'; the nostrils opening through horny tubes on top of the upper mandible. About fifty species form four families: albatrosses, shearwaters (2 families) and petrels.

Albatrosses (family Diomedeidae)

No birds are more nomadic than the albatrosses. They roam the southern oceans, gliding for hours on almost motionless wings, often travelling up to 9500km (5700 miles) from their breeding colonies. Most species are limited to the Southern Hemisphere, the area of calm water and windless skies known as the doldrums preventing them from flying further north. The magnificent wandering albatross (*Diomedea exulans*) has the largest wingspan of any bird, measuring up to 3·3m (11ft).

Shearwaters, petrels and fulmars (family Procellariidae)

Shearwaters are also excellent fliers, most possessing long, slender wings and bodies. In common with the rest of the family, the Manx shearwater (*Puffinus puffinus*) of northern Europe has remarkable powers of navigation.

Closely allied to the shearwaters are the fulmars. The northern fulmar (*Fulmarus glacialis*) is noted for its dramatic increase in distribution and numbers in the North Atlantic since the seventeenth century.

Storm petrels (family Hydrobatidae)

Storm petrels are the tiniest of all web-footed seabirds, although they are close relatives of the huge albatrosses. When feeding, they flutter over the waves resembling a gathering of butterflies.

Diving petrels (family Pelecanoididae)

The small family of diving petrels from the southern oceans are the most unusual members of the Procellariiformes, as they have short wings and squat bodies. Because of their similarity to auks, they are regarded as their southern counter-

parts. The flight is direct, with whirring wing beats reminiscent of that of bumble bees.

Pelicans, gannets and cormorants (order Pelecaniformes)

The Pelecaniformes is an ancient order dating back sixty million years. It consists of six families, five of which are seabirds, consisting of about fifty species. Generally they are large, fish-eating, web-footed birds. Like the order Procellariiformes, the greatest number of species are found in the Southern Hemisphere.

Tropicbirds (family Phaethontidae)

Tropicbirds have long, distinctive tail streamers, short wings and long bills, making them among the most attractive of water birds. Their flight is particularly graceful. Fish and squids swimming just below the surface are spotted by the hovering birds, which dive sharply down to catch them.

Gannets and boobies (family Sulidae)

Near relatives of the tropicbirds are the gannets and boobies. These streamlined birds also obtain fishes by plunging into the sea, but usually they dive from a much greater height

---

The flight of the albatross

Albatrosses are noted for their spectacular powers of flight. In daylight at least, they spend nearly all of their time in gliding over the oceans with little apparent effort.

Like other expert gliders of the sea, their wings are long, narrow and pointed. Even their heavy weight is used to advantage in flight. Although it causes drag, as the albatross gains speed, it results in a marked increase in momentum.

Wind does most of the work for the albatrosses. Indeed, these magnificent birds are unable to cross large areas of calm water. Waves are whipped up by even light winds. Friction with these waves reduces the flow of air at sea level. The air speed increases gradually with height, to reach its maximum at about 15m (49ft) above the surface. The albatrosses utilize this change in the rate of flow of air. With gathering speed, they dive down to sea level and turn along the troughs. Momentum from the dive and upcurrents from the wave crests enables them to rise again. As the birds ascend, they slow down until they reach a height of about 15m (49ft). Here, the prevailing wind has increased to its full strength and the birds turn and glide down once more.

In this manner, albatrosses 'sail plane' low over the waves, covering remarkable distances without a wing beat.

Opposite: The pink-backed pelican of Africa is one of six species. The pouch under the bill is not a store for fish, but a trap for catching fish. As a pelican jabs at a shoal of fishes, the sides of the lower half of the bill expand to make a broad scoop. The fishes are swallowed immediately and never carried in the pouch.

Left: Gannets fish by plunging into the sea from a height of 30m (98ft). As the bird drops headfirst, it folds its wings back to lessen the impact. In addition, the skull is strengthened to withstand hitting the water.

Below: Cormorants pursue fish under water, sometimes to considerable depths. They remain near sea coasts and freshwater lakes, returning to the shore after fishing. After a fishing trip, they stand with their wings outspread to dry.

of up to 30m (98ft). Plummeting down at a great speed, they can reach prey well below the surface and must stun their prey with the impact. Breeding colonies of the northern gannet (*Sula bassana*) are typical of those of the other species. Birds are densely packed together, one pair building its nest just beyond the reach of neighbours.

Cormorants (family Phalacrocoracidae)
Cormorants are large, bulky black or pied birds. They are expert divers and swimmers and are found throughout the coastal waters of the world. A few species also occur in fresh water.

Pelicans (family Pelecanidae)
Despite their ridiculous appearance, pelicans are very well adapted for swimming and flying. The large extendible pouch beneath the bill is used as an efficient net for catching fishes.

Frigatebirds (family Fregatidae)
The marauders of the tropical oceans are the frigatebirds. Using powers of rapid flight, they harass and then pirate food from boobies, pelicans and others. They are probably the most aerial of all seabirds. Indeed, if they land on water they have extreme difficulty in flying off again. Treetops or rocks are chosen as perches so the birds can easily take to the air.

whereas grebes occur worldwide except for Antarctica and the smaller oceanic islands.

Fishes are caught by pursuit, the divers being particularly proficient swimmers. A depth of 50m (164ft) can be reached, and dives may last as long as 15 minutes. The diet of the grebes is more varied than the divers, and includes other aquatic animals.

While divers breed on land using a scrape to lay eggs, the grebes build their huge weed nests on the water surface. When small, the young of both families are carried pickaback by their parents for warmth and protection. If alarmed, grebes may dive with the young still clinging to their bodies. Characteristic of breeding divers is their wailing, demoniacal calls which can be heard by day and by night.

Large wading birds (order Ciconiiformes)

Ciconiiformes are, in general, large birds with long legs and long bills, adapted for feeding on aquatic life by wading. Most of the 116 species live in the warmer temperate, subtropical and tropical regions of the world. Their preferred habitat is freshwater margins and lagoons, as well as marshes and swamps. They are gregarious birds, especially in the breeding season.

Herons and bitterns (family Ardeidae)

The Ardeidae consists of sixty-one species of herons, egrets, and bitterns, all of which are structurally similar. The 'powder downs' of their plumage are a notable characteristic of the family. These are areas of small friable feathers which can be crumbled into dust by the bill. When rubbed into the soiled plumage during preening, the powder soaks up fish slime and oil. It is then combed out using a serration on the middle toe.

They have two main techniques of feeding. One is to stand motionless until the prey comes within striking distance of the bird's dagger-like bill. The other is to wade through the water actively searching for food, sometimes moving slowly or making a quick dash. The long sinuous neck of these birds enables the sharp beak to act as an efficient hunting instrument. Contrary to popular belief, aquatic animals are seized and not speared.

Unlike the sociable, diurnal herons and egrets, the bitterns are largely crepuscular, secretive and solitary birds. The Eurasian bittern (*Botaurus stellaris*) has a typically cryptic plumage comprising beautiful patterns of black, brown and yellow, which imitate the colours of the dense reedbeds where they live. If surprised a bittern will stand rigid, its beak and neck pointing vertically upwards with its feathers tightly compressed against its body. If a breeze blows, it may actually sway with the reeds and some have been seen to carry on in this way for fifteen minutes.

Spectacular ornamental plumes are worn by both sexes of the egrets at the beginning of the breeding season. Little egrets (*Egretta garzetta*) were once threatened by persecution for their lovely, lace-like feathers.

One of the most cosmopolitan of all bird species is the cattle egret (*Bubulcus ibis*) which now breeds on all the continents except Antarctica.

Night-herons are relatively small, squat, short-necked members of the family. As their name suggests, they are usually nocturnal but this is possibly only to avoid the larger, more aggressive day-feeding herons.

The boat-billed heron (*Cochlearius cochlearius*), from the mangrove swamps of South America is now thought to be an aberrant night-heron. Structurally it only differs from the others in that it has a strange slipper-like bill.

Whale-headed stork (family Balaenicipitidae)

The whale-headed stork (*Balaeniceps rex*) from Africa is the sole member of its family. Its most obvious characteristic is a huge, bulging beak which may be used to actually dig for lungfish, one of its prey items.

Hammerhead (family Scopidae)

Like the whale-headed stork, the hammerhead (*Scopus umbretta*) is thought to be intermediate between herons and storks. It, too, is an African species and is the only member of the family Scopidae.

Storks (family Ciconiidae)

Some of the seventeen species of storks which form the Ciconiidae family are very large birds standing over 1·2m (4ft) tall. Usually they

feed in dry or damp grassland. They are strong fliers and are capable of feats of soaring; a few species undergo long migrations. As they lack a voice-box, they communicate by vigorous clattering of their bills during the nesting season.

Popular fables surround the white stork (*Ciconia ciconia*) of Europe and Asia. Often it chooses roof tops on which to build its stick nest, and may return to the same site year after year. The saddle-billed stork (*Ephippiorhynchus senegalensis*) from Africa is unusual among storks as it feeds by wading in shallow water.

You need to be a true bird lover to find a marabou stork (*Leptoptilos*

Marabou storks have the scavenging habits of vultures for they gather with vultures to feed on the carcases of dead animals. Rubbish tips and slaughterhouses attract crowds of marabous, and they are welcomed around towns and villages in Africa because they perform a useful cleaning-up service.

Nest of the hammerhead

A pair of hammerheads (*Scopus umbretta*) may spend six months building their nest. Several pairs may be found together in a loose colony. A site is chosen well above the ground at a height of 5-13m (16½-42½ft). It may be in the fork of a tree or occasionally in a rock fissure on a cliff face.

Basically this fortress-like structure is a closed ball 1-1·3m (3-4ft) in diameter, consisting of vast numbers of sticks. So rigid is the framework it can even bear a man's weight. Bright objects such as stones and buttons are added as decoration.

A very small, round entrance hole is made on the most inaccessible side of the nest. Birds enter by flying directly up to their dwelling, closing their wings at the last moment and diving into the hole.

Inside the nest are three chambers. The three to five white eggs are laid in the highest one. When the young grow too big for this chamber, they clamber down into the middle portion. The third section is in the form of a tunnel and is used as a lookout.

Other animals often appropriate these almost impregnable nests for their own use. Bees may take over an old nest and build a hive inside it. Birds such as barn owls also use them.

crumeniferus) attractive. It is generally considered an ugly bird, possessing a huge skin pouch and a massive bill. It feeds with vultures on the carcases of animals on the African plains.

Despite its noticeably down-curved bill, the wood stork (*Mycteria americana*) belongs to the same family. It flushes fishes and invertebrates to the surface by jumping about in the water.

Ibises and spoonbills
(family Threskiornithidae)

The thirty-one species of ibises and spoonbills both belong to the family Threskiornithidae. Although their bills are widely different in shape, the birds are closely related. Ibises typically have long, slender, curlew-like beaks, while those of spoonbills are flattened with a spatulate tip. The latter group sweep their bills back and forth like a scythe through the water to filter minute crustaceans.

Flocks of ibises often take part in group gliding. They alternately flap their wings in unison and then glide for a period. The sacred ibis (*Threskiornis aethiopicus*) was revered by the ancient Egyptians, and mummified birds have often been found in the tombs of the Pharaohs.

Flamingos
(family Phoenicopteridae)

Most remarkable of the Ciconiiformes must surely be the flamingos. There are five closely allied members in the family. They are most graceful birds, beautifully tinted with pink or red. Unlike the rest of this order, they have fully webbed feet and can swim with ease. The peculiarly shaped bill is a unique feature of the family. It is strongly down-curved, the lower mandible resembling a large trough and the upper mandible a smaller lid. Water is repeatedly taken into the beak and then expelled again by vigorous gobbling movements of the tongue and throat. A specialized filtering structure retains blue-green algae and diatoms which form the bird's diet.

Above: Flocks of flamingos standing in the shallow water are one of the great sights of Africa. The food of flamingos consists of tiny animals and plants which they sieve out of the water with their bills. The pink colour of their feathers comes from a substance in their food.

Left: The sacred ibis is so called because the Ancient Egyptians linked it with the god Thoth, who was depicted as having the head of an ibis. At one time the sacred ibis nested on the banks of the Nile. It appeared during the annual flood, reared its family and migrated away again as the water subsided, so it became linked with the essential, life-giving cycle of the Nile.

Flamingos are well known for the size of their nesting colonies, which have been known to reach 900 000 pairs in east Africa. The nests are simply cones of mud, 15-35 cm (6-14 in) high. Young birds can swim when a few days old.

Waterfowl (order Anseriformes)

Swans, ducks, geese and a group of most peculiar birds known as screamers, make up the large order Anseriformes.

There are only three species of screamers, placed in the Anhimidae family. All the remaining 140 species of the order are in the family Anatidae.

Although members of this family are superficially distinct, their structure and behaviour are very much alike. The majority have webbed feet, which are used as paddles when swimming. Their bills are generally broad and flattened with a rounded tip. The edges of the mandibles have small projections which form an efficient sieve, separating food from water and mud. Beaks of the fish-eating mergansers have developed enlarged serrations to enable them to grasp slippery, wet prey.

The plumage is very dense and incorporates a thick layer of down to give birds insulation when in the water. Waterproofing of the feathers is maintained by smearing the feathers with oil secreted from a gland situated at the base of the bill.

Most species swim and all except the swans can dive, although some do so only when necessary to escape danger.

They are gregarious birds and flocks often reach a colossal size, with occasionally entire populations concentrating together. Shelducks (*Tadorna tadorna*) from Europe gather in thousands in late summer on the sandbanks of the German Bight. Here these birds undergo a heavy moult. The simultaneous loss of some of their wing feathers forces them to remain flightless for a time. All the waterfowl undergo a similar moult and are usually retiring in their habits at this vulnerable 'eclipse' stage.

Not as silent as their name suggests, mute swans are a familiar sight on lakes and waterways in urban areas. At one time all British mute swans were the property of the Crown or certain privileged people.

Generally they are omnivorous, although mergansers feed exclusively on fish whilst sea ducks feed on crustaceans and shellfishes.

Only a few members of this order defend territories when breeding. The mute swan (*Cygnus olor*), for example, is very aggressive and will attack intruders fearlessly with a blow from its powerful wings.

Their nests are usually on the ground among marsh vegetation, dry land or even burrows in the case of the shelduck. Perching ducks and small mergansers use holes in trees, although they are incapable of making their own. Down from the breast of the female is used to line the nest and cover the eggs to provide warmth and camouflage when she is feeding. Sleeping bags and eider downs are packed with the famous soft down of the eider (*Somateria mollissima*).

With the exception of the sea ducks, most species inhabit fresh waters and marshes. They occur throughout the world, apart from the

Antarctic. Some species, such as the mallard (*Anas platyrhynchos*), are extremely numerous and widespread. This adaptable bird is found in desert, tundra, steppe and temperate regions of the Northern Hemisphere.

Geese and swans are long-necked, large members of the family, mute swans (*Cygnus olor*) weighing as much as 15kg (33lb). One of their most endearing features is that pairs frequently mate for life. The young remain with their parents after breeding and they migrate to their wintering grounds thousands of kilometres away as a family party.

The whistling ducks, of which the white-faced tree duck (*Dendrocygna viduata*) from Africa and South America is an example, bear some resemblance to geese. Both sexes are alike in plumage and calls.

Shelducks, dabbling ducks, diving ducks, perching ducks, sea ducks and the torrent duck (*Merganetta armata*) comprise the rest of the family. Despite wide variations in their appearance, they are thought to be closely allied.

The shelducks look rather similar to geese, but in general behaviour they are more like typical ducks. The females are exceptionally truculent, and encourage males to attack other birds. The delightful steamer ducks from South America are one of the shelduck group. Two species are flightless and swim rather like penguins.

Surface feeders or dabbling ducks include the elegant pintail (*Anas acuta*), garganey (*Anas querquedula*) and shoveler (*Anas clypeata*). The plant material on which they feed is reached by the birds upending from the water's surface. Pochards are heavily built diving ducks which prefer fresh water. Like the sea ducks, they drink very little or not at all.

Some species of perching ducks spend much of their time in trees and nest in holes above the ground. The mandarin (*Aix galericulata*) belongs to this group and is one of the world's most beautiful and ornate birds. Sadly, its population is now at a very low level in its native China.

Eiders and scoters are typical of the sea ducks and are truly marine species.

Stifftails are sprightly comical ducks which indulge in bizarre

The Egyptian goose looks more like a shelduck than a true goose. Its native home is in Africa, south of the Sahara but extending up the Nile to Egypt. It is often kept as an ornamental waterfowl on lakes.

Above: Shelduck live in estuaries and around coasts where they feed on marine snails and other invertebrates. They are unusual among ducks in that the sexes look alike and the drake remains with the family, accompanying the duck (female) when she leaves the nest to feed and escorting the ducklings until they have fledged.

Right: The brilliantly plumaged wood duck or Carolina duck lives in damp woodlands of North America. It nests in holes in trees, including abandoned squirrel and woodpecker nests. The ducklings must jump to the ground when they leave the nest to follow their parents to the water.

The white-faced tree duck, which lives in both America and Africa, is one of several tree duck species with unusual habits. The nest, which is either on the ground or in a tree, is not lined with down and the drake helps to incubate the eggs.

courtship display. The black-headed duck (*Heteronetta atricapilla*) is unusual as it lays its eggs in the nests of other species and so avoids the problems of parenthood. One of the few ducks adapted to live in fast-flowing water is the torrent duck (*Merganetta armata*) from the Andes. Its stiff tail feathers are used as a rudder and also help the bird to balance on slippery rocks.

Similarities in anatomy have resulted in screamers being placed in the same order as the other Anseriformes. Quite ugly in appearance, these large birds have chicken-like beaks, long thick legs and almost unwebbed feet.

Birds of prey (order Falconiformes)

Falconiformes, or raptors as they are sometimes called, form a successful and diverse order ranging in size from the tiny pygmy falcons, hardly bigger than sparrows, to the gigantic condors which can have a wing span of over 3m (10ft). With the exception of the Antarctic, they are found worldwide. There are five families which make up this order.

Their life-style is geared to hunting or scavenging. With the aid of sharply pointed talons, their feet form very effective killing weapons, crushing a victim as it is seized. The hooked beak is used to rip food into pieces, which can then be swallowed.

Many birds of prey build their own nests and these may be huge structures. Sometimes, particularly in the case of falcons, the vacated nests of other birds may be used. Because the eggs hatch at intervals of several days, the young are at different stages of development while in the nest. In certain species, notably the eagles, the result of this is that the larger chick is dominant and often persistently attacks the younger bird. This strange behaviour is thought to be related to the available food supply, the weaker chick only having the chance to eat and to eventually survive when there is enough food for both birds.

New World vultures (family Cathartidae)

The family of New World vultures includes the Andean condor (*Vultur gryphus*), one of the most superb fliers of all raptors. Like the other

149

The hooded vulture is one of several species of birds living in Africa which gather around dead animals. Being one of the smaller vultures it has to wait until other, larger birds have fed. Hooded vultures often frequent villages where they feed on refuse, and they follow farmers to eat insects as they are dug up.

vultures, they have developed very long, broad wings to enable them to soar and glide with minimum effort. They may travel 300km (180miles) in a day in search of the carrion on which they feed. Their heads and necks are covered only in bare, wrinkled and often warty skin to allow them to feed without fouling their feathers.

Kites, eagles, harriers, hawks, buzzards and Old World vultures (family Accipitridae)

This family totals over 200 species. The black or cinereous vulture (*Aegypius monachus*) is the largest of the vultures in this family and can drive any other bird from a dead animal. The lammergeier (*Gypaetus barbatus*) is perhaps the most dramatic because, although all birds of prey glide, it has perfected this skill and hardly moves it swings at all, as it flies around the slopes of the remote mountains where it lives. It sometimes feeds on bone marrow which it obtains by dropping bones from high above the ground in order to crack them.

Kites are also adept at soaring and gliding but as they are particularly lightweight birds, they do not need broad wings like the vultures. The black kite (*Milvus migrans*) is a common scavenger in Africa and Asia, hundreds often circling over the middle of Indian cities.

The sea eagles are closely related to the kites, although they are heavier with correspondingly broader wings to help keep them airborne. The bald eagle (*Haliaetus leucocephalus*) is the best-known as it is the national emblem of the United States. It is one of the many bird predators which are renowned for their aerial displays during courtship. A pair may interlock feet while high in the air and then tumble over and over together.

Harriers are about the size of kites and are extremely light-winged birds which hunt by quartering low over the ground in open country.

Raptors, which hunt in forests and well-wooded country, have evolved short, broad wings and long tails which enable them to reach remarkable speeds over short distances and to turn sharply to grab their victims. These are the sparrowhawks and goshawks, bold, fierce killers which feed almost exclusively on birds.

A less specialized group of predators is the buzzards. They are not as swift or as powerful as some but nevertheless they are very successful and are found widely throughout the world. The familiar common buzzard (*Buteo buteo*) of northern Europe spends hours at a time in graceful soaring flight. The honey buzzard (*Pernis apivorus*) is superficially similar to the buzzards, although it is related to the kites. It is unusual as its favourite foods are honeycombs and larvae of bees and wasps.

Some of the most imposing of birds are eagles, spectacular hunters and magnificent aerialists. The famous golden eagle (*Aquila chrysaetos*) is very strong; the largest birds from Asia have been known to kill wolves, although they usually feed on carrion or birds. The closely related imperial eagle (*Aquila heliaca*) is sadly now one of the scarcest of European raptors. Other members of this varied group are the extremely powerful harpy eagles, including the Philippine or monkey-eating eagle (*Pithecophaga jefferyi*) which, as its name suggests, feeds partly on macaques. The serpent eagles are well known for their skills in catching snakes and other reptiles.

Falcons and carrion hawks (family Falconidae)

There are about sixty species of falcons and carrion hawks, which form the other large family of bird predators, the Falconidae. Falcons are comparable in hunting ability to the eagles, but use quite different techniques. Their long, narrow wings are superbly designed for fast flight, enabling them to hunt by pursuit. The strange carrion hawks are related to the falcons, the common caracara (*Polyborus plancus*) being typical. It is an energetic, piratical bird which runs quickly over the ground and will eat almost anything.

Osprey (family Pandionidae)

The osprey (*Pandion haliaetus*) has been placed in a family of its own, as it is structurally different from other

The buzzard belongs to the Accipitridae or hawk family. They all have broad wings which distinguish them from the falcons which have slender, pointed wings.

birds of prey. It is an expert at catching fish. It is well adapted to seize and hold its slippery, wet victims, having two claws in front and two behind on each foot, as well as spine-like scales below its toes.

Secretary bird
(family Sagittariidae)

The ground-dwelling secretary bird (*Sagittarius serpentarius*) from the savannahs of Africa has long puzzled ornithologists but it is now thought to be related to the raptors. An impressive bird with long gangling legs, it can walk faster than a man can run but is also an expert in the air. It feeds on lizards, rodents and snakes and is known to tackle cobras over a metre (3¼ft) long.

Gamebirds
(order Galliformes)

Gamebirds are stocky, medium-sized, mainly terrestrial birds. In general they have short, rounded wings, powerful legs and feet and a short, stout bill. They occur worldwide with the exception of the Antarctic, and nearly all are non-migratory. Some species have been domesticated for food or kept in captivity because of their beautiful, elaborate plumage. There are six families.

Megapodes
(family Megapodidae)

The small family of fifteen megapodes are distributed from southeast Asia to Australia and the southwest Pacific. In most species, the strong feet and legs are used to rake vegetation, sticks and soil into a mound and the eggs are laid inside. Megapodes feed in the same way as hens, scratching at the soil and pecking among leaf litter for invertebrates and seeds.

Curassows and guans
(family Cracidae)

Curassows, chachalacas and guans are primitive gamebirds with forty-four members in the family. They are restricted to forests in the warmer parts of the New World. They are slim birds with a long heavy tail. Curassows and chachalacas feed mainly on the ground but guans are much more at home in the trees.

Grouse (family Tetraonidae)

Grouse are fowl-like birds with feathered legs. There are about seventeen species in the family. Most live in the higher latitudes of the Northern Hemisphere. In winter, many species develop a dense covering of stiff feathers on the toes. Buds and shoots form the major diet of these largely ground-feeding birds.

Opposite: The pale chanting goshawk is named after its melodious whistling calls. It lives in Africa where it spends much of its time on the ground, running at high speed after lizards and insects.

Left: The striated caracara, or Johnny Rook as it is known in the Falkland Islands, is one of the New World vultures and is related to the condors. It scavenges around colonies of penguins and other seabirds and is so inquisitive and tame that it can be approached easily.

Many of the grouse are cryptically coloured, but none is as well adapted as the rock ptarmigan (*Lagopus mutus*). When breeding, the plumage consists of warm browns to match its moorland or tundra habitat. As the vegetation dries in autumn, the bird's upperparts become greyer. In winter it is pure white and perfectly camouflaged among the snow.

Pheasants (family Phasianidae)

The pheasants belong to a large varied family of over 160 species, which also include quails, partridges, and peafowl. In size they range from the tiny short-tailed Chinese quail (*Coturnix chinensis*) which is only 13cm (5in) long, to the male blue peafowl (*Pavo cristatus*) which measures about 2m (6½ft) including his magnificent train. In common with the grouse, they fly swiftly, but usually only over short distances. Exceptions to this are the European (*Coturnix coturnix*) and Japanese quail (*Coturnix japonica*), which are the only long distance migrants in the order.

As in the grouse family, their nests are merely scrapes on the ground with a scant lining. The downy chicks are able to follow their mother soon after hatching and feed chiefly on insects. An interesting method of defence is used by some quails. Birds gather in a circle on the ground and if a predator approaches they spring into the air and scatter in all directions.

The Californian quail (*Callipepla californica*) lives in semi-desert and manages to live for months without drinking. It uses succulent vegetation as a source of water.

True pheasants must surely be among the most beautiful and ornate of birds as nearly all the males are brilliantly coloured. The hardy common pheasant (*Phasianus colchicus*) is the most cosmopolitan of this group. Our familiar domestic chicken is descended from the red junglefowl (*Gallus gallus*), an abundant pheasant in some subtropical forests of the Orient. The display of the male Peafowl (*Pavo cristatus*) is most spectacular. He raises his lacy feathers to form a giant fan of glistening blue, green and bronze colours.

Guineafowl (family Numididae)

Guineafowl are plump, medium-sized birds with the head and neck mainly bare of feathers. They have exceptionally powerful legs and feet which are well adapted for running and scratching in the soil. There are seven species in the family, which is virtually confined to Africa.

Incubator bird

Malleefowl (*Leipoa ocellata*), like the other megapodes, do not actually brood their eggs. Instead they use the heat derived from rotting plant material or the sun. A wide range of temperature is experienced during the day in the semi-desert areas where they live. The male, which undertakes most of the work, is therefore obliged to go to extraordinary lengths to maintain the eggs at a fairly constant temperature of 33°C (90°F).

In winter, he digs a hole about 5m (16ft) in diameter and 1-1·2m (3ft) deep and fills it with vegetation. He waits for a shower of rain to moisten the hole and its contents and then covers it with a layer of sandy soil. Cut off from the dry air, the plant material ferments and generates heat which is increased later in the year by the sun's rays. The mound has now been converted into an incubating oven for the bird's eggs. A remarkable number of up to thirty-five are laid, over a period of months. For each egg, the hen digs a hole and amazingly manages to place them all in the same plane in the mound. The first four eggs are laid in the corners of a square and the others are added in a regular way to form a circle. The male is able to test the internal temperature by using his bill to probe the mound.

Throughout each day for up to ten months he diligently tends the mound and regulates its temperature. If it rises too high, he digs into the top of the mound and allows some of the heat to escape. Sometimes he may scatter most of the material, only to rebuild it later in the day. In the autumn, when more heat is needed, he scoops the mound into a saucer shape to allow the sun to penetrate and warm the eggs. After struggling to the surface unaided, the newly hatched chicks run off into the undergrowth and have no contact with their parents.

Turkeys (family Meleagrididae)

The two turkeys of the Meleagrididae family are particularly large. A large wild male may weigh 10 kg (22 lb), but the female is only half his weight. Once abundant from Canada to Mexico, these birds were slaughtered by the settlers and are now much reduced in numbers. In spring, violent fights take place between males which may end in the death of one opponent.

Cranes, rails, crakes and bustards (order Gruiformes)

This is a diverse order whose members are linked by similarities of internal structure. It includes the cranes; rails, gallinules and crakes; and bustards.

Cranes (family Gruidae)

The tall elegant cranes occur throughout the tropical and temperate regions, apart from South America. Only fourteen species constitute the family and some of these are in danger of extinction. All have a strong bill which is used like a hammer to kill small animal prey. A specially modified windpipe with loops about 1·6m (5¼ft) long enables the production of exceptionally powerful trumpeting and whooping calls.

Dramatic courtship displays are characteristic of cranes. Males and females call exuberantly and dance together, leaping high into the air. The nuptial dance of the crowned crane (*Balearica pavonina*) from Africa is particularly spectacular. A nest platform of grass and reeds is made on marshy ground and two eggs are laid, although often only one young is reared.

Many species are migratory and travel together in large skeins, calling constantly. Flocks of demoiselle (*Anthropoides virgo*) and common

cranes (*Grus grus*) are seen each spring flying over the Himalayas sometimes as high as 7000m (23 000ft).

Rails and crakes
(family Rallidae)

There are 140 species of rails and crakes in the family Rallidae. Apart from the polar regions and deserts, they are found worldwide and are among the most widespread of land birds. Many small and even remote oceanic islands have their own species.

In appearance, they are rather like fowl with short rounded wings, large feet and legs and a small tail. The bill shape is variable. For example, spotted crakes (*Porzana porzana*) have a short, stout beak, while the bill of the water rail (*Rallus aquaticus*) is slender and decurved. Different again is the large conical beak of the purple gallinule (*Porphyrio porphyrio*).

The calls of many rails and crakes are distinctive. Some sound very unbirdlike; water rails can squeal like pigs, for instance. In spring, spotted crakes repeatedly utter a cry which resembles a whiplash. A var-

iety of food including insects, frogs, lizards and plants is eaten.

Despite their apparently weak flight and reluctance to fly when disturbed, many species can migrate over long distances.

Although the Rallidae are usually associated with marshland, they are found in a wide range of habitats including thick tropical mountain forests and dry grassy fields. Giant (*Fulica gigantea*) and horned coots (*Fulica cornuta*) occur in lakes at heights of over 4000m (13 000ft) in the Andes of South America.

In general they are monogamous and build a nest of marsh vegetation or grasses.

Rails and crakes tend to be dull coloured and cryptically patterned. They are secretive birds, often being most active at night. The less wary members of the family are more diurnal in their habits. Their toes are long and enable the birds to walk on floating vegetation. Vivid glossy colours of purple and green are typical of this group. The drab plumage of the familiar moorhen (*Gallinula chloropus*) is an exception. This bird is one of the most widely distributed and successful in the world. Coots

A native of India and Sri Lanka, peafowl have been kept in captivity for over 2000 years. The male, or peacock (shown here), displays a magnificent fan of plumes, each tipped with iridescent 'eye spots'.

are most unusual rails as they can swim and dive with ease.

Bustards (family Otididae)

Bustards are shy, terrestrial birds well adapted for life in semi-deserts and grassy plains. There are twenty-two species in the family, most of which are found in Africa. In length they measure 37-132cm (1-4¼ft) and include some of the heaviest flying birds. All species have long legs and usually run to escape danger.

During the breeding season males generally wear ornamental plumes. Some members of the Otididae such as the great bustard (*Otis tarda*) develop special throat pouches which they inflate and use as sounding boards. Males of this species, one of the largest of bustards, join in bizarre dances while hissing and barking together. The displaying male Bengal florican (*Houbaropsis bengalensis*) is reputed to jump to an amazing height of about 10m (33ft) to show itself above the tall elephant grass, which it inhabits at the base of the Himalayas. The breeding behaviour of males varies according to the species. Although some are promiscuous and leave all nesting duties to the hens, others remain close to their mates at this time. A shallow depression in the ground serves as a nest and one to five eggs are laid.

Long-legged and long-necked, the crowned crane is an elegant bird with a golden yellow crest. Throughout the year, but especially during the breeding season, the cranes gather for spectacular displays. They leap into the air, flying upwards and then dropping back to the ground.

Bustards are large birds which prefer to run rather than fly. Their plumage makes a very effective camouflage but the males of some species have white plumes which make a spectacular display in the breeding season.

Waders and jacanas (order Charadriiformes)

The large order Charadriiformes comprises the waders and jacanas, as well as the gulls, terns and auks which are considered with the seabirds. Waders are small to moderate sized birds, usually frequenting the vicinity of water, either inland or on the coast. Most prefer open habitats, relying for safety on cryptic coloration, mobility and their own wariness. They can run swiftly when necessary and most fly strongly. A variety of specialized bill shapes are used in different feeding techniques.

They are gregarious birds which often breed in colonies and form large flocks out of the nesting season. A scrape or depression on the ground serves as the nest. In most cases, the young can follow their parents and even feed themselves soon after hatching. Tropical species are sedentary in general, in contrast to those from higher latitudes which undergo long migrations.

There are ten families: painted snipes; oystercatchers; plovers; sandpipers; avocets and stilts; ibisbill; crab plover; stone-curlews; pratincoles and coursers; and seed snipes.

Oystercatchers are large waders which are pied or black in colour, with contrasting reddish legs. The family consists of about seven species, and representatives can be found on the shores of every continent except Antarctica. A specially adapted bill is used for opening the shells of bivalve molluscs, as well as for probing in mud and sand for other animals. In the breeding season, groups of oystercatchers take part in an elaborate piping ceremony. The birds run about with hunched shoulders, beaks pointing to the ground, uttering high-pitched incessant cries. If a nesting pair feels threatened they may move their eggs to a safer position. Another method of confusing predators is to use false brooding spots where no eggs lie.

There are about sixty-two species in the almost cosmopolitan family of plovers. The bill is usually straight and fairly short and stout. Some have sharp 'spurs' at the bend of the wing which can be used in defence. Their plumage consists of bold patterns of brown, grey, black and white. The familiar lapwing (*Vanellus vanellus*) of Eurasia feeds in a manner typical of the family. It first runs, stops sharply and remains motionless, bends down to pick up an insect and then dashes off in a new direction.

The largest family in the order, with approximately eighty-two members, is the Scolopacidae. Included in this diverse group are curlews, turnstones, sandpipers, dowitchers, woodcocks, snipes, godwits and phalaropes.

In length, they range between 13cm (5in) (stints) and 60cm (2ft) (curlews). Bill shape also varies widely, for example, a curlew's beak is long and sharply curved, while those of other species are less curved or straight. Apart from the turnstones, these birds probe with their bills to locate prey. Outside the breeding season, they are the most numerous waders of the shore. Many species have the ability to fly in close tight flocks, rising, wheeling and settling as one bird. As most breed in the far north, even in the Arctic, they undertake spectacular migrations and move as far south as the tropics.

Complex courtship displays are typical of the family. That of the great snipe (*Gallinago media*) may last through the night as birds sing together and males battle at traditional places. Curlews are best known for their evocative cries, heard most often in the breeding season. Unlike nearly all the other members of the order, the green (*Tringa ochropus*) and wood (*Tringa glareola*) sandpipers nest not on the ground but in trees, using old nests of other birds.

The beaks of the woodcocks and snipes are flexible and sensitive near the tip, forming most effective probing tools. In the nuptial flights of some of these species, specialized feathers vibrate in the air to produce mechanical sounds. As their name

The oystercatcher is a shoreline bird which uses its strong, chisel-shaped bill to smash open the shells of mussels, crabs and other hard-bodied animals. The methods for extracting the food are very precise; a hole is made in the weakest part of mussel shells and the muscles inside are severed. Crabs are flipped onto their backs and stabbed through the head.

Courtship display of the ruff

The ruff (*Philomachus pugnax*) is related to sandpipers but has quite different behaviour patterns to the rest of the family, especially when breeding. Each year, males and females only spend a few minutes together during mating. Otherwise the sexes do not associate, even wintering in separate flocks. Another unusual feature of ruffs is that cocks are 29cm (11 in) long, about 6cm (2½in) larger than hens.

Nesting takes place in the tundra of northern Eurasia and the damp meadows to the south. At this time, males develop a massive and elaborate neck collar and plumes of bright colours. Striking colour variation is found between birds, ranging from black, brown, red, yellow and white, so that individuals can easily be identified. The females or reeves, as they are called, remain a drab brown. The cocks gather on grassy mounds, especially in the early morning, and perform strenuous and aggressive 'lekking' rituals. They attempt to attract the reeves by showing off their magnificent plumage. Many also need to display vigorously to each other to maintain their status among the other males. Displaying birds erect their splendid ruffs, and droop and quiver their wings. When fighting, they kick and peck at each other, jumping up into the air at times. Bouts of aggression are often finished by birds suddenly freezing in position and then dozing for a time.

There is a well defined pecking order within males of the lek. Dominant birds, which tend to wear dark ruffs, are resident and have territories 60-90cm (2-3ft) across. Birds highest in the pecking order rarely need to fight. Surrounding them, satellite males, often wearing white ruffs, hold temporary territories. It is the dominant birds which copulate most frequently with reeves. Indeed, they often have a monopoly of the hens' attentions. When the latter are attracted to the scene, they wander into the lekking area and solicit males by pecking at their ruffs. Mating takes place immediately. Females are promiscuous and may fly from lek to lek before laying the eggs. Nest building, incubation of the eggs and caring for the young are all carried out by the females.

suggests, woodcocks are unusual among waders in frequenting damp woodland.

In the three species of phalaropes, the sex roles are reversed. The more colourful hen does the wooing then leaves the male to incubate the eggs and care for the young. Apart from the nesting season, they live mainly at sea and are expert swimmers. A thick, dense plumage traps bubbles of air and allows the phalaropes to float as lightly as corks on the waves. In more shallow water, small animals are flushed from the mud and sand by the birds pirouetting on the surface.

The two species of painted snipes superficially resemble snipe in shape but have brilliantly coloured plumage. As in the phalaropes, the sex roles are reversed, the larger hens fighting each other for the attention of males. During dramatic threat displays, females appear to be several times their actual size. The broad wings are spread and brought forward to beyond the tip of the bill, while the tail feathers are fully fanned.

Avocets and stilts are very long-legged, most graceful birds. Despite the difference in bill structure, the six species in the two groups are basically similar. Stilts probe for food with their straight needle-like bills, while avocets sweep their upcurved bills from side to side through the water. In common with many other waders, stilts may feign injury to distract predators. The race of black-winged stilts (*Himantopus himantopus*) from New Zealand may even play dead.

The curious and beautiful ibis bill (*Ibidorhyncha struthersii*) has a sharply decurved bill as its name suggests. It breeds above 3000m (10000ft) in the Himalayas and other mountain ranges nearby.

The crab plover (*Dromas ardeola*), which has no close relatives, lives along the sandy shores of the Indian Ocean and feeds largely on crabs. The birds dig nesting tunnels which can be a metre (3¼ft) long. Hundreds of pairs may nest together, turning the ground into a honeycomb.

The nine species of stone-curlews mainly live in dry, stony or sandy habitats. The plumage of sombre greys and browns merges well with the ground, concealing these 'goggle-eyed' nocturnal birds.

Although they are quite different from each other in appearance, the

eight species of pratincoles and eight species of coursers are closely related. Coursers, like most waders, are ground feeders and inhabit dry, stony areas. The Egyptian plover (*Pluvianus aegyptius*) is actually a type of courser, and interestingly is one of very few birds that depends largely on the sun's heat to incubate its eggs. These are buried in the hot sand which acts like an incubator. Pratincoles are the only members of the order which feed on the wing. The collared pratincole (*Glareola pratincola*) from southern Europe uses a graceful swallow-like flight in its pursuit of insects.

Seed snipes are terrestrial birds which resemble sandgrouse or pigeons in their dumpy bodies, small heads and short legs. The four species are all confined to South America.

Jacanas (family Jacanidae)

There are about seven species in the family, all inhabiting the tropical and subtropical regions. With the help of its remarkably long claws and toes, which distributes the jacana's weight widely, the bird can walk with ease on floating vegetation in the freshwater marshes where it lives.

A scant platform on floating aquatic plants forms the nest. As the eggs are frequently submerged, the outer layer is waterproof. They have a highly polished, almost varnished appearance.

Pigeons and sandgrouse (order Columbiformes)

Pigeons and sandgrouse comprise the Columbiformes. The unfortunate dodo (*Raphus cucullatus*), which has long been extinct, was also a member of this order. Drinking methods of the dodos were not recorded, but pigeons and sandgrouse imbibe water in a way most unusual for birds. The bill is held continuously under water and they apparently drink by sucking. Columbiformes are vegetarians, living on seeds, fruits and other plant material. The young are fed on 'pigeon's milk' secreted from the parents' crop.

Pigeons and doves (family Columbidae)

The large family of over 280 pigeons and doves are all similar in their habits and structure. They are plump birds with short necks, small heads and short bills. Their flight is strong and direct. Although they are

found throughout the temperate and tropical regions, about two-thirds of the species occur in the Orient and Australia.

Characteristic of pigeons are their soft, plaintive cooing calls which are repeated monotonously. Fruit and seeds form the major part of their diet. Pigeons are monogamous and the males are particularly attentive to their mates. The nest is usually in trees, although sometimes on the ground or cliff ledges.

The many varieties of domestic pigeon are descended from rock doves (*Columba livia*) and have been kept by man since Egyptian times. In southeast Asia and the Pacific, there are many species of colourful fruit pigeons. Their gaudy shades of green, yellow and orange form an effective camouflage for these arboreal birds. The gut of this group is specially adapted for digesting large fruits and seeds.

Sandgrouse
(family Pteroclididae)
Sandgrouse resemble grouse in their general appearance and terrestrial habits, but are actually related to pigeons. The sixteen species of Pteroclididae live in Eurasia and Africa in arid, open country. They have a chunky body, and short bill and legs. Insulation against the extreme temperatures of their environment is provided by a dense undercoat of down. Like many other seed-eating birds, they are nomadic. Often flocks of hundreds may be seen together.

Sandgrouse must drink at least once a day. As they live in dry habitats, they frequently need to fly long distances to find water. Traditional drinking sites are used, even when water is temporarily available much closer. The distance between feeding grounds and a source of water may be as much as 80 km (48 miles) and, although the birds' flight is very fast and direct, a round trip can still take over two hours.

In the early morning, sandgrouse fly off swiftly to a water hole, calling continuously as they fly. Hundreds or even thousands pitch to the ground together, often several hundred metres from the water. Only when the sandgrouse are satisfied there is no danger will they move in to drink. After just five or ten seconds they may suddenly take to the air to make their return flight.

Young birds are provided with

water in a most remarkable way. While drinking, the male crouches in the water and thoroughly soaks his belly feathers. When he goes back to the nest he stands upright while his chicks sit under him. They drink by stripping water from his wet plumage.

Parrots
(order Psittaciformes)
The 330 species of this chiefly arboreal order are easily recognized by several characteristics: all have a relatively large head, short neck and strong grasping feet with two toes in front and two behind.

The sharply decurved, hooked beak has a greater leverage than that of most other birds and can crush extremely hard objects. A macaw's bill can even crack brazil nuts or remove a man's finger. The tongue is thick and fleshy. Blunt-tongued birds like macaws feed on nuts, while parrots with brush-fringed tongues, such as lorikeets, drink fruit-juices and nectar. They are mainly coloured bright shades of blue, green, red and yellow. Their nesting behaviour is surprisingly uniform. The round white eggs are usually laid in unlined tree holes.

The colourful macaws from Central and South America are the most handsome and the largest of the order, measuring up to about 1m (3¼ft). In contrast, the tiny pygmy parrots are only about 9cm (3½in) long. In their feeding habits, pygmy parrots are reminiscent of woodpeckers as they creep about tree trunks searching for insects.

In the wild, cockatoos are noisy, gregarious birds which live in the treetops. The sulphur-crested cockatoo (*Cacatua galerita*) is the most familiar. Lories and lorikeets from the Australian region have particularly brilliant plumage and are nectar feeders. True to their name, the strange hanging parrots sleep upside down from perches, like bats. Budgerigars (*Melopsittacus undulatus*) of Australia are true parakeets. Large chattering flocks often travel together and gather to feed on grain in fields, like sparrows. Strangest of the group is the very rare kakapo (*Strigops habroptilus*) from New Zealand. It is flightless and can run rapidly on the ground. The bird is nocturnal, and hides during the day in holes, among rocks or under tree roots.

Cuckoos and hoatzins
(order Cuculiformes)
The Cuculiformes are most closely related to parrots. With the exception of the hoatzin (*Opisthocomus hoatzin*), sole member of the Opisthocomidae family, they have two claws in front and two behind, like the parrots. The largest and most widespread family of the order is the Cuculidae.

Cuckoos and roadrunners
(family Cuculidae)
The Cuculidae consist of about 127 species, which exhibit a wide diversity in structure and habits. Most species are coloured shades of brown and grey, although some like the emerald cuckoo (*Chrysococcyx maculatus*) have metallic green or bronze hues.

Although many are arboreal, there are also a number of exclusively terrestrial members of the family. The extraordinary roadrunner (*Geococcyx californianus*) from North America is one of this latter category. It has long legs and can run very quickly, although its flight is poor. Lizards and snakes, including rattlesnakes, form its diet. Even its appearance is unusual among cuckoos as it is coloured brown with black stripes. Coucals are also essentially ground cuckoos. They are dark, heavily built birds found in Africa, Asia and Australasia. They build a large domed nest and some species add a funnelled entrance.

Insects, especially their larvae, form the main food item of the Cuculidae.

Many species are nest parasitic. The eggs are laid in the nests of other birds, which then care for and feed the young. If the cuckoos are much larger than their hosts, then only a single egg is laid in a nest. Other members of the family, such as the yellow-billed cuckoo (*Coccyzus americanus*) of North America, build their own nests of loose twigs in trees or bushes. The eggs are incubated and the young reared by both parents.

Anis are gregarious cuckoos which live in South America. A communal

Opposite: The pintado petrel, is one of the many members of the petrel order that live in the Antarctic. They spend most of their time at sea, feeding on small marine animals, but return to the barren shores to nest.

Parrots live in tropical countries around the world. Many live in flocks in forests where they use their strong hooked bills to crack open seeds and nuts. They also eat fruit and insects.

nest is built, each female having a separate chamber within it, in which to lay her eggs.

Hoatzin (family Opisthocomidae)

The relationship of the hoatzin (*Opisthocomus hoatzin*) to other birds has long puzzled scientists. It is now generally thought to be most closely allied to the Cuculiformes but it has some structural affinities with the Galliformes.

The hoatzin lives in the flooded forests of South America and is quite sedentary. In many respects it is unique among birds. Unlike any other living bird, the young have claws on their wings which they use to grasp branches and to crawl along the limbs. Mature birds lose these claws but their wings still assist them in climbing. It also possesses an unusual digestive system. In all other vegetarian birds food is broken up in the gizzard, but the hoatzin has a specially adapted crop which performs this function. Once filled, the crop makes the bird top-heavy so it is obliged to lean on its breastbone when at rest.

Owls (order Strigiformes)

The owls, or Strigiformes, are largely nocturnal predators, easily recognized by their distinctive appearance. In general, they have big heads with no visible neck and short tails, giving them a rounded outline which is enhanced by their dense, soft plumage. About 130 species in two families make up the order: the barn and bay owls; and the wood, scops, eagle, fish, pygmy, little, hawk, eared and snowy owls.

Like the raptors, their powerful legs and exceptionally sharp claws are used to seize and kill their quarry. Their strongly hooked beaks are not adapted for tearing flesh, as in other birds of prey, owls usually preferring to swallow their victims whole.

The species which hunt after dark rely on their extremely acute senses of sight and hearing to locate their prey. Their large eyes are placed in the front of their heads, surrounded by a characteristic facial disc. Some species can capture animals by hearing alone if necessary. The barn owl (*Tyto alba*) is one of this category,

and recently its hearing has been studied in detail. It can locate sounds in the horizontal and vertical planes better than other animals whose hearing has been tested.

Another feature of the night hunters is their ability to fly silently so they can make a surprise attack. There is a velvet-like pile over the surface of the feathers, so their wing beats are virtually noiseless.

Typical of most owls is their beautifully patterned plumage, which is usually a mixture of browns and greys providing them with camouflage when they roost during the day. Some owls may use the nests of other birds, but most breed in holes.

The small family of barn and bay owls differ structurally from the rest of the Strigiformes in a number of minor ways, the most obvious being their heart-shaped faces. The barn owl occurs more widely than any other night bird, and often lives close to man.

The rest of the owls consist of one large family of about 120 species. It includes the wood owls which are typical nocturnal feeders. The tawny owl (*Strix aluco*) is one of the most familiar in the Old World.

Not all owls are active at night. The little owl (*Athene noctua*) is often seen in daylight, although it usually feeds at dawn and dusk.

The burrowing owl (*Athene cunicularia*), from the grasslands of the Americas, is superficially similar in appearance to the little owl (*Athene noctua*). As its name indicates, it breeds and roosts in burrows, often using the abandoned holes of prairie dogs.

The tiny, partly diurnal pygmy owls, are also chiefly insect eaters. They are, however, voracious little hunters and some species can take animals as big as themselves.

In contrast, are the massive eagle owls. The impressive northern eagle owl (*Bubo bubo*) occurs over a wide region of the world, and varies greatly in size and colour; while birds from the forests of northern Europe are large and dark, those from African deserts are a sandy hue and are much smaller.

Approaching them in size are the fish owls. They have been likened to a nocturnal osprey (*Pandion haliaetus*), which catches fishes in the same manner, using sharp, rough spikes on the under surface of their feet to help them grip efficiently.

Another method of feeding is used by owls which hunt in open country. These include the eared owls, such as the short-eared owl (*Asio flammeus*). Unlike the forest-dwelling species, it has long slender wings and quarters the ground like a harrier.

A young tawny owl demonstrates the flexibility of its neck. Owls' eyes are so large that they cannot swivel inside the skull and so they have to turn the whole head instead.

Pellets

Birds disgorge pellets as a means of removing any part of their diet which they cannot later digest. Many species, including raptors, fish eaters such as kingfishers, curlews and owls form pellets. The pellets are cylindrical capsules packed with bones, teeth, fur, feathers or the fragments of the external armour of insects. Those which have recently been ejected are covered in a shiny mucous secretion, which probably helps the pellet to move up the digestive tract. The pellets vary in size, texture and colour according to the bird which produced them, and thus can be identified with practice.

Because owls swallow their victims whole, their pellets contain all the indigestible parts of the body. Unlike other birds of prey, they cannot break down small bones and so parts of the skeleton such as skulls, lower jaw bones, beaks and limb girdles can easily be identified. Even worm casts and other invertebrate remains can be recognized.

Careful examination of the contents of pellets over a period of time can reveal the bird's diet. The best place to find pellets is in the vicinity of a roost or nest, where they form piles on the ground. Approximately two pellets are ejected each day by a fully grown owl, usually within twenty-four hours of the meal.

Nightjars and allies (order Caprimulgiformes)

The Caprimulgiformes are strange, crepuscular or nocturnal birds, the closest relatives of owls. In general, they have long pointed wings and gaping mouths to catch the insects on which they mainly feed. Their plumage is beautifully mottled, barred and vermiculated to merge with vegetation or bark and acts as effective camouflage while they roost during the day.

Nightjars (family Caprimulgidae)

The seventy species of nightjars form the largest family in the order, and are found widely throughout the world. With long, slender wings and tails, they are superbly built for agility on the wing as they chase flying prey. Characteristic of the family is the enormous gape which is used to catch insects in the same fashion as the diurnal swifts and swallows. The poor-will (*Phalaenoptilus nuttallii*), an American species, is the only bird known to hibernate. Although swifts and a few other species can survive short periods of cold in a torpid condition, the poor-will can remain in this state for three months.

Frogmouths (family Podargidae)

Closely related are the frogmouths from Australia and southeast Asia, but they feed in a different manner. Waiting motionless, they suddenly pounce on insects on the ground like some owl species. Their most distinctive features are the large hooked bill and huge mouth.

Oilbird (family Steatornithidae)

The curious fruit-eating oilbird (*Steatornis caripensis*) from the forest of South America is placed in its own family. It is outstanding for its ability to employ echo-location, in the same manner as bats, as a means of navigation in the pitch black caves where it roosts and nests.

Swifts and hummingbirds (order Apodiformes)

This order consists of two families, the swifts and hummingbirds which, although very different in appearance, are structurally similar in many respects. The wings have special adaptations which have led to these birds becoming aerialists *par excellence*.

Swifts (family Apodidae)

About eighty-six species constitute the Apodidae. In length they vary from 9-23cm (3½-9in). Swifts, the most aerial of all birds, are supremely adapted for a life spent almost entirely in the air. They feed and, apart from the breeding season, also sleep on the wing. Mating itself often takes place in flight. Their wings are slender, narrow and powerful, ideally suited for rapid aerobatic flight. The family contains the fastest fliers of all small birds. As swifts rarely land, their legs are extremely short. Although the bill itself is small, the birds have an extremely wide gape.

They usually feed by flying back and forth through concentrations of insects in the air, with the beak and gape fully open.

A few species of swiftlets can find their way in complete darkness by echo-location.

Leaves and grasses are collected on the wing and cemented together with saliva to make a typical swift's nest. That of the edible nest swiftlet (*Collocalia fuciphaga*) is constructed almost entirely of hardened saliva and has traditionally been regarded as a food delicacy in China. Young swiftlets can be safely left for days if necessary. The young bird's body temperature is dramatically reduced, and it lapses temporarily into a torpid state.

Hummingbirds (family Trochilidae)

There are just over 300 species of hummingbirds, which are all found in the New World.

Hummingbirds are tiny, fast moving and extremely active. Cuban bee hummers (*Mellisuga helenae*) measure 5·6cm (2¼in) in length, and are the smallest of all birds. The vivid iridescent plumage of the family also makes them among the most beautiful. Like flashing jewels, they dart among flowers in the tropical forests where they live. A bewildering array of plumage decorations are exhibited by the hummingbirds including gorgets, tufts, whiskers and tail streamers.

Nectar and tiny insects form their diet. All species have an elongated tongue which can be projected beyond the end of the bill. Some have a tongue with a tubular tip to suck nectar from flowers. Others have a brush-tipped tongue, which can also collect tiny insects. Within the group, the bill structure varies widely.

By nature, hummingbirds are exceptionally quarrelsome and pugnacious. If food becomes scarce they can, like swifts, become torpid until conditions improve.

A number of species undergo long migrations. The rubythroat (*Archilochus colubris*) of North America, perhaps the best known of the family, flies up to 800 km (480 miles) across the Gulf of Mexico without stopping.

Most hummingbirds are polygamous. Cock birds vigorously defend and advertise their territories, while the hens carry out all nesting duties. The nests are marvellous constructions, consisting mainly of fine plant materials. These are bound together with spiders' webs and saliva.

Above: The colourful hummingbirds are among the most skilful of all fliers. The wings beat at rates of up to 80 times per second, and hummingbirds can hover with ease while sucking nectar from flowers. They can even fly backwards.

Opposite: The nightjars are night-flying insect hunters. During the day they roost on branches or on the ground and their mottled plumage makes them very hard to spot.

Flight of hummingbirds

No other family of birds has mastered the same degree of skill in the air as have the hummingbirds. They have developed the technique of flying back and forth with ease, as well as up and down.

When feeding, they must be able to hover without changing position in order to extract nectar. To remove the bill and tongue from the inside of a flower, they also need the ability to fly backwards. Compared to the birds' size, the flying muscles are very large and constitute twenty-five to thirty per cent of the bodyweight while, in common with swifts, the bone structure of the wing is much reduced. These two adaptations, together with the hummingbirds' tiny size, allow them to beat their wings faster than any other bird. In normal flight, this rate reaches about seventy-five beats per second and appears as a blur to the human eye. It creates a humming sound, which gives the birds their name. Not all members of the family, however, can achieve such fast movements. For instance, the wing beats of giant hummingbirds (*Patagona gigas*) can be clearly seen.

When many species display, the males zoom up and down in front of females at an astonishing rate, their wings reaching 200 beats per second. While hovering, the body is held vertically and the wings move horizontally as the tips turn through a figure-of-eight. The attachment point of the wing bones to the shoulder girdle is particularly manoeuvrable and enables hummingbirds to fly in almost any direction.

Kingfishers, bee-eaters and hornbills (order Coraciiformes)

In general, the Coraciiformes are particularly colourful birds. One distinctive feature is that the three front toes are joined for part of their length.

Kingfishers (family Alcedinidae)

The eighty-five species of the family Alcedinidae, or kingfishers, are distributed worldwide, with the exception of the polar regions and some islands.

Characteristic of nearly all kingfishers is their brilliant plumage. Shades of blue, green, purple and red are dominant and are often enhanced by a metallic gloss. The legs, feet and bill of many species are also brightly coloured. Kingfishers are easily recognized as they all have the same general shape. The body is stumpy, with a large head, short legs and a long bill.

A few species, like the belted kingfisher (*Ceryle alcyon*) of North America, migrate, but most are fairly sedentary. Many eat fish exclusively. Other kingfishers live far from water and may take insects in flight or by pouncing to the ground. Shovel-billed kingfishers (*Clytoceyx rex*) from New Guinea actually dig for earthworms and have a specially flattened bill for this purpose. The clownish kookaburra (*Dacelo novaeguineae*) of Australia eats snakes and lizards. It is noted for its fiendish laughing calls and ability to imitate strange noises.

Kingfishers dig burrows in river banks, trees or even termite nests to serve as breeding sites.

Bee-eaters (family Meropidae)

There are about twenty-five species in the family Meropidae, or bee-eaters. Bee-eaters are beautiful, elegant, sociable birds. Most are found in the warmer areas of Africa and Asia. Their plumage is vividly coloured, predominantly with green, blue, red and yellow. They are slender in shape, with an elongated tail and pointed wings. The bill is long, thin and decurved.

As their name suggests, bees form a large proportion of their diet, although they do eat many other flying insects. These are caught in the air, either by pursuit or by brief sallies from a perch, like flycatchers. Often bee-eaters can be heard before they are seen as flocks are frequently noisy, uttering various trills and chirps.

Although essentially arboreal birds, in the breeding season they choose a bank of crumbling soil as a nest site. A burrow with an unlined chamber is excavated.

Hornbills (family Bucerotidae)

Most of the forty-five species of hornbills live in tropical and subtropical forests, and all are confined to the Old World. An immense bill and ugly casque are distinctive features of hornbills. The casque is usually hollow or is filled with a comb of cells. Its function, if any, is still a mystery. Another strange feature of hornbills is their long eyelashes. Some species are 1·5m (5ft) long, as large as some eagles, and the smallest measure about 37·5cm (15in). Generally, the plumage is black or dark brown with bold pale patches. The feathers are coarse and loose webbed.

Hornbills have a powerful flight, consisting of slow, heavy wing beats and alternate glides. A variety of loud calls including honking, squealing, and bellowing sounds are made. Casqued hornbills from Africa even bray like a donkey. Although most species feed on fruit and berries, a wide range of animal and plant items are eaten.

The spectacular giant hornbill (*Buceros bicornis*) of southeast Asia is the largest of the arboreal members of the family. Its feathers are often stained bright yellow by oil which the bird spreads on its plumage from its preen gland.

The ground hornbill (*Bucorvus abyssinicus*) has particularly strong legs and, as its name implies, it feeds largely on the ground. Grasshoppers, locusts and other insects form its diet.

The breeding habits of hornbills are extraordinary, and have led primitive peoples to regard the birds as symbols of purity and marital fidelity. Hornbills are believed to mate for life. They usually nest in tree holes which may be as high as 30m (98ft) above the ground. The female may enlarge the cavity before laying her eggs inside.

When she has finished laying, the male actually begins to construct a prison for his mate. Mud, droppings and regurgitated matter are used to

One of the strangest nesting habits in the bird world has been developed by hornbills. The entrance of the nest hole is walled up with mud and the female becomes a voluntary prisoner inside. She receives food from her mate through a narrow slit.

seal the hole, leaving only a slit in the centre. The female often helps him by plastering from the inside. A wall of brick-like consistency finally protects the nest, making it quite safe from attack by tree snakes and monkeys.

Barbets, woodpeckers, toucans and honeyguides (order Piciformes)

A unique feature of the Piciformes is the arrangement of the thigh muscles and tendons that move the feet. In common with parrots and cuckoos, they have two toes facing forward and two back.

Most species are arboreal, and are often non-gregarious by nature. Holes are used as nest sites for the white eggs. As in the order Coraciiformes, the young are blind on hatching and are reared in the nest.

Barbets (family Capitonidae)

The gaudy barbets are thickset birds with short necks, large heads and stout bills. The name barbet is derived from the beard of bristles around the base of the beak. None are migratory and their flight is generally weak. Many of the eighty species occur in Africa, although the family is found throughout the tropics of the Old and New Worlds, with the exception of Australia.

Adults may eat fruits, buds, flowers and insects. The young are usually fed on insects.

A distinctive habit of barbets is to sit for long periods on one perch, calling monotonously. Barbets excavate their own nest holes, usually in trees. Both parents feed and vigorously defend the young.

Toucans (family Ramphastidae)

The thirty-two members of the toucan family range from medium to large in size, and measure 30·5-61 cm (1-2ft). They occur in the tropical and subtropical forests of Mexico and South America, from sea level up to about 3200m (10 500ft).

The comic toucans are easily recognizable. All have a ridiculously large, but surprisingly lightweight, bill. In some species, it may even be as long as the bird itself. The function of the strange bill shape of toucans and hornbills is still unknown. Although toucans can deftly handle the fruit and berries which they eat, their bills do seem unnecessarily large for this purpose. The birds apparently use their bills in

The strange partnership between honeyguides and man

In parts of Africa, natives revere and protect the greater (*Indicator indicator*) and scaly throated honeyguides (*Indicator variegatus*). A mutually beneficial relationship, long disbelieved by naturalists, has developed between man and bird.

The inconspicuous honeyguide draws a hunter's attention by loud chattering and by flitting from branch to branch. The hunter follows the bird as he knows it will take him to a bees' nest nearby. Some tribes believe that if they ignore the honeyguide's lure then their gods will be angered. Apparently, the bird only starts to look for a bees' nest after it has enticed a native to follow it. Calling continuously, it leads him on an erratic trail. The bird usually finds a bee's nest after about half an hour, at which point the honeyguide suddenly becomes silent, often flying in small circles and returning to the same perch.

The nearby nest can easily be located by the hunter, who simply looks for a stream of bees emerging from its entrance. A termite mound or tree are common sites. He can then break into the nest without difficulty and remove the comb. A smoking branch is often used to fend off the bees. A part of the comb is always left for the bird, as the tribes believe if they fail to do this the bird will drive game away when they go hunting.

play, throwing berries from one to another.

Gregarious by habit, they live in small noisy flocks among the tree-tops. In the jungles, they are one of the noisiest birds, and utter varied bugling, yelping and croaking cries.

Honeyguides (family Indicatoridae)

The family of honeyguides has eighteen members, most of which live in the tropics of Africa, but two occur in southern Asia. The appearance of honeyguides is quite nondescript, but the family has some interesting characteristics. The birds are sparrow or starling sized, with a robust build. The beak in most species, is thick and strong, although in some it is small and slim or curved.

Honeyguides possess the ability, unique among birds, of digesting beeswax. Indeed, the larvae of a few insect species are the only other creatures which can obtain nourishment from this wax. Recently it has been discovered that special micro-organisms live in the birds' stomachs and are involved in the digestion of the wax. The diet is supplemented in many species by insects, especially bees which are caught by short flights from favoured perches. The honeyguides' particularly tough skin acts as protection against bee stings.

Another unusual feature of this group is their habit of nest parasitism, in which eggs are laid in the nests of other species. The nest holes of such species as woodpeckers, barbets and bee-eaters are used for this purpose. The honeyguide eggs are almost indistinguishable from those of the hosts. All are white and nearly spherical.

A newly hatched honeyguide is pink, naked and blind, like the other nestlings, but has needle-sharp tips to its bill mandibles. These are used to repeatedly bite its nest mates, which consequently suffer a horrible death. In this way, the surviving chick ensures the provision of an adequate food supply from its foster-parents. After about a week, the bill tips wear off, having served their gruesome purpose.

Woodpeckers (family Picidae)

There are about 210 species of woodpeckers, or Picidae, which occur in Asia, Africa, Europe and the Americas, but are not found in Australia. Essentially, woodpeckers are arboreal birds adapted for digging prey out of wood or from under bark. An extraordinary feature of the family is the extremely long and mobile tongue. The bones supporting it are also particularly long, and usually extend round the back of the skull, ending near the bill base. Muscles attached to these bones allow the tongue to be darted in and out remarkably quickly. Insects are caught on the sticky tip, which is often edged with barbs or bristles.

The bill of true woodpeckers is long and powerful and acts as a chisel. A specially modified skull allows the birds to safely pound their bills onto tree trunks. Bristle-shaped feathers cover the nostrils and so protect them from the sawdust created by this hammering. The wedge-shaped tail of stiff feathers provides an efficient brace when the birds are climbing up trees. Even the legs and claws are highly specialized. Woodpeckers are able to cling to and hop up vertical trunks, aided by very sharp curved claws and short, strong legs.

Wrynecks and piculets are two small groups which do not share some of these characteristics. Their bills are shorter and weaker and the tail feathers are soft.

Generally, the family Picidae are sedentary, as an adequate food supply is present all year round. Loud, harsh ringing calls are typical of the family. In spring, males of many species beat their bills violently and rapidly against tree trunks and branches. This drumming is the equivalent of other birds' songs.

Perching birds (order Passeriformes)

More than half of all living bird species belong to the order Passeriformes. Characteristic of all its members are their perching feet which have three toes in front and one behind. When the birds cling onto branches, their grip automatically tightens. All the species in this order are land birds, and are small to medium in size. They are often termed passerines or perching birds. The so-called 'songbirds' all belong to this order.

Lyrebirds (family Menuridae)

When lyrebirds were first described, naturalists compared them to the pheasants, but they are now recognized to belong with the perching birds. Only two members of the family exist and both live in the dense rain forests of Australia. By far the best known is the superb lyrebird (*Menura novaehollandiae*). The Prince Albert's lyrebird (*Menura alberti*) is rare and limited to a small area.

Males are about 1m (3¼ft) long, but this includes 60cm (2ft) of tail. The birds are famous for the two beautiful lyre-shaped feathers in the tails. Hens are the same size but lack these magnificent feathers. Their food consists of small crustaceans, snails, worms and insects taken from the forest floor.

Breeding takes place mainly in winter. The nests are bulky dome-shaped structures of sticks, mosses and other plant materials. At high altitudes, snow may actually cover the nest of the superb lyrebird. A single egg is laid, which is remarkably resistant to cold.

Larks (family Alaudidae)

The Alaudidae or lark family has eighty members, mainly concentrated in Africa, Asia and Europe. The flute-like songs of larks are famous; perhaps one of the most attractive is that of the European skylark (*Alauda arvensis*). Like many other larks, it usually sings on the wing.

They are predominantly small terrestrial birds which live in open country. Most species are coloured a mixture of drab browns and greys, which match their environment. The cup-shaped nest is always on the ground. Many species raise two broods in a year.

Swallows and martins (family Hirundinidae)

Swallows and martins are among the most familiar of birds. There are about seventy-five species, distributed almost worldwide, apart from the polar regions. In appearance they are slender, small passerines with long pointed wings and often a forked tail. The bill is small but a wide gape, aided by facial bristles, acts as an efficient aerial scoop for catching flying insects. Superficially they resemble swifts, although the families are not related.

They often breed in colonies and return to the same site year after year. A number of species, such as the purple martin (*Progne subis*) of North America and common swallow (*Hirundo rustica*) of Europe, now readily nest in buildings instead of tree holes or on cliffs. Some construct nests by gluing together small pieces of mud. Others use tunnels excavated in banks of loose earth.

Wagtails and pipits (family Motacillidae)

The Motacillidae consists of about fifty-four species of wagtails and pipits. With the exception of the polar regions, the family is found worldwide, although the wagtails are almost entirely confined to the Old World.

They are small and slender-bodied, with long legs and a slim pointed bill. In appearance and habits, pipits resemble larks. Most have a drab, streaked brown plumage. Wagtails are more colourful and possess a long tail, which they continually nod or wag up and down. Characteristically they are ground birds which walk and run but never hop. Almost all occur in open country, although wagtails show a preference for wet areas. Essentially they are insectivorous and capture prey on or near the ground.

Gregarious by nature, pipits and wagtails often form flocks in winter. Thousands of wagtails may roost together, frequently in trees or reed-beds. Their nests are open structures of dried grasses, usually built on the ground.

Shrikes (family Laniidae)

The seventy-two species of shrikes are concentrated in the Old World. Their main characteristics are their strongly hooked bills and bold predatory habits. Insects are their main food but they also eat small reptiles, mammals and birds. They usually hunt by swooping down on prey from an exposed perch. Some species frequently impale their victims on thorns and appear to store them in this way.

Generally shrikes are solitary birds found in areas with scattered trees and bushes, which provide prominent look-outs. The nest is often in a tree or bush and is built of leaves and twigs.

Wrens (family Troglodytidae)

All sixty-three wren species are found in the New World. One, the wren or winter wren (*Troglodytes troglodytes*), as it is called in North America, has also colonized Asia, north Africa and Europe.

Show-off birds

The mimicry and display of male superb lyrebirds (*Menura novaehollandiae*) are spectacular. The performances take place chiefly in autumn and winter, during the breeding season, but can occur at any time. Superb lyrebirds are polygamous, a male having up to three mates. He clears areas on the forest floor of all vegetation and uses his strong feet to create mounds about 15cm (6in) high and 90cm (3ft) in diameter. Care is taken to keep the soil of the mound surface clear.

Several mounds are made and used in turn as dancing platforms. Logs and low branches may also serve the same purpose.

During his dramatic display, the tail is raised and falls forward so the two lyre-shaped feathers lie parallel to the ground. His body is totally obscured by other tail streamers, which are fanned to form a lovely lace-like lattice. As he prances on the mound, he shimmers his splendid plumage. The dance is accompanied by an equally impressive vocal performance. The male is a remarkable mimic and intersperses his own loud calls with those of other forest birds. Other sounds have been attributed to them, such as the imitation of car horns, dogs barking and rustling of birds' wings, but these are heard less often. Females are attracted to the mounds and mating occurs nearby.

Wrens are small, active, inconspicuous birds which are often brown in colour. Apart from the cactus wrens, they have a stocky build and short tails. The slender bill is adapted for an insectivorous diet. Generally they are birds of the undergrowth and can be found in habitats as varied as rain forests and semi-deserts. All are vigorous songsters and may sing throughout the year.

The nest is built by the male and is usually a complex domed structure of woven plant material and hair. In many species, the male also constructs several other nests. Up to ten of these have been recorded for the wren. These may serve as roosting sites and also help to maintain the pair bond.

Mockingbirds and their allies (family Mimidae)

Mockingbirds, thrashers and catbirds form the Mimidae family. There are over thirty species, including such familiar North American birds as the catbird (*Dumetella carolinensis*), northern mockingbird (*Mimus polyglottos*) and brown thrasher (*Toxostoma rufum*). All are restricted to the Americas and adjacent islands.

They measure 20-30 cm (8-12 in) in length, and are generally coloured shades of grey and brown. The tail is long, while the wings are short and rounded.

Mockingbirds are noted for their varied musical songs. They are solitary and aggressive birds, defending territories even outside the breeding season and are found in gardens, bushy grassland or forest edges. Their diet consists of invertebrates, fruits and seeds, which are collected on the ground. Most species build rather bulky open nests of twigs lined with hair and grasses in thick foliage.

Thrushes (family Turdidae)

The Turdidae include some of the best songsters of the bird world, such as the nightingale (*Luscinia megarhynchos*) and the hermit thrush (*Catharus guttatus*). Robins, chats and the so-called true thrushes all belong to this family. Familiar members are the robin (*Erithacus rubecula*) and blackbird (*Turdus merula*) of Europe and American robin (*Turdus migratorius*) from North America. There are over 300 species which occur worldwide, apart from Antarctica and some islands.

Thrushes can be found in habitats ranging from bare deserts to tropical rain forests. Although they are chiefly insectivorous, many also eat fruit. Most species feed on the ground, others feed in trees but none take prey in flight.

Nearly all the thrushes build a neat cup-shaped nest, frequently of stems and leaves.

Babblers (family Timaliidae)

Babblers live in the forests and bushy grasslands of Africa, southern Asia and Australia. The 275 species constitute a remarkably diverse family, within which are species similar to wrens, tits, thrushes, small crows and others. Some are sombrely dressed like the jungle babbler (*Turdoides striatus*), while others, such as the so-called pekin robin (*Leiothrix lutea*), have brightly coloured plumage. Their bill shapes are strikingly varied. The long thin curved beak of the slender-billed scimitar babbler (*Xiphirhynchus superciliaris*) and the stout jay-like beak of the laughing thrushes are just two examples. Generally, the bill and legs are strong and the plumage is soft and fluffy. They are weak fliers.

Most are highly sociable and forage together in small, noisy, skulking flocks. The cup- or dome-shaped nests are usually built on or near the ground in wooded areas.

Old World warblers (family Sylviidae)

The approximately 350 members of the Sylviidae are found mainly in the

Old World, although three species breed in North America. Many species living in the temperate region migrate. Some populations travel huge distances, for example the Arctic warblers (*Phylloscopus borealis*) from Scandinavia fly as far as Indonesia in winter. The goldcrest (*Regulus regulus*), the firecrest (*Regulus ignicapillus*) and kinglets form a small and unusual group of the family.

Most of this family are small inconspicuous birds, generally coloured shades of brown, green or grey. In habits they are usually shy and non-gregarious. Warblers occur in many different habitats including woods, bushy areas, reedbeds and tall grasslands. Warblers are mainly insectivorous, and collect food items by picking directly from the vegetation.

Their finely woven nests may be domed or cup-shaped. They are often placed among thick vegetation or suspended from stems or branches. Tailorbirds make remarkable nests by sewing together the edges of large leaves.

Old World flycatchers (family Muscicapidae)

There are approximately 300 species of flycatcher; they are found throughout the Old World and on some Pacific islands. True to their name, flycatchers feed by capturing insects in flight. They habitually make short sallies in the air from a favoured perch. Bristles on the upper mandible help them to catch their prey.

Generally they are small or fairly small birds which are often brightly coloured. Undoubtedly, the most beautiful are the paradise flycatchers, which occur from Africa east to Australia. In the breeding season, males of some species carry two extremely long, ribbon-like tail feathers.

Flycatchers weave a neat cup-shaped nest of lichens, mosses and hairs. Both sexes share the nesting duties but the females work the hardest.

Nuthatches (family Sittidae)

There are about twenty-five species of nuthatches, mainly concentrated in the Old World. They are noted for their ability to move in all directions on branches and trunks of trees. They can even walk upside down with ease, aided by their strong claws and long toes. Unlike the woodpeckers, their tails are soft and are not used as a brace. These rather small arboreal birds have short tails and powerful bills. In general they are coloured blue-grey above and paler below. As the name suggests, nuts are a favourite food item on the menu of nuthatches.

A tree hole serves as a nest site. Some species excavate fresh holes, some use old ones and others even plaster up holes which are too large, to make them smaller.

Titmice (family Paridae), Penduline tits (family Remizidae) and Long-tailed tits (family Aegithalidae)

There are over sixty species of tits. They are found in Europe, Asia, Africa and Central and North America. All are small, active and acrobatic birds. They have a stubby body with a large head and short bill. Often they join in small feeding parties which search noisily for food together. Predominantly they eat insects, which they collect from bark and the undersides of foliage. In winter the diet may be supplemented by seeds.

Many species, like the blue tit (*Parus caeruleus*), build a cup-shaped nest. The long-tailed tit (*Aegithalos caudatus*) of Eurasia and Africa makes a lovely ball-like structure lined with a remarkable number of feathers. The penduline tit (*Remiz pendulinus*) also from Eurasia and Africa suspends its unusual flask-shaped nest from branches. Some species like the black-capped chickadee (*Parus atricapillus*) actually excavate their own nest hole from soft wood. Tits are mostly found in areas of scattered trees, although some will visit gardens.

Sunbirds (family Nectariniidae)

In total there are about 120 species of the tiny sunbirds. All occur in the warmer forested areas of the Old World, with the greatest number in Africa. In many ways, sunbirds are reminiscent of the hummingbirds from the New World. Both families are largely nectar feeders and exhibit brilliantly coloured plumage, often with a metallic lustre. However, sunbirds do not share the hummingbirds' remarkable flying powers and perch on or beside flowers as they feed. The tongue is tubular, with a forked tip for extracting nectar.

The lesser grey shrike and its relatives behave like miniature birds of prey. They hunt small animals, mainly insects but also rodents, birds and reptiles. The prey is struck with the claws and killed with a bite. Surplus food is impaled on a thorn for later use, a habit which has earned shrikes the nickname of 'butcherbirds'.

Spiderhunters are an unusual group which have drab plumage and a longer, stronger bill than the rest of the family. They build an open nest and actually sew the rim to the underside of a leaf. In contrast, the other sunbirds make a purse-like nest of fine plant materials and spiders' webs which they hang from a branch.

Honeyeaters
(family Meliphagidae)
The Meliphagidae, or honeyeaters, is one of the dominant families of Australian birds. About half of the 170 species occur there and the rest are distributed throughout the southwest Pacific region.

A characteristic feature of honeyeaters is their extensible tongue. It has a brush-like tip and sides which

curl to form a tube for sucking-up nectar and tiny insects. While feeding, the birds' plumage continually brushes against the nectar-producing flowers. In this way, they play a major role in pollination in the brushlands and eucalyptus forests where they live. They are small to medium in size with a slim, down-curved bill. Frequently they feed together in small, noisy, quarrelsome flocks. Many are sombrely dressed but some are strongly marked with black, white and red colours. Although they usually have harsh and or metallic calls, there are exceptions. The tui (*Prosthemadera novaeseelandiae*) of New Zealand is regarded as one of the country's finest songsters. Nearly all species make a flimsy, open nest which is suspended from a small branch or leaves.

Buntings, American sparrows, cardinals and grosbeaks
(family Emberizidae)
There are over 320 species of cardinals, grosbeaks, buntings and American sparrows. The family is found in the Americas, Europe, Asia and Africa. A typical example is the red cardinal (*Cardinalis cardinalis*), a familiar bird of North American suburbs and gardens, with all red plumage.

All are stocky, and are small to medium in size with robust conical bills suited to their seed-eating diet. Buntings and American sparrows are generally patterned black, white and brown. Essentially they are terrestrial birds found in a wide range of habitats. Outside the breeding season, most species are gregarious. By contrast, the cardinals and gros-

beaks of the New World are mainly unsociable, arboreal, brightly coloured birds. The cup-shaped nest is usually built on or near the ground, although cardinals and grosbeaks frequently nest in trees.

Tanagers (family Thraupidae)

Tanagers are finch-like birds characterized by their gaudy colours. They constitute a large family of about 215 species occurring chiefly in the tropics and subtropics of the Americas. Nearly all are arboreal. Tanagers are not conspicuous, despite their bright colours, as they are quiet birds, the majority having weak, pleasant songs. Insects supplemented by fruit and berries form their diet. Most species build an open nest placed high in the trees, although a few also construct a roof to their nests.

Wood warblers (family Parulidae)

The Parulidae, or wood warblers, is a family of small, dainty, insectivorous birds. There are about 113 species all confined to the New World. They live in widely different habitats such as tropical and coniferous forests, as well as marshes and deserts. The plumage is extremely varied. Most species are brightly coloured or strikingly marked, like the American redstart (*Setophaga ruticilla*) and black-and-white warbler (*Mniotilta varia*).

They have exploited a wide range of feeding niches. The voice is well developed in the family and, although the songs are not particularly musical, they are persistently repeated. Their nests may be open or domed and are built on the ground, in bushes or in trees.

Icterids (family Icteridae)

The family Icteridae exhibit a greater degree of diversity than any other family of birds. They range throughout the Western Hemisphere but are concentrated in the tropics. There are over ninety species, including some of the more familiar North American birds, such as grackles, American orioles, meadowlarks and cowbirds, as well as the less well known tropical caciques and oropendolas.

The birds vary between 15-53cm (6-21in) in length. Although the predominant family colour is black, many species are patterned brown, orange, red, yellow and white. As the icterids have exploited widely different feeding niches, their bills are of varying proportions and lengths. However, they are essentially conical and pointed. Many species are arbor-

Opposite: The nightingale is famous for its sweet song which is heard mainly at night. Why it should sing at night is not known, however.

eal and representatives occur in almost every type of forest. Some, like the meadowlarks, are found in prairies, while others are found in marshes or semi-deserts.

The diet is also varied, although all eat insects to some extent. Most are gregarious and some species form large feeding or roosting flocks.

Orioles are noted for their lovely flute-like songs. Other icterids have a large repertoire of loud calls and whistles.

Breeding habits are equally diverse. They may nest in colonies or in solitary pairs, on the ground, in marshes or in trees. The majority of nests are open but others are roofed. A hanging pouch-like nest is typical of the American orioles. Oropendolas and caciques construct long sleeves of woven grasses. Usually they are colonial and suspend their nest high in the trees. Cowbirds are notorious nest parasites, laying their eggs in the nests of other birds.

Finches (family Fringillidae)

The 126 members of the Fringillidae are small, chiefly arboreal birds. They occur in Eurasia, Africa, the Americas and also Australasia since being introduced there.

Finches are well adapted for a seed eating diet. The strong, conical bill and large jaw muscles can easily crack or crush hard seeds. Hawfinches (*Coccothraustes coccothraustes*)

Right: The black redstart is a relative of the thrushes whose name means 'red-tail'. Originally a bird of sea cliffs, it is now a town-dweller which nests on industrial sites.

The nest of the social weaver

The social weaver (*Philetairus socius*) is a soberly dressed and sparrow-sized bird, which lives in the arid areas of South Africa. This rather nondescript species builds a huge and complex communal nest, which may be as high as 3m (10ft) and up to 5m (16½ft) in diameter. The hammerhead (*Scopus umbretta*) and monk parakeet (*Myiopsitta monachus*) of Argentina are the only other birds which make nest structures of comparable size. From a distance, the nests have been mistaken for native huts.

As many as 100 to 300 pairs join together to create their dwelling. The flock usually returns to the nest to roost, even outside the breeding season.

An isolated grassland tree is generally chosen as a site, but telegraph poles have also been used. The massive dome-shaped roof is constructed first. Grass stems are arranged vertically so that the canopy resembles thatch and likewise efficiently repels water, providing total protection against the occasional heavy rains of the area. Underneath the roof, each pair uses grasses to weave its own nest chamber. Vertical walls divide the superstructure into numerous apartments, one for each pair. Despite the birds breeding at such close quarters, sexual partners remain faithful to each other and to their nesting compartment. The tenement nest may last as long as twenty years.

have particularly powerful and massive beaks. Crossbills (*Loxia curvirostra*) are most unusual, as their bill mandibles cross over to form an efficient tool for extracting seeds from pine cones.

Within the family, nesting habits are fairly uniform. Although some species form loose colonies, most breed solitarily. A neat cup-shaped nest is built in trees or bushes.

Sparrows, weavers and their allies (family Ploceidae)

The Ploceidae consists of over 141 species of small, seed eating birds with short thick bills. The family is found naturally in the Old World, and is well developed in Africa.

A well-known member is the house sparrow (*Passer domesticus*), the most successful town dweller of all birds. Perhaps the most destructive bird species, the red billed quelea (*Quelea quelea*) from Africa, also belongs to the family. Huge bands of these birds devastate crops in the manner of locusts.

The voice is unmusical and consists of a variety of chirping and chattering sounds. In general they are gregarious, especially the weavers which form large flocks throughout the year. Most live in open country but others occur in forests, on rocky hillsides and in high mountains.

Sparrows are soberly dressed, mainly in browns and greys, but the male weavers are often splashed with bright colours of red, orange and yellow.

Sometimes sparrows breed in colonies, but weavers always do so. Invariably, the nests are roofed. Those of sparrows are usually built in holes in trees or buildings, whilst the elaborate constructions of weavers are suspended from branches.

Starlings (family Sturnidae)

These medium-sized passerines have a stocky build with a short tail, strong legs and bill. Generally their plumage is very dark and glossy, with a metallic sheen. In habits they are often highly gregarious, and may be seen in immense flocks.

The 110 species live in a wide range of habitats, many occurring in forests or on agricultural land. Although some starlings are omnivorous, others have a more limited diet, feeding on insects or fruit.

The Sturnidae is naturally restricted to the Old World but the common starling (*Sturnus vulgaris*) has become widespread in North America since its introduction there.

Many are remarkable mimics of other bird calls and songs, as well as other sounds. Indian hill mynahs (*Gracula religiosa*) are renowned for their ability to imitate the human voice.

Tree holes usually serve as nest sites.

The clamour of thousands of starlings is a familiar sound in towns and city centres. As the birds use buildings rather than trees, they cause considerable damage by fouling masonry with their droppings. At the end of the last century, they first started to roost in urban areas and now many cities hold large congregations all year round.

In summer, many use reed beds but later move to evergreen thickets and trees such as rhododendrons and pines, which provide more protection. Although the largest roosts can hold as many as five million birds, the majority are much smaller. They also cause damage in the country, and whole plantations may be killed by the birds' excreta.

Usually starlings fly about 15 km (9 miles) each evening but may travel up to 50 km (30 miles) to reach the larger roosts. About an hour before sunset, the more distant birds start to fly in. As others join them, they eventually form an enormous mass of birds. Swirling flocks repeatedly fly over the roosting site before landing. The starlings create a din of high-pitched squealing, which may carry on throughout the whole night.

Orioles (family Oriolidae)

Although the twenty-four species of orioles predominantly live in the tropics and sub-tropics of the Old World, one species, the golden oriole (*Oriolus oriolus*), is a summer visitor to Europe. Orioles are arboreal by habit and spend most of their time in the forest crown. They are medium-sized birds with robust bills and pointed wings. The males of many species are brightly patterned with yellow and black. Females are less colourful and are usually a greenish-yellow.

These wary and usually solitary birds are often more easily heard than seen. Many have a melodious song and make loud liquid whistles. They build a finely woven cup-shaped nest of grasses, often placed high above the ground.

The courting structures of bowerbirds

In the breeding season, male bowerbirds stimulate their mates by constructing and decorating a bower.

The simplest is made by the tooth-billed bowerbird (*Archboldia dentirostris*) and consists merely of a cleared area of the forest floor. Almost daily he scatters fresh leaves on his stage and removes the old ones. A rather more complex affair is made by Archbold's bowerbird (*Archboldia papuensis*). He hangs a curtain of bamboo strands and ferns around a mat of twigs on the ground. At the edges he places berries, snail shells and pieces of bark. Several species, including the smallest, the golden bowerbird (*Prionodura newtoniana*), build huge roofed structures, often called 'maypole bowers'. These may be up to 3m (10ft) in height and are the result of years of work. The walls and ground are covered in bright ferns, mosses, flowers and berries.

Probably the most intricate bowers are constructed by the avenue builders. Twigs and sticks are meshed together to form the floor. In the centre are placed two parallel walls of upright sticks, just far enough apart to let the bird walk through easily.

Regent (*Sericulus thrysocephalus*) and satin bowerbirds (*Pfilonorhynchus violaceus*) actually paint the interior walls of their bowers with bluish or greenish pigments mixed with saliva. They use leaves or a piece of bark to daub on the paint and are among the few bird species which use tools. All manner of objects such as pebbles, shells, leaves and flowers are added as decoration.

Bowerbirds (family Ptilonorhynchidae)

The eighteen species of bowerbirds are restricted to the forests of New Guinea and Australia. These wary birds have skills as architects and decorators shared by no other birds. The male constructs a bower, which may be a remarkably elaborate structure, and this is used as a stage to attract a mate. As in the birds of paradise, the hen incubates the eggs and rears the young unaided.

Males exhibit a variety of colours and plumage patterns, although the females are quite drab in appearance.

Birds of paradise (family Paradisaeidae)

The most colourful and ornate of all birds must surely be the birds of paradise. Most of the forty-three species are found in the forests of New Guinea and lead a sedentary way of life.

A bewildering array of extraordinary plumes decorate the adult males. They expend their energy in spectacular courtship displays in an effort to attract as many mates as possible. In contrast, females are drab and inconspicuous. The majority of species are polygamous, the males taking no part in nesting duties.

Although other species have developed special feathers for the attraction of a mate, none can rival the splendid plumes of the birds of paradise. Their courtship displays, like their elaborate plumage, are diverse.

The standard-winged bird of paradise (*Semioptera wallacii*) is noted for two white pennant-shaped feathers which extend from the bend of each wing. When courting, the bird raises them to form a 'V' over its back.

One of the species which joins in communal displays is the blue bird of paradise (*Paradisaea rudolphi*). Each male maintains his own perch within an arena. During his noisy, elaborate performance he hangs upside down and spreads his gorgeous blue plumes about him. Some, like the four species of six-winged birds of paradise, take part in spectacular dances. In this group the males meticulously clear an area of the forest floor to use as a display arena. They wear six elongated feathers, like hatpins, on the head, and during the dance these are swung and rotated.

Males of other species have strictly individual display perches or territories which they defend against intruders. The magnificent bird of paradise (*Diphyllodes magnificus*) clears the ground around a sapling and plucks leaves overhead to let in a shaft of light through the forest. He dances up and down the sapling, spreading his yellow crest like a huge fan and expanding his glossy green chest feathers.

Crows (family Corvidae)

There are over one hundred members of the Corvidae or crows. The family is almost cosmopolitan although absent from New Zealand and most islands in the Pacific.

Crows are renowned for their bold, inquisitive and aggressive behaviour, and are the heaviest and most bulky of the passerines. Their learning ability is considerable and their behaviour is highly adaptable. Both features suggest that crows have a high degree of intelligence compared with other birds. Despite persecution by man throughout much of their worldwide range, they continue to prosper. A number of species co-exist with man in cities, but most live in woodlands or bushy grasslands. Many have a highly varied diet. Typical crows are largely black with strong bills and legs. The largest of the family, the raven (*Corvus corax*), belongs to this group. The nests are usually large structures of sticks and branches built in trees.

Choughs are most unusual crows, often living above the tree-line in mountain areas of Europe and south-west Asia. Flocks frequently take part in aerial acrobatics high in the air. Nutcrackers are found in the coniferous mountain forests of North America and Europe. These handsome birds store quantities of pine cones and nuts. It has been shown that they have a surprising memory for relocating these food caches.

Jays and magpies are particularly beautiful birds. Eurasian jays (*Garrulus glandarius*) largely eat acorns and, like nutcrackers, are also notorious food storers. Blue jays (*Cyanocitta cristata*) are commonly found in the suburbs of North American cities. The noisy, wily magpies are notable thieves and are especially fond of removing bright objects. Grey jays (*Perisoreus canadensis*) from North America have no hesitation in entering camps to steal.

Mammals

The unique features of the mammals are that they have hair (even baby whales have a few bristles on the throat), and that they feed their offspring on milk manufactured in the mother's body. The name mammal comes from the Latin *mamma*, meaning breast. There are about 4000 species of mammal alive today – fewer than the reptiles or birds – and about two-thirds of all mammals are rodents – the rats, mice and their relatives.

Mammals may be divided into three main groups, depending on the way they reproduce. The first group is the monotremes – consisting of the platypus and the echidna – which are egg-laying mammals; the second group, the marsupials – such as the kangaroos and the opossums – give birth to tiny, partly developed offspring which develop in the mother's pouch; and the third group – the placentals, sometimes called the true mammals – give birth to well-developed young.

The placentals form the largest group. The developing baby or embryo grows inside the mother's uterus or womb and is nourished by means of a placenta. This is a mass of tissue in which blood vessels from mother and embryo intertwine. The embryo is attached to the placenta by the umbilical cord. Food and oxygen are transferred into the embryo's body and waste products are passed back into the mother for disposal. Some placentals are born when they are still not fully developed. Baby mice and rabbits are born blind and naked, and they have to be kept warm by their mothers. Others, such as horses and sheep, can walk almost as soon as they are born.

Both mammals and birds evolved from the reptiles, and in both groups their bodies have become more efficient through the development of warm-bloodedness. However, the course of evolution has taken different lines. Most mammals still run on four legs like their reptilian ancestors and have a tail for balance, but the limbs are brought under the body to give greater support and agility than in the sprawling reptile.

The scales of the reptile have been replaced by hair which usually forms a thick covering called fur. There are two kinds of hair: short, dense underfur and long, sparser guard hairs. The guard hairs form a waterproof covering over the underfur, which traps a layer of air next to the skin to keep the animal warm. Hair sometimes has other functions. A lion's mane and a man's beard are sexual characteristics; whiskers are organs of touch; while the spines of hedgehogs and quills of porcupines are hairs modified for defence.

The ability to regulate their body temperature is one of the main reasons for the mammals' success. A high body temperature enables the muscles, nerves and other parts of the body to work more efficiently. Mammals are 'warm-blooded' and keep their temperatures constant despite wide changes in the temperature of their surroundings. The fur acts as an insulator to prevent heat loss in cold weather and if the mammal gets too hot, it sweats or pants to cool down. The high body temperature is maintained by generating heat in the body. The large amounts of food and oxygen needed for this process are made available by efficient blood and breathing systems. Some mammals, especially small ones, are less efficient at maintaining an even body temperature. They often avoid the cold weather or a shortage of food by hibernating. This is more than a long sleep. Their breathing and heart-beat slow down, the body temperature drops and they become virtually cold-blooded, in order to save energy.

The Australian platypus must count as one of the strangest of all mammals. It is one of only two kinds which lay eggs and it has a leathery 'duck's-bill' for gathering food. The male has a poison spur on each ankle, but its function is not known.

Mammals may have four kinds of teeth set into the sockets in their jaws. The incisors in the front of the mouth are for grasping and biting. Next comes the canines, one in each corner of the mouth, for stabbing. The premolars and molars, called the cheek teeth, are set in the side of the mouth. They have points, called cusps, for chewing. The arrangement of teeth depends on a mammal's diet. Carnivores have long canines, or fangs, for stabbing prey, while cattle and horses have large, flat cheek teeth for grinding tough plant food. Some whales and anteaters have no teeth at all. Most mammals have two sets of teeth; the milk teeth appear usually just after birth and they are replaced by the adult teeth before the mammal has grown up.

The large brain is another important feature of the mammals. Their active way of life requires good sense organs with a well-developed nervous system to analyse their input and order quick reactions. Some mammals have small brains which are hardly more advanced than those of reptiles, but most have a considerable mental capacity compared with other groups of animals. The folding of the cerebral hemispheres is a sign of intelligence and reaches its peak in the human being, the most intelligent animal of all.

Monotremes (order Monotremata)

The monotremes are unique among the mammals because they lay eggs instead of giving birth to live young. Nevertheless, they are true mammals because their bodies are covered in hair and they suckle their young with milk. They are the most primitive mammals alive, for they have several features which are otherwise found only in reptiles. The first stages in the development of the embryo is the same as in a reptile egg, and the young has an egg-tooth on its snout to help break out of the shell. The bones of the shoulders and the structure of the ear mechanism are also reptilian. Full mammalian characters include the possession of a diaphragm, the structure of the red blood cells and the well-developed cerebral hemispheres of the brain. Living monotremes are found only in Australia and New Guinea.

The platypus (*Ornithorhynchus anatinus*) is one of the strangest-looking mammals. When the first skin of a platypus arrived in London in 1797 it was thought to be a fake, made by sewing a duck's bill onto the body of some other mammal, and the specimen still bears the marks where an attempt was made to prise the bill off with a pair of scissors. A platypus is about 50 cm (20 in) long and has a

streamlined body covered with fine, dense fur. The feet are webbed for swimming, and the ears and the small eyes are set in a furrow which closes over when the platypus is under water. A platypus can remain submerged for about ten minutes while it searches for crustaceans, molluscs and aquatic insects. It finds its prey by touch, the bill being soft, rather than horny as in a duck, and set with large numbers of tactile sense organs. Young platypuses have a small number of teeth but these are replaced in the adult by horny plates which are used to crush prey.

The male platypus has a poison spur on the ankle of each hind leg. The poison is painful, but not fatal to humans. Courtship takes place in the water and the female digs a long burrow, up to 30 m (98 ft) long with a nest chamber at the end. After laying two, sometimes three, soft-shelled eggs, she blocks the burrow at intervals with soil. The eggs hatch after ten to twelve days, and the newborn babies are naked and blind. The mother has no teats but the milk oozes through patches on her abdomen where the babies lick it up.

The two species of echidna or spiny anteater live in continental Australia, Tasmania and New Guinea. They resemble hedgehogs with long spines set in a coat of coarse hair. A large echidna is 46 cm (1½ ft)

long and weighs 4·5 kg (10 lb). The diet consists of ants and termites which are swept up with a sticky, whip-like tongue that thrusts 18 cm (7 in) beyond the pointed snout.

The female echidna lays a single egg which is incubated in a pouch on her belly. After hatching, the baby remains in the pouch but, after its spines begin to grow, it is placed in a burrow.

Marsupials (order Marsupalia)

The best-known of the marsupials are the kangaroos of Australia. Marsupials get their name from the Latin *marsupium*, meaning a pouch, and marsupials are often referred to as pouched animals. They are among the most primitive of the mammals, only slightly more advanced than the egg-laying mammals or monotremes. The pouch, which is found only on females, is formed by a fold of skin on the abdomen and is used as a nursery for the babies. The opening of the pouch may be forward, towards the head, or backward.

Although the great majority of marsupials are found in Australia, they also live on adjacent islands such as Tasmania to the south, and New Guinea to the north. A few species also live in South America and one, the Virginian opossum

Wallabies are a type of small kangaroo. They are marsupial mammals which give birth to their young in an undeveloped state and rear them in a pouch on the mother's body.

(*Didelphis marsupialis*), has extended into southern North America.

In spite of the name, not all female marsupials have a pouch but they all have a double womb, which no other mammal has. All marsupials are alike, moreover, in other features of their anatomy, and especially in the undeveloped state in which they are born.

Some species of marsupial may be as small as mice, while others may be very large – the great grey kangaroo (*Macropus major*) is 2 m (6½ ft) tall, for instance. Most share with the kangaroo the long, powerful hind legs, long strong tail and small forelegs; and they progress by leaps. When standing still their stance is upright, the body being supported on a tripod formed by the hind legs and tail. It would clearly then be a disadvantage for them if the pouch opened backwards, towards the ground. In the rest of the marsupials, like the Tasmanian devil (*Sarcophilus harrisi*) and the wombat (*Vombatus hirsutus*) which have legs of more or less equal length and which progress by running, it is an advantage that the pouch should open backwards, otherwise there would be the risk that its opening might catch in vegetation.

Most remarkable of all is perhaps the marsupials' method of birth. The babies are born at an early stage of their development – a sort of very premature birth – and they are then still very small. The newborn baby of a 2 m (6½ ft) kangaroo, for example, is no bigger than a haricot bean. Its brain is not fully developed, yet its senses of smell and touch are already working well. Its forelegs are longer and stronger than its hind legs. The moment it leaves the opening of the mother's birth canal it clings to her fur and makes its way through the fur into the pouch. There it takes one of the teats that are in the pouch into its mouth and begins to feed. A special muscle in the mouth ensures such a grip on the teat that it is difficult to remove a baby once it has taken hold. The baby remains in the pouch until it has grown to the point of being a small, fully formed version of its mother. Even when it is old enough to move about on its own it still uses the mother's pouch for resting. The baby kangaroo for instance, known as a joey, continues to suck, putting its head in the pouch to find a teat: and it also jumps back into the pouch in times of danger.

Marsupials were formerly worldwide. We know this from their fossils. They evidently died out through competition with the true mammals except in Australasia, and to a lesser extent in South America, because these areas became separated in geological times from the main land masses, before the true mammals had had time to spread into those areas. Consequently, when Europeans first discovered Australia they found only marsupials, the two egg-laying mammals, a few rodents, some bats (which had flown across the sea) and the dingo (which had been introduced by earlier settlers).

Being free to evolve, undisturbed by the presence of the superior true or placental mammals, some species became tree-dwelling, such as the koala (*Phascolarctos cinereus*) and the tree kangaroos, and others took to burrowing. This is what happened to the true mammals, also. So we find counterparts between the two groups. There is, for example, a marsupial mole (*Notoryctes typhlops*), very like the true mole in appearance and habits, but the female has a pouch. Very small marsupials are like mice and rats except that they are pouch-bearers and usually have markedly longer legs, for leaping. Marsupial mice and rat kangaroos have the same appearance and habits as true mice and rats do in deserts elsewhere in the world.

A group of marsupials which are of larger size than the marsupial moles, rats and mice are the bandicoots. They include the rabbit bandicoot (*Thalacomys lagotis*) which eats vegetation and has long rabbit-like ears. Corresponding to the badger of other parts of the world is the wombat, the two being very alike in size, build and habits. Larger still are the wallabies and kangaroos which represent the deer and cattle elsewhere that live by grazing and browsing in the forests and on the plains. The koala (*Phascolarctos cinereus*) is a bear-like marsupial which lives in trees. It eats mainly the leaves of gum trees.

The marsupials so far mentioned by name are either total vegetarians or feed on plant food which may or may not be supplemented with insects or other small invertebrates. Inevitably, there came into being the meat-eating species, the counterparts of the cats and dogs among true mammals. Notably there was the Tasmanian wolf (*Thylacinus cyno-*

cephalus), so-named because it looked like a wolf. This animal is now almost certainly extinct. Other flesh-eaters are the Tasmanian devil and the native cat (*Dasyurus quoll*), the latter looking more like an overgrown stoat, yet sufficiently cat-like to have been given that name.

In the trees live the phalangers, remarkably like squirrels and, in New Guinea and northern Australia, the cuscuses, monkey-like in appearance and given that name because the noises they make sound like 'cussing'.

There is even an anteater, the numbat (*Myrmecobius fasciatus*) which specializes in eating termites and, like the anteaters in other parts of the world, has a long snout and a long slender tongue for extracting the insects from their nests.

Finally, there are the various opossums. The true or original opossum is an animal native to America, the size of a cat but looking like a rat. When Australia was settled by Europeans they named some of the animals they saw 'opossums' although, as was later realized, they are phalangers. American and Australian opossums belong to different families and Australian zoologists today prefer to call the Australian species possums, and the American species opossums.

Also known as the Australian teddy bear, the koala is a slow-moving but very capable tree-climber. It has sharp claws and strong toes for gripping and moves up the trunk in a series of short jumps. After leaving the pouch, the baby is carried on its mother's back for another six months.

Insectivores (order Insectivora)

These mammals are the oldest and most primitive of the placentals. They have the full set of five toes on each foot and they walk with the sole pressed to the ground; their brains are small and simple but the part concerned with smell is well-developed; and they have many similar-shaped teeth with sharp cusps. The name insectivore implies that these animals are insect-eaters and that their teeth are suited for crunching hard-bodied prey. This is true of many insectivores, but some species eat worms, molluscs, frogs and even plants. Of the 370 or so species, not one is larger than a rabbit, and 265 are shrews.

The shrews look rather like small mice, with long, pointed snout, small ears and pin-head eyes. The Etruscan shrew (*Suncus etruscus*) is the world's smallest mammal, at a weight of 2 g. The hero shrew (*Scutisorex congicus*) of Africa has an extraordinarily strong backbone and is said to be able to survive being stood on by a man. Characteristically shrews are quick, jerky and nervous in their movements. They are active throughout the day and night, with only short periods of rest, and they need to find their own weight in food every day to provide the necessary energy for their rapid way of life. Like rabbits and hares, the common shrew (*Sorex araneus*) eats its own droppings to gain extra vitamins which would otherwise have been lost. Although shrews are normally solitary and aggressive towards other shrews, the young may stay with their mother after they are weaned. Some species have the habit of forming caravans in which the young form a chain behind their mother, each holding the tail of the one in front. The elephant shrews (Macroscelididae) have large ears and a long pointed snout.

The eleven species of hedgehogs belong to the Old World, some of them living in deserts. Their characteristic spines are modified hairs which are continually being shed and regrown. The spines can be erected or laid back by muscles in the skin, while a special band of muscle enables the hedgehog to roll up tightly and draw the coat of spines around its soft underparts. Although many animals kill and eat hedgehogs despite the spines, none does so regular-

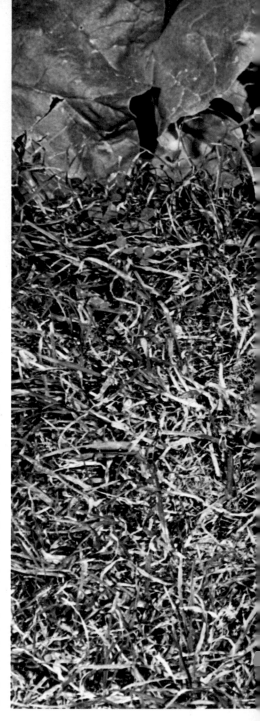

ly. Baby hedgehogs are born with a set of soft spines hidden under the skin.

The moles are designed for burrowing underground. The body is torpedo-shaped, the short neck making head and body almost continuous. The fur has no 'set' and brushes equally well in any direction, so there is no danger of impeding progress during tunnelling, and there are no external ears. The forelimbs have become strong shovels operated by powerful muscles. The mole digs through soft soil with a breaststroke action, but in harder soil it braces itself with both hind feet and one forefoot and digs with the other forefoot. Excess soil is removed by excavating a vertical shaft to the

---

Hibernation

For the European hedgehog, hibernation starts about October, although young animals are active until later. The hedgehog retires to a nest of leaves in a sheltered place and goes into a deep sleep. Its body temperature falls from 34°C (93°F) to that of the environment, its heartbeat slows from 190 to 20 beats per minute and breathing drops to ten per minute. In effect, the hedgehog is living more slowly, so conserving its body reserves until food becomes plentiful again.

Energy is, of course, still being used to maintain life processes during hibernation, and the hedgehog will lose approximately one-third of its body weight over the course of the winter. It must, therefore, enter hibernation with plenty of fat to see it through to spring. If a hedgehog cannot put on sufficient weight in autumn it will not survive the winter.

Hedgehogs and other hibernating animals have two kinds of fat. White fat accumulates under the skin and around the abdominal organs as in other animals, while brown fat forms lumps or pads, mainly around the shoulders. Brown fat is energy-rich and can liberate large amounts of heat rapidly. It is used to warm the hibernating animal if the outside temperature drops too much and, at the end of hibernation, it raises the body temperature as the animal rouses. Brown fat also occurs in other animals, especially in babies (including humans), where it helps to keep the body warm during the critical period immediately after birth.

surface and raising a molehill. The mole's tunnel system acts as a trap for worms and insects, which the mole collects on frequent patrols. Worms not eaten immediately are sometimes stored, the mole first immobilizing them by biting the front end.

The star-nosed mole (*Condylura cristata*) of North America is similar to the mole (*Talpa europaea*) of Europe and Asia but it has twenty-two fleshy tentacles on the tip of its snout. The golden moles (family Chrysochloridae) of Africa are different in several ways and they dig with snouts that end in a leathery pad.

The desmans are aquatic relatives of the moles and live in rivers in Russia, Spain and Portugal. They resemble large shrews.

Madagascar is the home of the tenrecs, a group of insectivores which have evolved in isolation to form a number of different types. Some of the twenty species look like shrews, others have spines like hedgehogs and can roll up for protection, while the rice tenrecs burrow in marshy ground. The water tenrec (*Limnogale mergulus*) has webbed hind feet and hair-fringed forefeet and tail. It lives near water and feeds on small fishes, aquatic insects and water plants. The tenrecs' nearest relatives are the rare solenodons of the West Indies, and the otter shrew (*Potamogale velox*) of Africa which swims by means of a flattened tail.

A bristling carpet of needle-sharp spines greets the enemies of the hedgehog. Each spine is controlled by a muscle and can be made to lie flat, or stand erect when the hedgehog is alarmed. Further provocation makes the hedgehog roll up into a ball.

Bats (order Chiroptera)

The bats are unique, since they are the only true flying mammals, but they are also interesting for their hibernation, echo-location system and diverse feeding habits. As with the birds, the forelimbs have been modified into wings. The bat's wing consists of a thin, elastic web of skin which is stretched between the body and the fore and hind limbs. It is supported by four fingers and becomes stretched taut, like an umbrella, when the forelimb is fully extended. The thumb is left free and bats may crawl or even run on all fours, with the thumbs supporting the wings.

There are some 750 species of bats, making them the largest group of mammals after the rodents, and they fall into two groups. The Megachiroptera are the fruit bats or 'flying foxes' of the Old World tropics. They eat fruit, pollen and nectar. The Microchiroptera also live mainly in warm countries, but they are found all over the world, except in polar regions and remote islands. Their diet is mostly insects. In cooler parts of their range microchiropteran bats hibernate for the winter. They select a place which has a cool, even temperature and a high humidity. During hibernation the heartbeat almost stops and the body temperature drops to that of the surroundings. In this way, the bats survive the winter months on the fat stored in their bodies. Hibernation is not continuous and all bats wake up at intervals, and may even move to a new roost.

Almost all bats are nocturnal, and in this way they avoid birds which could either compete for the same food or prey upon them. Microchiropteran bats are not blind and they may use their eyes to find their way around the countryside, but the main sense for finding their insect prey and detecting obstacles in the dark is echo-location, or sonar. The bat emits a stream of clicks and listens for the faint echoes which give it the position of prey or obstacles ahead of it. The clicks are essentially ultrasonic, which means that the pitch is too high for the human ear to hear. They range from 15 to 150 kHz (1 kHz = 1000 cycles/second). The upper range of human hearing is 20 kHz, so some bats can just be heard by humans.

There are two main systems of echo-location. Most bats 'shout' through their open mouths. When searching for food, they emit clicks at a rate of three or four a second. Once an insect is detected, the clicks speed up and finally there is a 'buzz' of 200 per second as the bat attacks. The 'leaf-nosed bats', like the horseshoe bats of the genus *Rhinolophus*, 'snort' through their noses. These bats emit long whistles instead of clicks and the intricately folded noseleaves make a megaphone to beam the sound. A bat's sonar is so effective that it can detect a tiny insect from about 50 cm (20 in) away, and the bat can avoid wires which are as fine as a human hair.

Except for a few species which live in caves and use audible clicks for navigation, megachiropterans or fruit bats do not possess echolocation and they rely on vision. They have exceptionally large and sensitive eyes, but they also have a good sense of smell. In the tropical forests where fruit bats live, crops of fruit ripen in succession to provide a continuous source of food all the year round. Fruits eaten by bats have a strong smell which attracts the bats; they also hang on long stalks so that they are easy to reach and they remain on the tree instead of falling when ripe. The bats eat only ripe fruit which they crush and press with the tongue to extract the juice. The flesh and seeds are spat out and, as the bats carry the fruit before eating it, they help to disperse the seeds. Some fruit bats are pollen- and nectar-eaters and they act as pollinators. They have long tongues for reaching into flowers, which attract the bats by opening at night and also by giving off a very strong-smelling scent.

Although most insect-eating bats hunt in open spaces for flying insects, a number of species pluck insects and other small animals from foliage or land to pick them off the ground. The pallid bat (*Antrozous pallidus*) of America even catches scorpions. Some bats hunt bigger prey such as lizards, mice and even other bats. Several species catch fishes, and two American bats specialize in fishing. Their echo-location detects the ripples of a fish swimming beneath the surface and the bats then catch the prey with the long claws of their hind feet. One Central American bat catches frogs. It perches above a pond and waits for the frogs to start calling. Then it glides down, guided

---

Gliding mammals

The bats, birds, the prehistoric pterosaurs and the insects are the only animals capable of sustained, flapping flight, but several groups of animals have evolved the ability to glide. These include fishes, frogs, lizards and snakes, as well as some mammals in addition to bats. These are the marsupial flying phalangers of the Australian eucalyptus forests, with one species, the sugar glider (*Petaurus breviceps*) reaching New Guinea and Tasmania; the flying squirrels of North America, northern Europe and Asia; the scalytails, another family of rodents (Anomaluridae), of Africa; and the colugo or flying lemur of southeast Asia, which is not a lemur but has an order of its own, the Dermoptera.

The 'flying mammals' are supported in the air by webs of skin stretched between the front and back legs, which are sometimes extended to the tail and neck. Gliding is slow, never more than about 16 kph (10 mph), but it enables the mammals to travel quickly from tree to tree in search of food. The giant flying squirrel (*Petaurista petaurista*) can ride on air currents, and may travel over 4 km (2½ miles). Gliding makes these mammals very vulnerable to attack by birds of prey, but this they avoid by being active at night.

190

by the sound of the frog and without using its echo-location so that the frog is not alerted.

The three species of vampire bats of the genus *Desmodus* are the only blood-sucking mammals. They live in Central and Southern America and usually attack cattle and horses, but humans also become victims. The vampire uses its razor-sharp incisor teeth to make a cut, so delicately that the victim is not aroused, and laps the blood that flows out. An anticoagulant in the saliva prevents the blood from clotting until the bat has finished feeding.

Bats, the only truly flying mammals, roost in quiet caves, buildings and hollow trees. These fruit bats rely on good eyesight rather than echo-location to find their way about.

191

Monkeys, apes and their relatives (order Primata)

Man is a primate, related to the monkeys and apes. Although we think that our intelligence puts us at the top of the evolutionary 'tree', the structure of the body shows that primates are fairly primitive mammals, in that they have features of the earliest mammals. The five fingers and toes on each limb are the basic vertebrate pattern which was first adopted by the amphibians and has been reduced in many mammals, to the single hoof of a horse for instance. Many other mammals have also lost the collarbones.

The first primates were small shrew-like mammals, not far removed from the very first mammals. They lived in trees, were probably active at night and scampered along the branches like squirrels. Gradually, eyesight became more important than smell, the snout shortened and the eyes moved to the front for good stereoscopic, or three-dimensional, vision. This is useful for judging distances when leaping from branch to branch. The primates have also developed large brains and include the most intelligent animals.

The tree shrews (family Tupaiidae) are probably similar in habits to the early primates, although they are now usually thought not to be primates. They are small, squirrel-like animals that live in the forests of southeast Asia and eat fruit and small animals.

The primates are divided into the prosimians (which means 'before the monkeys'), or lower primates; and the anthropoids (meaning 'monkey-like'), or higher primates.

Prosimians (suborder Prosimii)

The prosimians include the bushbabies, lemurs, lorises and tarsiers. They are found mainly on the islands of Madagascar where there are no monkeys or apes. Elsewhere, they have survived the arrival of the modern, diurnal anthropoids because they are active only at night. Most live among vertical branches, feeding on insects, so they do not compete with their more vegetarian relatives.

There are twenty-one species of lemurs on Madagascar. The cat-sized ringtail lemur (*Lemur catta*) is the most familiar, because it is often seen in zoos and is active by day. Groups feed together, and walk with their black-and-white ringed tails held in the air. The indris (*Indris indri*) is the largest lemur, and the sifakas (genus *Propithecus*) are a striking white, orange and maroon colour. These last two animals leap rather than clamber. The sportive lemur (*Lepilemur mustelinus*) is so-called because it boxes its opponents. The aye-aye (*Daubentonia madagascarensis*) is now one of the rarest animals. It is not only strange-looking; it has the unusual habit of extracting insect grubs from inside trees. It digs a hole in the timber with its teeth, then squashes the grub and picks out the remains with a long finger.

Outside Madagascar, the bushbabies (genus *Galago*) live in Africa. They spend the day in hollow trees and feed at night on insects, fruit and the gum that oozes from the bark of certain trees. Bushbabies are good jumpers, as are the tarsiers (genus *Tarsius*) of southeast Asia. The tarsiers have huge eyes that cannot move in their sockets and, like owls, they have to turn their heads to look over their shoulders. By contrast, the lorises of Asia, and the potto (*Perodicticus potto*) and angwantibo (*Arctocebus calabarensis*) of Africa creep slowly and deliberately. One finger or toe is reduced to a stub, so that the hand or foot forms a pincer to give a firm grip on the branches.

Monkeys and apes (suborder Anthropoidea)

With the exception of the tarsiers, the prosimians rely largely on their sense of smell to find food and keep in touch with each other, whereas the monkeys developed their eyesight and are less reliant on smell. They are diurnal animals, except for the night monkeys or douroucoulis (genus *Aotus*) of South America. Most live in the trees but the baboons are ground-dwellers. There are two main kinds of monkeys: the New World and Old World monkeys.

The New World monkeys have flat noses and round heads. All have long tails and, in some species, the tail is used as an extra 'hand'. It is prehensile, and can grasp a branch to support the monkey's weight, or even to hold food. The capuchin monkey (genus *Cebus*) was once well

which are not his offspring. The colobus and guereza monkeys (of the genus *Colobus*) of Africa differ from the langurs in having a very short thumb, and several are strikingly coloured. The black-and-white colobus (*Colobus polykomos*) is threatened because it is hunted for its fur.

The macaques are the commonest monkeys of Asia. They also live in Africa; the Barbary ape is the only monkey in North Africa. The rhesus monkey (*Macaca mulatta*) is well known because it is widely used in medical research. The 'rhesus factor' in blood is named after the monkey. The pig-tailed macaque (*Macaca nemestrina*) is trained to climb palm trees and throw down coconuts, and the crab-eating macaque (*Macaca fascicularis*) lives in mangrove swamps, feeding on shellfishes. The Japanese macaque (*Macaca fuscata*) is the most northerly distributed of the monkeys, and has a shaggy coat to keep it warm in winter snows. Several incidents have demonstrated how quickly these monkeys learn. One troop discovered some volcanic springs, the monkeys soon learned to take hot baths. Another troop was being studied by scientists who gave them food. First the macaques learned to wash dirt from the sweet potatoes they were given, then they discovered that they could separate sand from rice by throwing it into the water. The rice grains floated and the sand sank. In each case, one particular female first learned the trick, and the other macaques then copied her.

The guenons of Africa include the vervet monkey (*Cercopithecus aethiops*), which is also called the green monkey and is responsible for the rare and fatal 'green monkey disease'. It is one of the few guenons to live in more open country, and it has a long tail which acts as a radiator to help it keep cool.

The baboons (*Papio hamadryas*) are monkeys which have taken to living in open grassland. They feed on the ground but retire to trees when attacked, and for safety at night. Baboons live in troops presided over by dominant males. When on the move, these males accompany the females. The infants are kept in the centre, with younger adults surrounding them. Baboons have long razor-edged canine teeth and a troop can defend itself against most predators, although a lone baboon may fall victim to a predator such as a leopard. The mandrill (*Mandrillus sphinx*) and drill (*Mandrillus leucophaeus*) are forest-dwelling baboons of west Africa, similar to other baboons except that they are better climbers.

Opposite: The mandrill, and its close relative the drill, are colourful baboons. They live in the rainforests of west Africa rather than on the open savannahs like other baboons.

Below: The vervet or green monkey is one of the guenon group of monkeys, and is found throughout Africa in savannah country. It lives in troops and feeds on the ground on plants and insects, then retires to a tree to sleep at night.

There are only nine species of apes. They have no tail, the big toe is separated from the others, the arms are long and the brain is larger than in monkeys.

The forests of southeast Asia are the home of six species of gibbons (genus *Hylobates*) which have extremely long arms, and can swing through the trees at an astonishing speed. They live in groups made up of an adult pair, together with their offspring. They rarely come to the ground and they feed on fruit, leaves, flowers, insects and birds' eggs.

The orang-utan (*Pongo pygmaeus*), whose name means 'man of the woods', lives in the rainforests of Borneo and Sumatra. Males grow much larger than females and develop huge crescent-shaped swellings on the sides of the face. Small family parties spend their time in the trees where they search mainly for fruit, but leaves, insects, birds' eggs and honey are also eaten. At night, the orangs sleep in nests which they rapidly make each night by bending branches into a platform. Orangs tend to walk along branches rather than brachiate on account of their large size, and old males eventually take to living on the ground on their own.

The gorilla (*Gorilla gorilla*) is the largest of the apes. There are two races: lowland gorillas and mountain gorillas. A male stands 1·7 m (5½ ft) on his hind legs and weighs up to 200 kg (450 lb). When fully adult, he develops a silvery 'saddle' on the back. Despite their massive strength, gorillas have proved to be inoffensive vegetarians. They live in troops which sometimes intermingle peacefully, and they will even accept humans into their company. Normally an old male will lead his troop away from danger but, if cornered, he can be very dangerous and cause

Orang utans, one of the great apes, are also one of man's closest relatives in the Animal Kingdom. Unfortunately they have become rare in their rainforest homes in Borneo and Sumatra, due to tree-felling programmes.

Above: A peaceful family of gorillas in a forest clearing in Central Africa. There is always plenty of food in the lush undergrowth for these huge apes, so life proceeds at a leisurely pace. Under the leadership and protection of an adult male they are seldom threatened by other animals.

Overleaf: Unlike the heavier gorilla, the chimpanzee is a good tree climber, but it still spends much of its time on the ground in large troops. Chimpanzees are very inquisitive and search everything and anything for edible titbits.

nasty wounds by biting and scratching. Smaller gorillas can climb well and move by brachiation, but they usually live on the ground and walk on all fours, using the soles of the feet and the knuckles of the hands.

The chimpanzee (*Pan troglodytes*) is our closest relative and, with the gorilla, is thought by some zoologists to belong to the same family, Hominidae. Like gorillas, chimpanzees spend most of their time on the ground, progressing by 'knuckle-walking', but they can also brachiate in the trees. The range of the chimpanzee extends across the forest belt of Africa. They live in troops of up to eighty animals, but these tend to split into smaller groups and there are no leaders. The day is spent foraging for food, and the chimps move around the forest in search of trees with ripe fruit, and other food. Bees' nests are raided for honey and termites' nests for the termites themselves. Both are collected by poking into the nests with a stick and then sucking it clean of the honey or insects which adhere. Although chimpanzees are generally unaggressive, they sometimes attack and kill members of another troop, and may even, as a troop, kill small antelopes.

Talking to chimpanzees
Captive chimpanzees have taken part in many experiments to demonstrate their intelligence, and some of the most remarkable results have been in the field of communication between the chimpanzee and their human companions. After attempts to teach chimps to talk failed because they do not naturally communicate orally, a chimpanzee called Washoe was successfully taught American Sign Language, (Ameslan) which is a language specially developed for communication with deaf people. Instead of spelling out words on the fingers, Ameslan uses gestures for words like 'eat', 'open', 'listen', 'box', 'door', 'sorry' and 'more'. Washoe quickly learned a large number of words and started to string them together like 'listen-dog' when she heard a dog barking. She had been taught to signal 'open' when she wanted to go through a door and then used the gesture to ask for a tap to be turned on. Since the breakthrough with Washoe, several chimpanzees have learned to 'speak' with Ameslan, not only to humans but to other chimpanzees, and they have been assisted by a device in which a keyboard can be punched to illuminate 'words' on a screen.

Pangolins
(order Pholidota)

Pangolins, or scaly anteaters, are not closely related to other mammals. The hair, except on the underparts, has been converted into flat, horny scales which overlap like the tiles on a roof. There are seven species, four living in Africa and three in Asia. They are nocturnal and feed on ants and termites, tearing open the nests with sharp claws and licking up the insects with their long sticky tongues. Pangolins are toothless and crush their food with horny projections in the stomach. When alarmed, pangolins roll into a tight ball.

Some species of pangolin live on the ground and sleep in burrows during the day, but they can climb trees if necessary. Other species are arboreal and sleep in the fork of a branch. They have longer tails than the ground-dwelling species, and use them to give extra support when climbing. A pangolin climbs a tree trunk by hitching itself upwards alternately, first with its front and then with its back legs. The tail is pressed against the trunk so that the scales provide extra support. The tip of the tail can also be wrapped around branches, and the arboreal pangolins can hang from a branch by their tails and 'climb up themselves' if they cannot find a secure footing.

Edentates
(order Edentata)

For a long time the anteaters, sloths, armadillos, pangolins and the aardvark were classed together in a single order, the Edentata, or toothless ones. They differ widely from each other, but had in common the fact that they were without incisor and canine teeth in the front of the mouth. Now the pangolins and the aardvark have been placed in orders of their own. Even so, the three groups left are still very different from each other in appearance and internal anatomy.

Anteaters
(family Myrmecophagidae)

The anteaters have a long slender muzzle with a tubular mouth opening at the tip. The third toe of each front foot bears a large claw for digging out insects, which anteaters then pick up with a long sticky tongue. Anteaters have no teeth. The great anteater (*Myrmecophaga jub-ata*) is 1·2 m (4 ft) long, with a tail of the same length. This tail bears a curtain of long hairs that can be brought forward to cover the body. There is a dark band of hair running diagonally across each side of the body.

The tamandua (*Tamandua tetradactyla*), only half the size of the great anteater, lives in trees, feeding on tree ants. Its tail, coated with short hair, can be wrapped round a branch to assist in climbing. The single baby is carried about by the mother, clinging to her tail until able to look after itself.

The little or two-toed anteater (*Cyclopes didactylus*), with buff or golden fur, is the size of a rat. It can wrap its tail round a branch and, gripping with its hind feet as well, can hold on tenaciously with its body at right angles to the branch. It uses the two long, strong claws on each forefoot to tear open bees' nests for the grubs.

Sloths (family Bradypodidae)

Sloths also live in trees, but they feed on leaves, chewing them up with their peg-like cheek teeth. Everything a sloth does is in slow motion. The long coarse hairs covering the almost tailless body are grooved. Green algae live in the grooves, giving the sloth an overall greenish colour. While it is at rest, a sloth looks like a growth of lichen. Its colour and extremely slow movements make it hard to see, but its chief enemy, the jaguar, manages to seek it out.

There are two kinds of sloth, the three-toed and the two-toed sloths (*Bradypus tridactylus* and *Choloepus didactylus*). The front legs of the three-toed sloth are shorter than its hind legs, and it has a black and orange patch on its chest. It also has three large hook-like claws on each foot. The two-toed sloth has legs of equal length and only two hooked claws on each front foot. Both species hang upside-down from branches, and the hair on their bodies is so arranged that rain falling on the belly is thrown off from the back and shoulders, the reverse of what happens in normal mammals. The single baby clings to its mother, resting on her belly as she hangs hammock-like from a branch.

Sloths rest clinging upright to a vertical branch or a tree trunk. They seldom descend to the ground, but when they do they drag themselves

along using the claws on their front feet as grapnel-hooks. They have been seen to swim with a powerful overarm stroke.

Armadillos
(family Dasypodidae)

Armadillos are more numerous than either sloths or anteaters. They live on the ground and dig holes in the ground for shelter. The muzzle is not so tapering as in the anteaters, and the tongue, which is forked, is shorter and not so slimy. The food of armadillos consists mainly of ants, beetles and worms, but they sometimes eat roots, fallen fruit and even carrion. Like the sloths they have peg-like cheek-teeth, but otherwise the two have little in common. Armadillos wear a protective armour consisting of bony shields covered with horn and supported on a strong internal skeleton. There is one large shield on the front part of the body and another on the hind part, with a

variable number of narrow band-like shields between the two. The top of the head is covered with a shield and the tail is protected by a series of rings. The outer surfaces of the legs are also protected by plates. The undersurface is covered with soft skin and sparse hair; to protect this vulnerable part an armadillo clings closely to the ground when attacked. One species, the apara (*Tolypeutes tricinctus*), can roll itself into a tight ball.

There are three kinds of armadillos. The first have seven to ten or more hinged bands round the body and long donkey-like ears. The largest, the giant armadillo (*Priodontes gigas*), is 1 m (3¼ ft) long, with a tail 50 cm (20 in) long, and feeds mainly on termites. The nine-banded armadillo (*Dasypus novemcinctus*) is the most common and has spread up into the southern United States as far as Texas. It has been seen to cross rivers. All armadillos are heavy for

Anteaters are completely toothless mammals which feed on termites and ants. They rip open the insects' nests with their sharp claws and lick up the inhabitants with a long, sticky tongue.

their size and the nine-banded is known to swallow air to inflate its intestine to give buoyancy for swimming.

The second kind of armadillos have only three to six bands and include the six-banded (*Euphractus sexcinctus*), the apara, and the hairy armadillo (*E. villosus*); all are medium-sized with smaller ears than the first kind. The hairy armadillo has a thick growth of hair springing from between the joints in its armour and almost hiding its scales.

The third kind includes only one species, the fairy armadillo (*Chlamyphorus truncatus*), which is only 15 cm (6 in) long, cylindrical in body and mole-like with its large digging claws. It is protected by twenty or so horny plates across the back and its rear end is flat and protected from attack by a scaly plate.

In spite of their heavy armour, armadillos are not safe from dogs, coyotes and peccaries. In fact the main value of the armour is that it allows them to take refuge in thorny scrub where animals with soft skin cannot penetrate.

Rabbits, hares and pikas (order Lagomorpha)

These mammals used to be classified as rodents with the rats and mice because of their gnawing habits. They are now placed in a separate order known as the lagomorphs. All members of the order have two pairs of incisors in the front of the mouth, with a gap, known as the diastema, between these and the cheek teeth. The skin of the lips can be drawn in across this gap so that the animal can chew inedible matter without the chips entering the mouth. Rabbits and hares differ from rodents in having a smaller pair of incisors behind the main incisors in the upper jaw. Also, the rodents have enamel on the front only of the incisors, whereas rabbits and hares have enamel on both sides. Like the common shrew and some rodents, the rabbits, hares and pikas practise the habit of refection, which means eating their food twice. The droppings produced after a meal are soft and moist, and the animal immediately eats them. During the second

passage through the animal, vitamins formed by bacterial action are absorbed into the body. The next droppings are hard and dry and are not re-eaten.

In Britain the name 'rabbit' is reserved for those lagomorphs with shorter ears that burrow in the ground, while 'hare' is reserved for those longer-eared species that do not burrow but seek safety in the speed of their running. In America no such distinction is made and the names are used indiscriminately. Thus, the largest lagomorphs in North America have very long ears and are known as Jack rabbits.

The European rabbit (*Oryctolagus cuniculus*), originally a native of southwest Europe, has been taken to other parts of the world, notably to Australia, where it multiplied rapidly because of the absence of natural enemies to become an unmitigated pest. It was a pest elsewhere also, feeding on grass needed for farm stock and on vegetable crops. Its habit of living in colonies and burrowing extensively in the ground reduced the amount of arable land available to farmers. Trapping, shooting, ferreting and gassing failed to do more than keep their numbers within bounds and, in Britain, rabbits ate a third of the farm crop each year until the introduction, in the 1950s, of the disease known as myxomatosis. The rabbit was also a pest to forestry, eating the bark from the lower parts of trees.

The European or brown hare (*Lepus capensis*), like the rabbit, is brown or fawn above with white underneath. Its hind legs are markedly longer than the forelegs and, like the rabbit, it has a very short tail. It is a speedy runner and is adept at jinking. That is, it will suddenly change direction or turn completely about without loss of speed when chased.

Lagomorphs live mainly in the Northern Hemisphere, although the true hare is found throughout Africa as far south as the Cape. Rabbits do not live as far north as hares, one species of which – the Arctic hare (*Lepus arcticus*) – lives in the far north. This species survives the polar winter by digging through the snow to reach plants underneath and shelters in a burrow dug in the snow. It is white all year round, but newborn babies are brown.

There are several species of Jack rabbits (genus *Lepus*) in North America, living on the western plains in large numbers. They are a familiar sight to travellers by road and rail. The Jack rabbit is probably the most speedy of all hares. It does great damage to crops, especially where its natural enemies, the coyotes, wolves and eagles, have been destroyed. Various forms of Jack rabbit are also found across northern Asia, in China and India and also in Africa from Egypt to the Cape.

The snowshoe rabbit (*Lepus americanus*), commonly found in the backwoods of Canada and the United States, is so-named because in winter, when it turns white, the hair on the soles of its feet grows long, forming dense mats or 'snowshoes'. It feeds mainly on bark and twigs. Like some of the small rodents, it is subject to fluctuations in numbers. Its normal litter is three to four young, but in years of plenty there may be ten in a litter. So the numbers build up until there is a crash and many die. The martens, lynxes and foxes which feed on them, and which formed the basis of a fur trade, also rise and fall in numbers

about every ten years as the numbers of snowshoe rabbits, which form their diet, rise and fall.

Another familiar hare is the cottontail or briar rabbit (*Syvilagus floridanus*), a species very common in thick woodlands and swamps as far south as Brazil. The smallest of the true hares, they have short ears and a short tail as well as short hind legs. Unable to run fast, they rely on dodging into the nearest cover to escape their enemies.

In the colder parts of Europe and Asia the brown hare is replaced by the varying hares, especially on mountains. In Scotland the varying hare is also called the blue or mountain hare (*Lepus timidus*). Its ears are smaller than those of the brown hare, and the smaller surface thereby exposed to the air reduces heat-loss from the body. Varying hares change their coat from white in winter to brown in summer. The white winter coat is good camouflage in the snow, but a white coat also lowers the loss of body-heat. Tests have showed that the whitening of the hairs occurs in response to a lowering of the

Above: The jack rabbits of North America are really hares. They live above ground and do not burrow. The long ears act as radiators and help to prevent them overheating in the hot sun.

Opposite: There are twenty species of armadillos ranging from Argentina to the United States. The body armour is a good defence against small predators, but not against larger predators such as coyotes and jaguars.

temperature and reduction in the hours of daylight.

Not all lagomorphs live in areas of abundant vegetation. The red rock hares of the genus *Pronolagus* of South Africa, with thick coats and bushy tails, live among rocks. The black-necked hare (*Lepus nigricollis*) of India lives on rubbish accumulated on the outskirts of villages. Some species live in the deserts of Saudi Arabia and the Sahara.

The many varieties of domestic rabbit, with their different coloured coats, are all derived from the European rabbit. The most colourful wild species, and the most colourful of all lagomorphs, is the rare Sumatran hare (*Nesolagus netscheri*) which has a coat blotched with brown, black, chestnut and pale grey – more like a tortoiseshell cat in appearance.

The pikas (family Ochotonidae) live in Asia, with two species in North America. They look like small rabbits with short ears. One species has been found at 5330 m (17 500 ft) in the Himalayas. Pikas cut vegetation and leave it to dry in the sun before storing it as winter food.

Rodents
(order Rodentia)

The rodents comprise more species than any other order of mammals. At least 1600 are known to exist. Because of their wide distribution, great numbers and the powers of rapid multiplication that some of them possess, as well as for their destructive feeding habits, rodents are of utmost significance to man. To a large extent man is to blame for the problems they cause him since he has created special opportunities for the enormous increase of some rodents by his large-scale cultivation and storage of foodstuffs, and by his almost total elimination in places of most of their natural enemies in the interests of farmcrops and game preserves.

The outstanding feature of rodents is their incisor teeth. All of them have one pair of chisel-like incisors situated in the upper jaw and one pair in the lower jaw; both pairs grow continuously at the roots. They are kept in check by continual use, wearing away at the cutting edge as fast as they grow. Rats are now known to grit their teeth when they are not gnawing anything, which probably helps to keep them down to a suitable length. Should a tooth become damaged or displaced, the opposite tooth continues to grow in a curve, finally hampering feeding, or growing up and round the head, locking the jaws or even entering the skull and killing the animal. Enamel is found on the front of the incisor only so the rear surface wears away more rapidly, resulting in a chisel-like edge. These remarkably sharp cutting teeth enable a rat to chew through lead pipes, tin cans and even concrete. They explain the beaver's ability to fell trees and the porcupine's ability to chew glass bottles.

Rodents, like the rabbits and hares, have no canine teeth. Instead, there is a gap, known as the diastema, between the incisors and the cheek teeth used for chewing. A special fold of hairy skin can be drawn in on either side, sealing the gap and cutting off the rest of the mouth from the incisors. A rat can therefore chew a lead pipe without getting lead poisoning and a squirrel can easily discard pieces of nutshell. Some rodents, the gophers and hamsters for instance, have cheek pouches for carrying food.

The many different kinds of rodents differ greatly in size and appear-

ance. The smallest mouse is not quite as small as the shrew, which is the smallest of all mammals. The largest rodent is the capybara of South America, the size of a small pig and up to 54 kg (120 lb) in weight. Most are terrestrial, many live in trees and a few are aquatic or amphibious. A very few are mole-like, living underground. Of those that live in trees, some have membranes on the side of the body and are able to glide from tree to tree. These include the flying squirrels and the scalytails. Rodents are found worldwide, only the uninhabitable polar ice-caps are without them, although house mice and rats have accompanied men accidentally to the research stations on Antarctic islands. Even Australia, with its otherwise unusual fauna, has some native rats. The order Rodentia is divided into three suborders.

Squirrels and squirrel-like mammals (suborder Sciuromorpha)

The Sciuromorpha are absent only from Madagascar, Australasia and the polar regions. Most species are sufficiently similar to be recognized as squirrels, except the beavers and gophers, although even they are so alike in their internal anatomy as to leave no doubt of their relationship to the typical squirrels.

The typical squirrels include species as small as mice and as large as a cat. They are active by day, feeding on nuts, seeds, fungi, occasional insects and the eggs and young of small birds. They build nests in trees or use holes in trees for shelter or to bear their young. They do not hibernate; even in cold latitudes at most they only partially hibernate. Being active by day some are brightly coloured, although commonly they are grey or brown; a few species have several colour phases. The fox squirrels of North America show colour phases so different that it was once believed they represented three different species.

The most brilliant coloration, and the greatest variety of species, live in the extensive forests of southeast Asia, including the Malay Archipelago. The Prevost squirrel (*Sciurus prevosti*) of Malaya is a striking black, white and red animal. Other species in the area may be black, white or red. The palm squirrels of the genus *Funambulus* of India have pale longitudinal stripes down the back.

Closely related to the true squirrels are the flying squirrels. Even the true squirrels, like the grey (*Sciurus carolinensis*) and the red (*Sciurus vulgaris*), will take long flying leaps from tree to tree. By the addition of a wide flap of skin stretching from wrist to ankle on both sides of the body, a flying squirrel can extend the range of each leap considerably, sailing through the air as if on a hang glider.

In contrast to the flying squirrels are those that live mainly on the ground. Since they no longer need a long tail for balancing, this organ is shorter than in tree squirrels. Some ground squirrels have taken to a diet of insects and have weak incisors, since they are no longer used for opening nuts, and their muzzles have become more pointed for probing the leaf-litter in search of their food. The tongue also is long and protrusible. A ground squirrel from the island of Celebes (Indonesia) has, in addition, strong claws on the front feet and is altogether very like the anteaters. The best-known ground squirrels are the North American chipmunks and prairiedogs. The latter are heavily built, with short legs and a short tail.

Still larger relatives of the ground squirrels are the marmots. These are mostly mountain dwellers and include the well-known woodchuck (*Marmota monax*) of North America, up to 60 cm (2 ft) long and a fair match for a small dog. Another relative is the beaver (*Castor fiber*) of North America and Europe. Stoutly built with a flat, scaly tail and webbed hind feet, it is aquatic, damming rivers to create beaver ponds. The dams, made of branches and logs cut by the animals, are waterproofed with mud and stones. The beaver eats bark of saplings and lives in lodges, made of small branches and mud, in the middle of the ponds. Beaver fur was once highly prized. Trapping led to so great a reduction in numbers that beavers are now protected in many places.

Other members of the Sciuromorpha are the gophers and kangaroo rats of North America, and the mountain beaver or sewellel (*Aplodontia rufa*) of the Rocky Mountains.

Rats and mice
(suborder Myomorpha)

The Myomorpha include more species and larger populations than all other rodents put together. They are also the most troublesome. Three species especially have made them notorious, the house mouse (*Mus musculus*), the common rat (*Rattus norvegicus*) and the ship rat (*Rattus rattus*), sometimes spoken of as the brown and black rats respectively. All three are believed to have come originally from central Asia, from where they spread through Asia and Europe by their own efforts and throughout practically the whole of the rest of the world in cargoes carried by ships.

Mice and rats have become essentially scavengers but can readily turn to stored foods, especially grain. In their original native state they probably fed on grass seeds but, as man learned to grow cereal crops, he made life too easy for them. They grew exceedingly in numbers and migrated to new lands, eating into man's stores and fouling more than they ate. The rat also carried fleas that spread bubonic plague, the devastating disease, known as the Black Death, that centuries ago killed a vast number of the inhabitants of Europe. Even without their plague-carrying propensities and the damage they cause to crops and food stores, rats are a great nuisance for the damage they do to buildings, and mice are only a little less troublesome, especially when they themselves occur in plagues, the plague of huge numbers.

The mice-like rodents can be divided into two groups: the true mice, and the voles. The latter have a blunter muzzle and smaller eyes and ears than true mice. Field voles of the genus *Microtus* show cyclic rises and falls in their populations. At times their numbers rise to plague proportions, until the grass in fields seems almost to be on the move with so many field voles. Then they fight among themselves, they fail to breed, food becomes scarce and finally disease breaks out and the numbers fall catastrophically. Then, with more food the survivors breed more frequently, have bigger litters and there is another population explosion.

The most famous instance of this kind of population explosion is that of the Norwegian lemming (*Lemmus lemmus*), another vole. Lemmings live in the mountains of Scandinavia and in some years they are so numerous that many migrate to the lowlands in search of food. There used to be stories of columns of them rushing down into the sea in a sort of mass suicide, thousands being drowned. It is not as simple as that, but certainly they do swarm over the countryside and many are drowned. It is now believed that mild winters are the cause of these phenomenal increases in their numbers, because the lemmings then go on breeding through the winter and so the population builds up to plague proportions.

One of the biggest population explosions, though from a different cause, concerns the golden hamster (*Mesocricetus auratus*). All the millions now kept as pets came from a mother and twelve babies dug out of the sand in Syria in 1930.

The deserts of the Old World are inhabited by small rodents which are adapted for life in dry conditions. They are the ecological equivalent of the kangaroo rats in America and several small marsupials in Australia. The gerbils, now familiar as pets, and the jerboas which hop like kangaroos, are found in the deserts of North Africa. Desert rodents share several habits. They spend the day in a burrow, emerging at night when it

---

Mouse and rat plagues

From time to time, in Europe, North America and, especially Australia, plagues of house mice are reported. Typical of these is one that occurred in South Australia during World War I, in a year of abnormally large grain harvests. Haystacks were ruined, horses eating the contaminated hay died, and much of the grain was eaten and fouled. The numbers of mice were enormous. In one wheatyard 70,000 were killed in one day. Another farmer put down poison and picked up 28,000 mice the next day. Finally, epidemic disease killed off the mice.

Similar stories could be told for the common rat in Europe and for the ship rat in North America, where it is the most common of the two rats. This is despite the relentless war that has been going on for centuries against mice and rats. Some years ago in Britain, so-called rat weeks were held when, for a week at a time, an intensive campaign would be waged, aimed at killing as many rats as possible. Within a short space of time there would be as many rats as before. The reason soon became apparent: if most of the rats were killed, leaving only a few survivors, the survivors then had more food per head, the females had bigger litters, there were more survivors among the babies and so the population quickly increased to what it had formerly been.

About the same time as the rat weeks were held, a bounty was paid per tail, in the hope of eradicating that other pest in Britain, the grey squirrel. This failed for the same reason.

Lemmings have a reputation for rushing over cliffs and drowning, but this is a myth; the lemmings' real importance is in forming the food supply of many predatory animals living in the Arctic.

is cool. They store food for the long periods of drought when nothing is growing, and they survive on a minimum of water. Some species never need to drink. The springhare (*Pedetes capensis*) of the drier parts of Africa is another kangaroo-like rodent with well-developed hind legs and a long hairy tail.

Porcupines and cavies (suborder Hystricomorpha)

The third group of rodents, the Hystricomorpha, contains some of the largest: the porcupines, the coypu (*Myocastor coypus*), the cavy or wild guinea pig (*Cavia porcellus*) and the capybara (*Hydrochoerus hydrochaeris*). The last of these is 1·2m (4ft) long, semi-aquatic and looks like a pig. The coypu is nearly as long, with a long scaly tail, and looks like a giant rat. It was once ranched on a large scale for its fur, known as nutria.

Porcupines are familiar animals with their coats of long quills, except that in some the quills are short and hidden in the fur. Most porcupines live on the ground, eating plant food, but the Canadian porcupine (*Erethizon dorsatum*) and the South American coendou (*Coendou prehensilis*) climb trees, the coendou being able to wrap its tail round a branch to assist it in climbing.

Prairie dog towns

Prairie dogs (*Cynomys ludovicianus*) live in large colonies or 'towns' consisting of a mass of burrows excavated in the ground. In 1901, one town was estimated to cover an area of 160×280 km (100×240 miles) and to contain 400 million prairie dogs. As the prairies were settled and opened up for farming and ranching, the prairie dogs were regarded as a pest and their numbers have become greatly reduced.

Around the mouth of each prairie dog burrow there is a mound of soil which was once thought to be a protection against floods or a raised sentry post. Experiments have shown that the shape of the mound causes the wind to set up a circulation of air in the burrow. The burrow is a roughly U-shaped tunnel, with side-chambers, and an entrance at each end. Without some form of air circulation, the prairie dogs would be unable to survive in the burrow. A breeze of about 45 cm per second (1 mile per hour) is sufficient to set up a draught and completely renew the air every ten minutes.

Flesh-eating mammals (order Carnivora)

The order Carnivora includes all the flesh-eating mammals, although some mammals outside this order also eat flesh, and some within it are not strictly flesh-eaters. The aardwolf (*Proteles cristatus*), for instance, is a relative of the hyaenas which eats only termites, and the giant panda (*Ailuropoda melanoleuca*) eats mainly bamboo shoots. The bears, the largest of the Carnivora, are omnivorous; they eat a wide variety of plants and small animals. There are seven families of carnivores.

The Carnivora are built as hunters. Many are fast runners: the dogs having staying power while the cats are sprinters. The martens, genets and cats are good climbers and hunt their prey in the trees. The otters swim after fish with graceful undulations of the body and the stout tail. Many carnivores are adept at digging, either to unearth their prey or to excavate shelters. Killing prey requires strength and agility, and a carnivore tackling prey perhaps larger than itself needs split-second reflexes and timing, because a moment's hesitation may lead to it being injured or even killed by its victim. The prey is caught and killed with the claws and teeth. Running and digging carnivores have blunt claws, but the cats keep their claws in protective sheaths until needed for seizing prey or climbing trees. The teeth are used for both seizing and killing. Compared with other mammals, a carnivore has large canine teeth, or fangs, which stab and hold the prey. Cats use their long fangs to pierce the vertebrae of their victim and sever the spinal cord. Two cheek teeth on each side of the mouth are specialized for shearing flesh. Called the carnassial teeth, they are blade-shaped and they work like scissors.

Carnivores are found all over the world, except in Antarctica, although some like the dingo, found in Australia, have been introduced by man. The polar bear (*Thalarctos maritimus*) and the Arctic fox (*Alopex lagopus*) live in the far north, where they may be found on icefloes far from land, and the tiny fennec fox (*Fennecus zerda*) lives in the Sahara Desert. It has huge ears which not only give it a good sense of hearing but act as radiators to help it keep cool. The largest carnivore is the Kodiak bear, a race of the grizzly bear (*Ursus horribilis*) – a record specimen weighed 751 kg (1650 lb); and the smallest carnivore is the least weasel (*Mustela rixosa*) which weighs 50 gm.

Dogs (family Canidae)

The dog family includes the wolf, jackals, foxes and domestic dog. Some species live solitary lives but others live in groups. The wolf (*Canis lupus*), which was once found across Europe, Asia and North America, lives in families consisting of a mother and her offspring. There is often a male living with them, and other adult wolves also join the pack. During the winter two families may

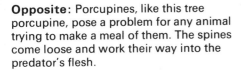

Opposite: Porcupines, like this tree porcupine, pose a problem for any animal trying to make a meal of them. The spines come loose and work their way into the predator's flesh.

Left: Supremely adaptable, the wolf has made a home in every sort of landscape from dense forests to the open Arctic tundra. However, wolves take to hunting domestic animals too readily for their own good, and they have been wiped out in many of their former haunts.

join up, but a pack larger than ten or more wolves is unusual. Each pack has a home range where it hunts along well-established trails. The main prey is deer, but small animals such as mice and hares, even fruit, are also eaten. Prey is most often found by accident but a wolf can scent a moose from a few hundred metres distance.

Unlike the wolf which is now extinct or very rare over much of its former range, the red fox (*Vulpes vulpes*) is flourishing despite persecution and the spread of civilization, through its ability to make use of any source of food, from earthworms to the contents of dustbins. It has even become a pest in some large cities. The same ability enables the Arctic fox to survive in the harshest polar weather. Snug inside its thick, white winter coat, it survives on any prey or scraps it can find, and follows polar bears to pick the remains of their kills.

The African hunting dog (*Lycaon pictus*) live in packs which hunt zebras and antelopes. They share their prey and take food back to the

den for the pups and the adults which remained behind to guard them. The three species of jackals live in pairs and hunt hares and gazelles or search for mice, insects and fruit. They also feed on carrion.

Bears (family Ursidae)

The bears are the least predatory of the carnivores. They have blunt teeth for chewing plant food but they also eat small animals and occasionally kill large animals such as deer. The exception is the polar bear which has sharp teeth and hunts seals. It is a good swimmer, using its front legs as paddles while its hind legs trail behind, but it has to come onto the ice to catch seals, which it

Attractive-looking, but a stern adversary in real life, the brown bear eats mainly vegetable food. Although normally walking on all fours, bears can stand upright and they use their paws to gather berries, turn over stones and flip fishes out of water.

kills with a blow from a massive paw. Bears do not hibernate properly, as is often thought, but they do spend the winter sleeping in a den. The cubs are born in the den when they are still very small and helpless. By spring they have grown sufficiently to leave the den with their mother.

Zoologists are not fully agreed whether the giant panda (*Ailuropoda melanoleuca*) is a bear or a member of the racoon family. It lives in the remote bamboo forests of China and its diet is almost entirely bamboo shoots. Very little is known about the habits of wild giant pandas and there are fears for its survival. Bamboo plants only flower at rare intervals but, when they do, all the plants in one area flower together and then die. When this happens, large numbers of giant pandas die of starvation if they cannot find alternative food.

Raccoons (family Procyonidae)

The raccoon (*Procyon lotor*) of North America is famous for its black 'robber-mask', the use of its fur to make the coon-skin hat of the American frontiersman, and its habit of washing its food – although it seems that food washing only takes place in captivity when the raccoons are 'pretending' to hunt for food. Raccoons eat a wide variety of animals and plants and they frequently forage in shallow water for crayfish and

The polar bear leads a nomadic life wandering among the ice floes and tundra in the Arctic Ocean. It is well designed for life in the harshest conditions. The soles of the feet are fur-covered for insulation and for giving a good grip on the ice, and its body is kept warm by a thick coat of fur and a layer of fat.

molluscs, feeling for them with their deft fingers. The coati (*Nasua narica*) of Central America lives in groups of females and their young, the adult males living separately. The kinkajou (*Potos caudivolvulus*) has a long prehensile tail and eats large amounts of fruit.

Weasels, skunks and badgers (family Mustelidae)

The family of weasels, otters, badgers and skunks is a large group of mainly short-legged, long-bodied animals, many of which are trapped for their fur. In the northern parts of their range, weasels and stoats turn white in winter. The weasels, martens, polecats and minks are typical of the family. They are efficient hunting animals which run down their prey and kill them with a bite to the neck. A stoat (*Mustela erminea*) can catch and kill a rabbit larger than itself. These animals are good climbers, especially the martens. The

minks are good swimmers, but they are not so aquatic as the otters. An otter has a flattened head, with the nostrils, eyes and small ears set high so that the senses are still alert when the otter is almost submerged. The nostrils and ears close when the otter dives. Its feet are webbed and used for swimming slowly and manoeuvring, but fast swimming is achieved by flexing the body and tail up and down. Although the fur is waterproof, otters do not spend long periods in the water, except for the sea-otter (*Enhydra lutris*) of the west coast of North America.

The sea-otter is one of the few animals to use a tool. Its diet is fishes, crabs, sea urchins, abalones, mussels and other shellfishes, which it finds by diving to the seabed to depths of as much as 50m (164ft). The food is brought to the surface, tucked under the left foreleg and the sea-otter then floats on its back, so that it can use its chest as a table. Crabs are pulled apart and the legs are devoured while the crab continues to crawl about on the sea-otter's chest. Shellfishes have to be smashed open and the sea-otter brings a flat stone to the surface and rests it on its chest for use as an anvil. The abalone or mussel is held between the paws and pounded against the stone until its shell cracks.

All mustelids have glands at the base of the tail which secrete odour for marking their territories, but the skunks of North America have developed the glands so that they can squirt an evil-smelling fluid at enemies over a distance of 3 m (10 ft). The bold black-and-white pattern of the fur is a warning to would-be attackers.

The badgers are heavy-bodied, bear-like animals. The European badger (*Meles meles*) feeds on earthworms, insects, plants and occasionally mammals and birds. The American badger (*Taxidea taxus*) is more carnivorous. Badgers live in extensive burrow systems occupied by small parties. The honey badger or ratel (*Mellivora capensis*) lives in Africa and Asia and is famous for its association with the honeyguide, a small bird. The ratel tears open bees' nests and shares the feast with the honeyguide.

The wolverine or glutton (*Gulo gulo*) is the largest member of the weasel family and lives in Arctic regions. It weighs up to 30 kg (66 lb) and is powerful enough to kill reindeer and elks.

The slender, streamlined body of the otters makes them one of the most graceful of animals. Propelled through the water by rhythmic movements of the body, otters can easily chase and capture fishes.

Civets and mongooses (family Viverridae)

There are seventy-two species of civets, mongooses and related animals living in tropical Africa and Asia. Two, the Egyptian mongoose (*Herpestes ichneumon*) and feline genet (*Genetta genetta*), live in southern Europe and some mongooses have been introduced to other parts of the world. It is not easy to distinguish these animals from the weasels and martens. Both have short legs and long bodies, but the former have tapering heads with no 'forehead' between the cranium and the snout. Many species are nocturnal and are expert tree climbers. Mongooses are famous for fighting snakes which they attack with such lightning speed that the snake does not have time to strike. For this reason, mongooses were introduced to Jamaica and elsewhere to get rid of snakes but, as mongooses also eat birds including poultry, they have become a pest. Mongooses also like eggs which they crack open by throwing them between their legs to hit a stone.

Some mongooses live in troops of a dozen or so animals. They rest in a communal burrow and forage together in search of insects and other small animals. There is safety in numbers because many pairs of eyes can watch for eagles, and they can bunch together for protection. In a troop of the dwarf mongoose (*Helogale parva*) only one pair breeds but young adults help by baby-sitting to guard against attacks by large carnivores. Sick members of the troop are guarded and allowed to share food by healthy companions.

Hyaenas (family Hyaenidae)

Hyaenas are not very attractive animals with their low hind quarters, unkempt coat and skulking nature, and they used to have a reputation for being cowardly scavengers that gathered with the vultures around lions' kills. It is now known that they are hunters in their own right. There are three species: the spotted hyaena (*Crocuta crocuta*) and brown hyaena (*Hyaena brunnea*) of Africa, and the striped hyaena (*H. hyaena*) of Africa and Asia. Spotted hyaenas live in bush country and grasslands where they roam in packs. The pack has a territory or hunting ground which it defends against other packs. Hunting takes place mainly at night when the hyaenas chase and pull down wildebeests and other antelopes.

Suricates are mongooses which live in southern Africa. Each colony of about two dozen animals lives in a system of burrows which they leave during the day to search for plant and animal food, including small snakes.

Right: Built like an outsized tabby, the European wildcat is like a domestic cat in many of its habits. Being solitary and nocturnal, it is not often seen.

Below: The lynx is easily recognized by its tufted ears, cheek ruffs and short tail. It is a forest dweller that preys on deer, hares and other mammals and birds. A lynx travels many kilometres on its hunting trips and catches its prey with a sudden sprint.

Opposite top: The leopard is recognized by its spots. They are arranged in rosettes, as are those of the jaguar, but the jaguar's rosettes have a central spot.

Opposite bottom: This tiger is not showing the cats' traditional dislike of water. They like to avoid the heat of the tropical sun and often sit in water to keep cool. Tigers range from cool Siberia to the humid forests of southern Asia.

Their powerful jaws can crunch the largest bones and by morning hardly anything is left of the victim.

Cats (family Felidae)

The cat family is the most specialized of the carnivores. All cats are flesh-eaters, and very rarely eat plants. The number of teeth is reduced and they rely on large carnassials for slicing meat into pieces suitable for swallowing. The tongue is roughened with rows of backward-pointing projections and it acts as a rasp for scraping meat off the bone. Cats hunt either by lying in ambush or sneaking stealthily towards their victims. In either case, there is an explosive dash and pounce, and the victim is usually killed with a bite to the neck.

Most of the thirty-five species of cats are about the same size as a domestic cat, which is probably descended from the bush or cafer cat (*Felis cafer*) of Africa. The puma or cougar (*Felis concolor*) of America, the caracal (*Lynx caracal*) of Africa and Asia and the short-tailed lynx (*L. lynx*) of Europe and America are medium-sized cats.

Five species are known as the 'big cats'; they all have the ability to roar. The snow leopard or ounce (*Felis uncia*), the most beautiful of cats, is confined to the mountains of central Asia. The leopard (*Panthera pardus*) used to be widespread in Africa and Asia, but has disappeared from large areas. The leopard is a very agile and powerful climber, and carries its

prey into trees so that it cannot be eaten by other predators. The jaguar (*Panthera onca*), which ranges from the southern United States to Argentina, is spotted like the leopard; but the two can be distinguished by the central spot in each rosette of spots on the jaguar's coat. The jaguar is found on mountains and open plains but it can be found mainly in forests, preying on peccaries, capybaras and many other animals including turtles and fishes.

The tiger (*Panthera tigris*) was once found across south and east Asia but has been hunted until it became very rare. It is extinct in Bali and has almost disappeared from other places. In India, however, the Government has set aside reserves for the Bengal tiger and its numbers are now increasing. Apart from hunting, tigers became rare because their prey, especially the blackbuck and deer were disappearing. Attacks on cattle and sometimes humans also hurried their demise.

Learning to hunt

The overwhelming majority of animal species have nothing to do with the rearing of their offspring. They lay their eggs and then abandon them to fend for themselves. A minority stay with them and keep guard (the Nile crocodile, for instance), but the mammals and many birds go a step further and feed the growing young. The food supplies the young animal with energy until it can feed itself, and childhood is prolonged in animals which have to learn specialized feeding habits. This is the case with hunting animals.

A young carnivore learns its hunting skills by playing with its brothers and sisters, with its parents or with 'toys'. By playing at hunting, it devel-

ops the necessary co-ordination for running, pouncing and killing, and it gains confidence for the time when it has to face live prey. It also has to learn what to hunt.

Domestic cats introduce their kittens to live prey. When the kittens have reached a certain age, the mother brings back captured animals. At first she makes mock attacks on them, and allows the kittens to take a turn. A lioness has been seen wounding a wildebeest and then allowing her cubs to finish it off. After the kittens are four or five weeks old, the mother leaves the prey to the kittens and does no more than keep a watch on the proceedings. The kind of prey the mother brings will also influence the young carnivore's own choice of prey in later life.

The lion (*Panthera leo*), still common in Africa but now restricted to the Gir Forest of India in Asia, is an unusual cat because it is sociable. Lions live in prides, consisting of several females with their cubs, with one or more males in attendance. Each pride has a hunting territory which is defended by the males, while the females do the hunting. The hunting strategy is to lie in ambush or stalk, using cover to get as close to the prey as possible before launching an attack. Large prey is grabbed with the paws and killed by a bite to the neck or muzzle which causes suffocation. Two or more lionesses will hunt together but they do not deliberately drive victims towards each other, however.

The cats have been persecuted for their soft, beautifully marked fur, but the lion escaped this persecution because its fur is harsh and without markings. Nevertheless, lions have disappeared from much of their original range. They are restricted to Africa and small parts of Asia.

The cheetah (*Acinonyx jubatus*) is an unusual cat in several respects. It has been exterminated through most of its original range in Africa and Asia and is now found mainly in east Africa. It lives in open country, hunting by day for gazelles and impala. Cheetahs are built for speed and unlike other cats they cannot sheath their claws. Its maximum speed is around 96kph (58mph) but most attacks still end with the prey escaping.

Seals (order Pinnipedia)

The seals are marine mammals, although some swim upriver, and three species live in lakes. Unlike the cetaceans and seacows, however, seals must leave the water to give birth to their young. There are three families of seals which are descended from land-dwelling carnivores. The true seals (family Phocidae) are distantly related to the otters. They have no external earflap and they swim with their hind flippers, using the foreflippers for steering. A true seal is clumsy on land and moves by hitching its body forwards, sometimes using the foreflippers as props. The eared seals (family Otariidae) include the sealions and fur seals, and are distantly related to the bears. They have small earflaps, and they swim with their foreflippers. They can turn their hind flippers forwards, lift the body clear of the ground and bound overland at a considerable speed. The walrus (family Odobenidae) is related to the eared seals but it lacks an external ear.

Most seals live in the cool waters of the Northern and Southern Hemispheres. Although the Californian sealion (*Zalophus californianus*) lives off California and the Galápagos, which are hot places, the sea is kept cool by currents from polar regions, and there is only one truly warm-water group of seals, the monk seals (*Monachus*) of Hawaii, the Mediterranean and, until they were wiped out, the West Indies. For most of the year seals live in the open sea where they feed on fishes, squids, crustaceans and various bottom-dwelling marine animals. Once a year the adults gather to breed. In some species, this can involve thousands of seals thronging the beaches. The males, or bulls, set up territories and the females, or cows, come ashore to bear their single pups. Mating takes place shortly after the birth of the pups. Other species, especially those that bear their pups on icefloes, do not gather in such dense groups.

Gathering to breed has made seals very vulnerable to human hunters who are able to walk among them and club them indiscriminately. One species, the West Indies monk seal (*Monachus tropicalis*), has been wiped out and other seals nearly shared this fate. Luckily they were protected in time; some have made a remarkable recovery and are now abundant again.

Built for diving

Like the whales, the seals are divers. They can stay under water for long periods, due to the special structure of their blood system. A seal's blood, like a whale's, is very rich in haemoglobin, the red pigment that carries oxygen from the lungs to the tissues, and the muscles contain large amounts of a similar substance called myoglobin. The seal also has a much larger volume of blood than a land animal, but the increased capacity to carry oxygen does not account for the ability of seals and whales to dive for such a long time. They have to conserve their oxygen supplies with the strictest economy. As soon as a seal dives, its heartbeat slows from about 140 beats per minute to from five to fifteen beats a minute. The blood is diverted from the skin and digestive organs, which are not concerned with diving, and is directed to the brain and nervous system which are easily damaged by a lack of oxygen. The muscles can continue working without oxygen but, like an athlete after a race, a seal has to pant after a long dive to get its breath back, and renew its supply of oxygen. The record for diving is held by the Weddell seal (*Leptonychotes weddelli*) which can dive to 600 m (1970 ft) and can stay submerged for over an hour.

The eyes of a seal are well adapted for seeing in dim light, but the way in which they find food at great depths where it is pitch-dark is unknown. Some species, such as the Californian sea-lion can avoid obstacles by echo-location; the sense of touch may also be important.

The pup of the harp seal is fed by its mother for only a few weeks but it grows a thick layer of blubber which will keep it nourished until it goes to sea and learns to hunt for its own food. The white coat is shed before it leaves the ice where it was born.

True seals (family Phocidae)

The largest of the true seals are the two elephant seals of the genus *Mirounga*, one living around the Southern Hemisphere, and the other off California. A large bull weighs over 2 tonnes, but the bulk is only one reason for its common name. The bull has a short trunk which can be inflated to make a cushion which hangs over the mouth and is used when threatening other bulls.

The coat of a newborn elephant seal pup is black, but most true seals are born with a fluffy white coat, and baby harp seals (*Pagophilus groenlandicus*) in particular, are killed for the sake of this coat. The white coat is shed and replaced by the adult coat when the pup becomes independent of its mother. This occurs when it is about three or four weeks old. The common seal (*Phoca vitulina*) is unusual because the white coat is shed before the pup is born. Common seals are born on rocks and sandbanks and they have to swim as soon as the tide comes in.

The Antarctic is the home of four true seals which live among the ice. The Weddell seal bears its pups on the solid ice around the coast, so it is the world's most southerly mammal. A population of fifteen million makes the crabeater seal (*Lobodon carcinophagus*) the most abundant seal. Its teeth are set with many points, or cusps, which form a sieve when the mouth is closed and function like the baleen of whales for filtering shrimplike krill from the water. The leopard seal (*Hydrurga leptonyx*) eats mainly krill and fishes but it also hunts penguins and young seals. The Ross seal (*Ommatophoca rossi*) was once thought to be very rare, but it is merely seldom seen since it lives among thick icefloes where ships rarely venture.

Eared seals (family Otariidae)

The most familiar of the eared seals is the Californian sealion which is seen in circuses and zoos. Like other seals it is very inquisitive and playful, so it is easy to teach it to perform tricks. They can also be trained to help divers. Most eared seals live in the Southern Hemisphere and none lives in the north Atlantic. The main difference between sealions and fur seals is that the latter have a very dense coat of underfur which gives them their name.

Young eared seals spend more time with their mothers than do true seals. A true seal does not leave her pup until it is weaned, but eared seals leave their pups on the beach while they go feeding and come back to feed them at intervals. The pups are usually weaned when over four months old and a few stay with their mothers for a year.

Walrus (family Odobenidae)

The walrus (*Odobenus rosmarus*) lives in the Arctic Ocean. Old animals become almost hairless but they are kept warm by a layer of blubber. The upper canine teeth have become long ivory tusks which are used for helping the walrus climb onto an icefloe and are thought to be used for searching for food in the mud. Their food is mainly clams, which are held by the lips and bristly moustache. The bodies of the clams are sucked out without the shells being swallowed.

Whales, dolphins and porpoises (order Cetacea)

The whales, dolphins and porpoises are often collectively called cetaceans. The name whale is usually used for species over 6·5 m (21 ft) in length, but the pigmy sperm whale (*Kogia breviceps*), among others, is smaller, whereas the killer whale (*Orcinus orca*) grows to 9 m (nearly 30 ft) and is a member of the dolphin family. In North America especially, some small cetaceans are called porpoises rather than dolphins, instead of restricting this to the six members of the porpoise family Phocaenidae.

The cetaceans are more completely adapted to life in water than any other mammal. They cannot come on land – as is shown by the deaths of whales which become stranded – although killer whales have been seen running onto rocks to attack seals and even dogs. The cetacean's body has been redesigned for an aquatic existence, so that it has come to outwardly resemble a fish. The body is streamlined, lacking hair, external ears or any structure which would impede passage through the water, and the whale is propelled by strokes of the flat tailflukes which beat up and down, rather than from side to side as in fish. The forelimbs have become flippers for steering and the hind limbs have disappeared. The flexible skin improves streamlining by changing shape to prevent turbulence over the body surface and so reducing drag. The result is that some cetaceans can swim at high speed. The record is held by the pilot whales (genus *Globicephala*), timed at 49kph (29mph). Many dolphins and porpoises 'hitch a lift' with ships by positioning themselves so they are carried along in the bow wave.

Walruses like to bask in the Arctic sun and they gather in masses on suitable beaches or on ice floes. While basking, they digest their meals of shellfish which they have gathered from the muddy seabed.

Cetaceans give birth to a single calf which is usually born tail first, rather than headfirst as is more usual in mammals. If it was born headfirst, it might drown before it could reach the surface and take its first breath. This breath is also needed to fill the lungs and make the calf buoyant. Sometimes it is helped to the surface by its mother or another adult.

Air breathing is a link with the cetaceans' terrestrial ancestors. They must still come to the surface at intervals to breathe through the blowholes, which are really nostrils that have moved to the top of the head. In the space of a few seconds, the lungs are emptied and refilled. As the air rushes out, the pressure drops and it cools rapidly. The water in the air condenses into a cloud of vapour called the blow. The presence of cetaceans, and sometimes even the identity of the larger whales, is given away by the blow. Cetaceans breathe slowly and blow only a few times every minute. When they are swimming near the surface, they blow three or four times before submerging for five or ten minutes. The sperm whale (*Physeter catodon*) feeds at great depths and submerges for over half an hour at a time. When it surfaces it has to remain breathing for many minutes, as if panting, to regain oxygen. There are two major groups of whales.

Whalebone whales (suborder Mysticeti)

The whalebone whales have no teeth, but they have rows of bristly plates called whalebone or baleen hanging from the upper jaws. The plates are used to strain small animals from the water. According to the species, the whale either takes a gulp of water by dropping the floor of its mouth to suck water in, or ploughs forwards so that water is continually swilling through the mouth. The water is channelled out of the sides of the mouth and the small animals are strained on the baleen plates, then scraped off with the tongue and swallowed. The main food of whalebone whales is small crustaceans, such as copepods and krill, which live in huge swarms, but in some parts of the ocean they feed on shoals of herring and other fishes.

The blue whale (*Balaenoptera musculus*) is the largest animal in existence. It can weigh over 100 tonnes, and can reach a length of 30 m (98 ft). The record is held by a female killed by whalers which measured 33·27 m (109 ft) in length. The fin whale (*B. physalus*), the sei whale (*B. borealis*), Bryde's whale (*B. edeni*) and the minke whale (*B. acutorostrata*) are smaller. They grey whale (*Eschrichtius robustus*) of the north Pacific is unusual because it feeds by ploughing through the seabed to stir up the mud and strain out molluscs and crustaceans. The humpback whale (*Megaptera nodosa*) is distinguished by very long flippers, fleshy knobs on its head and a distinctly 'humped' back. The remaining whalebone whales are the right whales, of the family Balaenidae. They are slow-swimming animals which were easily caught by the whalers and they floated when dead. The name 'right' whale derives from the fact that they were the right whales to hunt. The bowhead (*Balaena mysticetus*) of the Arctic Ocean is the rarest whale, having been overhunted for many years.

With the exception of Bryde's (pronounced Breuder's) whale and the pigmy right whale (*Neobalaena marginata*) which live in warm seas around the world, each species of whalebone whale exists in northern and southern populations, although the grey whale has only a northern population. Each population spends the summer in polar waters, either Arctic or Antarctic, where the whales feed on the swarms of marine animals. They migrate to warmer seas in the winter where the calves are born. A newborn whale calf has very little blubber to help it keep warm but it rapidly develops a layer as it feeds on its mother's rich milk, and is ready to accompany her to the polar feeding grounds in the summer.

Toothed whales (suborder Odontoceti)

The toothed whales are more numerous than the whalebone whales. There are sixty-six species, which include the dolphins and porpoises, the sperm whale, killer whale and the narwhal. Some species, like the whalebone whales, are extremely rare. The diet of toothed whales is mainly fishes and squids and many species have rows of uniform peg-shaped teeth for grasping such slippery prey, but the beaked whales (family Ziphiidae) have only two teeth, which protrude from the lower jaw like tusks.

The sperm whale (*Physeter catodon*) is the largest toothed whale,

---

Communication in whales

At one time scientists thought that whales were deaf, although whalers knew that they could be scared by a sudden sound and that species of whales could be recognized by their calls. Records have now been made of the calls of many cetaceans. The best-known are the 'songs' of the humpback whale. These are made only by male humpbacks and the function is not known but, since sound travels very well in water and the whales must therefore be able to hear one another over hundreds of kilometres, it seems likely that they can identify each other as individuals. It is also possible that dolphins 'talk' to each other by whistling.

The toothed whales also have a system of echo-location or sonar, similar to that employed by the bats. A stream of clicks comes from the air passages leading to the blowhole and is beamed forwards through the snout. Echoes are picked up by ears and translated by the brain to give a 'picture' of what lies ahead of the cetacean. So sensitive is this method that captured dolphins have been trained to distinguish between similar-sized plates of copper and aluminium by using their sonar.

males reaching a length of 20 m (66 ft) and females 17 m (56 ft). The head of a sperm whale is unique. It makes up one-third of the body length and the snout is enlarged to make a 'tank' that holds the spermaceti. This is a wax which is liquid at body temperature and is thought to help the whale regulate buoyancy when it dives. Spermaceti was once a very valuable product which was used for lubricants and lighting, and sperm whales were at one time the main quarry of whalers. Sperm whales also yielded ambergris, a resinous substance formed in the intestine, which was used as a base for perfumes. Sperm whales feed on squids which they find at great depths. One specimen was found entangled in a submarine cable at a depth of 1135 m (3723 ft).

The pilot whales of the genus *Globicephala* are best known for the hunt which takes place in the Faroe Islands, where schools of pilot whales are driven onto the shore and killed for food. The killer whale (*Orcinus orca*) is the only cetacean that eats warm-blooded prey. Its main prey is fish, but seabirds, seals and less frequently other cetaceans are also eaten. There are no authentic records of unprovoked attacks on humans, however, despite the fact that they may attack boats, mistaking them for other whales.

Pilot whales and the killer whale are large dolphins and, like the smaller dolphins, they live in large groups called schools, or small family groups called pods. Dolphins are found in all seas, and some live in rivers. An increasing number are being kept in captivity and they are proving to be sociable and intelligent. Some have been trained to help human divers. In the wild, dolphins co-operate by herding shoals of fishes, and even support injured fellows.

The narwhal (*Monodon monoceros*) and white whale or beluga (*Delphinapterus leucas*) live in the Arctic Ocean. The tusk of the narwhal is an enormous tooth which grows out of the upper lip. It is found only in males and its function is not known.

The killer whale is found throughout the oceans of the world. They live in small groups that include one or two old males which are recognized by the very tall dorsal fin. Killer whales are often kept in captivity where they have been found to be friendly and intelligent.

Opposite: A full-grown African elephant eats over 250kg (550lb) of grass, leaves, bark and fruit every day and, where elephants are common, they significantly alter the countryside. Bushes and low trees are eaten down to the roots and tall trees are killed by having the bark removed or are pushed over. Gradually the woodland changes into open grassland.

Seacows (order Sirenia)

Of the five modern species of seacows, one is extinct and the remainder are seriously threatened. The seacows are distant relatives of the elephants, and they are divided into two groups: the manatees and the dugongs. They are placid, slow-moving animals which graze on aquatic vegetation in shallow water, and they have no means of defence. Seacows are wholly aquatic. They have streamlined bodies, about 3 m (10 ft) long and 450 kg (990 lb) in weight. They are hairless but have a thick layer of blubber under the skin. The forelimbs have been converted to flippers and there are no hind limbs. Propulsion comes from beats of the tail which is flattened into broad flukes like a whale's.

The three species of manatee (family Trichechidae) live on the tropical coasts on each side of the Atlantic and one species has spread to the cooler waters of the southeast United States. Manatees are also found inland in large rivers. The manatees in the Florida Everglades face dangers from motorboats and from other forms of disturbance, however.

Much of a manatee's life is spent in feeding. The flippers and prehensile lips are used for stuffing the mouth with leaves of aquatic grasses, mangrove shoots and other water plants. In Guiana manatees have been used to clear waterways choked with dense growths of water hyacinth and they will even eat lawn clippings.

A single calf is born in the water after about one year's gestation. The mother pushes it to the surface for its first breath. While small it will ride on her back and, although it takes solid food at one month, it is not weaned until two years old.

The dugong (*Dugong dugon*) has a wide range covering the east coast of Africa, across the Indian Ocean to Australia, the Philippines and China, although it is rare or extinct in many places. It is distinguished by its notched tail flukes which look like a whale's, whereas the manatees have a single lobed fluke, like a spatula. Dugongs live in shallow water, feeding on eelgrass and other marine plants, although seaweed is only eaten as a last resort. Dugongs live in large herds where they have not been persecuted, but they are difficult to study and little is known of their breeding or other habits.

Steller's seacow (*Hydrodamalis stelleri*) was unique among mammals in that its main food was seaweed. Unlike other seacows it lived in cold water and was found only in the Bering Sea. It was discovered in 1742 and hunted so ruthlessly that it was extinct by 1768.

Aardvark (order Tubulidentata)

The aardvark (*Orycteropus afer*) whose name means 'earth-pig', looks like a grotesque hog 2 m (6½ ft) long and up to 70 kg (154 lb) in weight. Its long narrow head has a pig-like snout, small mouth and long ears. The tail is long, strong and tapering and all four feet bear stout digging claws. The body is grey, and almost hairless except on the hindquarters. The aardvark is found in Africa wherever there are termites; it rips the termite nests open with its claws, then sweeps up the exposed insects with its long sticky tongue. It is active mainly by night, spending the day in an enormous burrow large enough for a small man to crawl into. Such is the aardvark's digging power that it can excavate faster than a gang of men can dig. Aardvarks live solitary lives, only coming together to mate.

Elephants and hyraxes (order Proboscoidea)

Apart from the great size of the elephant its most striking feature is its trunk. This is in reality an enormously elongated nose which is used also for picking up food, wrenching off branches, for drinking, bathing and taking dust baths as well as for testing the air for scent of danger and caressing in courtship. The pair of tusks growing from the upper jaw are incisors. The only other teeth are three molars each side, top and bottom. When worn out these are replaced by a new set. This can happen five times in a lifetime. The tusks are used for defence, for prising up roots for food and digging for water.

There are two living species: the African elephant (*Loxodonta africana*) and the Indian elephant (*Elephas maximus*). The former is the larger, and is the largest living land animal. A male may reach 3·3 m (11 ft) in height and weigh 6 tonnes. The smaller male Indian elephant may grow to 3 m (10 ft) in height, the female being rather shorter. The two

species are very alike, but the African elephant has much larger ears, a sloping forehead, hollow back and two 'lips' at the end of its trunk. The Indian species has smaller ears, a domed forehead, a convex back and only one 'lip'. The ears are used as radiators for losing heat, and the smaller ears of the Indian elephant are due to the fact that it lives in the cool of the forest whereas the African elephant lives exposed to the sun in open country.

For thousands of years Indian elephants have been caught, tamed and used as beasts of burden, and now there are few wild ones left. The African elephant has not been tamed, except on rare occasions, but it has been exploited for its ivory – its tusks being much larger than those of the Indian elephant.

Elephants live in family groups presided over by an old female. She is accompanied by her youngest mature daughter and both their young offspring. Each calf is suckled for about four years and is dependent on its mother's protection for several more years, when the next calf shares her attention. Young bulls leave the family at maturity and either live alone or in bull herds, and only join temporarily with the family herds.

The food of elephants is mainly grass in the wet season, together with herbs, the leaves of trees, fruit and bark. As much as 270 kg (594 lb) is needed each day by a bull, and elephants can cause considerable damage by knocking over trees or removing the bark. Food is chewed by six teeth on each side of each jaw but only a small part of the total grinding surface is in use at any time. As the front teeth are worn down those behind them come into action. When all the teeth have worn out, the elephant cannot feed properly and dies, at a maximum of sixty to seventy years.

Hyraxes or dassies are the coneys mentioned in the Bible, and their nearest relative is the elephant. Although they look more like rodents, the relationship is borne out by details of their internal anatomy. They are rabbit-sized and live in southwest Asia and over much of Africa, among rocks, but one species, the tree hyrax (*Dendrohyrax arboreus*), as its name suggests, lives in trees. All feed on plants, and the rock hyraxes deposit their excrement in carefully chosen sites called latrines

where it is collected and used in the making of perfumes.

Odd-toed ungulates (order Perissodactyla)

Horses, donkeys and zebras are clearly related, but it may come as a surprise to find that tapirs and rhinoceroses are also included in this order of mammals. Nevertheless, despite the obvious differences in their appearance, all are more closely related to each other than to any other group of animals in the structure of their teeth and hoofs. All are terrestrial and herbivorous, and all have one, three or four toes on the forefeet and one or three on the hind feet, either enclosed in hoofs or in hoof-like nails. All have a simple stomach, and horns, when present, grow on the muzzle. In every way, therefore, they differ from the cloven-hoofed animals, that other large group of hoofed mammals known as the Artiodactyla.

Horses (family Equidae)
Although the domestic horse (*Equus caballus*) is now worldwide, its wild ancestors have dwindled. The tarpan of Europe is extinct and the Mongolian wild horse, or Przewalski's horse, survives in small numbers only. It is a similar story for the domesticated ass. It has been taken over a large part of the world and used either as the donkey or its hybrid, the mule, whereas wild asses have greatly decreased in numbers.

There are two kinds of wild ass (*Equus asinus*): the Asiatic and the African. The Asiatic ass was formerly found from Syria to Mongolia, but today they are everywhere much reduced in numbers or even extinct. In Africa they have become extinct in Algeria, but the Nubian wild ass is still plentiful in areas between the Upper Nile and the Red Sea.

For thousands of years wild horses and wild asses have been hunted for their flesh and their foals captured for domestication. With the invention of firearms capture and killing became much easier and their numbers dropped. The striped horses, known as zebras, escaped this fate for a long time. They were numerous on the plains of Africa south of the Sahara, until that part of the continent was exploited by Europeans. Then they were shot for sport or for their hides. Today, as their habitat is encroached upon for agriculture and the other effects of the advance of civilization, they are being further reduced in numbers.

Every zebra can be identified by the pattern of its stripes, just as people can be identified by the whorls of their fingerprints, and the patterns also identify the species. The plains or Burchell's zebra (*Equus quagga*) has stripes meeting under the belly and forming a Y on the flanks. Grévy's zebra (*Equus grevyi*) has narrow stripes and a white belly. The mountain zebra (*Equus zebra*), now very rare, has a 'grid-iron' pattern on the rump. Whether the stripes are a form of camouflage is still in dispute, but zebras are sometimes difficult to see.

The earliest horses, long since extinct, had five toes on each foot. Their descendants not only grew larger, from the size of a hare to that of present-day horses, but their legs grew longer and they lost first two toes, then two more, until only one was left. The lower part of a horse's leg is in reality an elongated middle finger with an enormous nail, which we call a hoof. On rare occasions a horse is born with three toes on each foot.

Tapirs (family Tapiridae)

The tapir is very different in appearance. It is round-bodied, with a round head ending in a slightly trunk-like snout. Its legs are short and it has four toes on each front foot and three toes on each hind foot. Tapirs are forest-dwelling, fond of water and shy, so they are seldom seen, although they are as big as a donkey. Their only enemies are the tiger in Asia and the jaguar in South America. The most interesting point is that there is one species in Malaya and several species in Brazil on the other side of the world. They were obviously once more widely distributed, but have died out except in these two regions. The Brazilian tapirs are blackish-brown; the Malayan tapir (*Tapirus indicus*) is white except for its forequarters and legs, which are black.

Tapirs show how the reduction in the number of toes seen in the horses occurred. They are nearer to their ancestors than the horses, having lost only one toe on the front feet and two toes on the hind feet. They are less speedy since they do not have the lengthening of the leg of horses, asses and zebras that endowed them with speed for escaping enemies.

Rhinoceroses (family Rhinocerotidae)

The rhinoceroses have three hoofed toes on each foot, and they have one or two horns composed of a highly compact, solid mass of hairy tissue which is smooth on the outside. They, too, are disappearing like the other members of the Perissodactyla, but the reduction in their numbers comes from a different cause.

History of the domestic horse

The horse seems to have been domesticated later than cattle and dogs. It was originally hunted for food, and probably first kept for its meat. Domestication started in central Asia and was an event which has been described as the 'proudest conquest of man' because of the influence the horse has had on human history and development. It has provided transport for people and loads, a weapon-platform for warriors, sport and recreation, meat, leather and milk. Even the manure is used for cultivating mushrooms. The course of the domestication of horses and the evolution of the many breeds is shrouded in mystery. It can be assumed that the first domestic horses were something like the tarpan, which finally became extinct in 1851, and Przewalski's horse, a wild horse that only narrowly survives in the wild but can be seen in zoos. It is likely that several varieties of wild horse developed in different circumstances, like the small, neat-hoofed ponies of northern Europe and the broad-hoofed horses from the soft marshes of the Camargue.

There are five species still in existence. All of these are in danger of extinction, or are so reduced in number that only rigid protection can ensure their survival. These are the Javan (*Rhinoceros sondaicus*), now down to just a couple of dozen individuals, the Sumatran (*Dicerorhinus sumatrensis*), the white rhinoceros (*Ceratotherium simum*) and the black rhinoceros (*Diceros bicornis*) of Africa, and the great Indian rhinoceros (*Rhinoceros unicornis*).

The white rhinoceros weighs over 3 tonnes. The bodies of the great Indian and Javan rhinoceroses appear to be covered with sheets of granular armour plate because of the deep folds in their thick, tough hides. The Indian and Javan rhinoceroses have only a single horn, while all the others have two. 'Black' and 'white' are misleading names for the African species. White comes from the Afrikaans word for wide and refers to the square-lipped mouth used for grazing grass. The black rhinoceros has a pointed upper lip for tearing leaves from trees.

All rhinoceroses look fearsome although they are fairly peaceful and even timid unless meddled with.

Their size, strength and weight, and their ability to use their horns as weapons means, however, that they have few natural enemies. The reduction in rhinoceros numbers is due to the fanciful belief held among some Asian peoples that rhinoceros horn has medicinal properties, especially when used as an aphrodisiac. The use of the horns, too, as ornamental daggers by the Arabs also poses a serious threat. In both cases, large numbers of rhinoceros are slaughtered simply for their horns. Here again, modern weapons have helped to intensify slaughter. Large sums of money are paid for a horn, and a poacher killing a rhinoceros has virtually a small fortune on his hands.

Even-toed ungulates (order Artiodactyla)

The cloven-hoofed mammals are often called the even-toed mammals because their weight is borne on two central toes, each capped by a horny hoof. Most also have another small pair of toes, called false hoofs or dew claws. These do not usually touch the ground but give extra support when walking on soft ground or

Above: The warthog lives in a burrow or under rocks and comes out during the day to feed on grass, fruit and roots. It defends itself very vigorously with its tusks when attacked, and will even turn and charge at leopards.

Opposite: The existence of the five species of rhinoceros has been put in jeopardy by the value placed on their horns. Although dangerous under certain circumstances, they are normally quite tranquil animals.

scrambling on rocks. The only other feature these mammals have in common, apart from their cloven feet, is their herbivorous diet. Otherwise, the Artiodactyla are a large group of diverse land animals, a few of which are partly aquatic. They include the pigs and peccaries, hippopotamuses, camels and llamas, deer, giraffes, cattle, sheep, goats and antelopes.

Pigs and hippopotamuses (suborder Suiformes)

The wild pig (*Sus scrofa*) from which the farmyard hog was domesticated, is found across Europe and Asia, deriving a living from eating almost anything, plant or animal, that it can pick up or root out of the ground with its mobile snout. It lives in forests and depends for its safety on speed and the ability to dodge into cover or on defending itself with its tusk-like canine teeth. Perhaps the oddest of all pigs is the babirusa (*Babyrousa babyrussa*) of the island of Celebes. Its skin is nearly hairless and its legs are long and deer-like, giving it great speed and agility. Its four tusks curve over its face. The upper canines do not enter the mouth but grow upwards through the bone

of the jaw and then curve backwards to form arcs in front of the eyes.

Africa has several pigs, including the warthog (*Phacochoerus aethiopicus*). The bush pig or red river hog (*Potamochoerus porcus*) and the forest hog (*Hydrochoerus meinertzhageni*) resemble the wild pig except for their broad faces which are ornamented by large warts and long snouts. Even their ugliness is exceeded by the warthog, probably the ugliest of all mammals, its ill-proportioned face being further disfigured by large tusks and two large excrescences strengthened by gristle.

The wild pigs of South America and southern North America are known as peccaries and live in herds. The white-lipped peccaries (*Tayassu pecari*) especially are feared by man and beast. They will stand in formation champing their tusks and making determined charges at hunters, horses and dogs alike.

Hippopotamuses (*Hippopotamus amphibius*) are not as numerous as they used to be in the rivers of sub-Saharan Africa. The name means 'river horse'. Out of water a hippopotamus looks more like a pig with its huge barrel-like body, broad, heavy head and tremendous mouth. The old males are 4·3 m (14 ft) long and weigh 4 tonnes. Coming out on land at night to feed on tall grasses, it lumbers along on its short, stout column-like legs. Yet it can run at speeds of up to 48 kph (29 mph) and when swimming under water it is extremely graceful. A hippopotamus can change its buoyancy so that it can walk on the bottom. The pigmy hippopotamus (*Choeropsis liberiensis*) of west Africa is even more pig-like in appearance than other hippopotamuses.

Hippopotamuses live in colonies in rivers and lakes. The females live together, usually around a sandbank. The males each mark a territory on the boundary of the females' territory. A male straying into another's territory is challenged, the occupier opening his huge mouth wide, as if yawning. If the intruder does not retreat at this stage a terrific fight ensues. A male straying into female territory must behave himself. He must show no sign of aggression and if one of the females should rise to her feet he must lie down or several females will attack him at once. A female enters a male's territory only to breed. He then treats her with respect.

Right: The hippopotamus spends the day keeping cool in the water and comes on land at night or in overcast weather when it will not get too hot. It follows regular trails for as much as 10km (6 miles) to its grazing grounds where it will consume 200kg (440lb) of grass.

Opposite: The Arabian camel plays a vital part in the economy of the desert. The Arabic language has 1000 words dealing with camels. As well as carrying people and goods on journeys, it is used for pulling ploughs and provides meat, milk and hair.

There is a single baby at a birth and it can run or swim at five minutes old. At first the mother allows it to ride on her back. From the first she disciplines it, making it walk at heel on land or swim at her shoulder in the water. This is to protect it from the males. If she moves on to land to feed or into a male territory to mate, she leaves her youngster in the care of another female, a baby-sitter.

Camels and llamas
(suborder Tylopoda)
One does not normally think of the camel and its South American cousins, the llamas, as hoofed animals, but anatomically they are justifiably included in the Artiodactyla.

The feet, like everything else about the camel, are adapted for life in deserts; each foot has two toes with prominent nails and a tough padded sole – ideal for walking on sand. Equally, the camel's heavy brows and long lashes protect the eyes from blown sand, and the slit-like nostrils can be closed to keep out sand. Also, large horny pads on the chest, elbows and knees take the camel's weight when it is resting in a crouched position, preventing the abrasion of the skin by the sand.

Tough lips, powerful teeth and a complicated stomach enable it to eat dry vegetation, and a camel can store fat in its hump against times of scarcity. There is no truth in the often-repeated story that it can store water in its stomach or its hump.

What it can do is go for days without water and then, when water is available, drink up to 140 litres (30 gallons) straight off, storing the water in its body tissues.

There are two species of camel: the Arabian or one-humped camel (*Camelus dromedarius*), known as a dromedary when used for riding, and the bactrian or two-humped camel (*Camelus bactrianus*) of Asia. The Arabian camel has been domesticated for at least 4000 years but is now unknown in the wild. There are still a few wild bactrian camels in the Gobi Desert.

Camels are known, from fossil remains, to have originated in North America. From there, one branch of the family found its way into Asia to give the only two surviving species of true camel. The other branch spread south to South America, splitting into numerous species, only two of which survive today. These are the vicuna (*Lama vicugna*) and the guanaco (*Lama huanacos*). The domesticated llama and alpaca are derived from the guanaco. All four are humpless and smaller than the true camels, but otherwise resemble them closely in their anatomy.

Ruminants
(suborder Ruminantia)
The largest and by far the most important group of cloven-hoofed animals is the ruminants. These also include a few species of small, hornless, deer-like chevrotains or mouse-

deer of the family Tragulidae which are about 30 cm (12 in) high at the shoulder. Those living in southeast Asia, including southern India, live among rocks and are adept at keeping out of sight. The water chevrotain (*Hyemoschus aquaticus*) of west Africa, on the other hand, lives in and by streams in forests. At the first sign of danger it takes to the water and is an excellent swimmer and diver.

All ruminants chew the cud. Chevrotains have only three stomach compartments but the remaining ruminants have four compartments. They eat grass or other vegetation, which they swallow after a little chewing. Then, with the first compartment of the stomach full they rest and ruminate, bringing a small amount of food back into the mouth at a time to chew thoroughly, after which it is swallowed and passed through the remaining stomach sections in turn for complete digestion. The ability to chew the cud means that the animal can take in a large amount of green food, quickly if necessary, in exposed situations, then retire to a sheltered place to complete the chewing process at leisure.

The ruminants differ widely in size and shape, from a chevrotain to the lofty giraffe. They have, with a few exceptions, the same pattern of teeth. That is, the six lower incisors and the canines lie in a row, projecting forward and all looking alike. These bite against a hard pad in the upper jaw, which is without incisors and canines. The cheek teeth have flat surfaces patterned with ridges and hollows for grinding fibrous

vegetation. Chewing is done with a sideways movement of the jaw.

Most ruminants also have horns. In deer the horns are usually referred to as antlers. They are bony outgrowths from two knobs on the forehead, and are shed and re-grown each year. Each time they are renewed they usually grow bigger. Except for reindeer and caribou, only the males bear antlers. They are used only for fighting in the breeding season and as symbols of superiority. Deer use their front hoofs against enemies, although the usual protection is in running at high speed.

The smallest deer, such as the pudu (*Pudu pudu*) of Chile at 35 cm (14 in) high, and the musk deer (*Moschus moschiferus*) and muntjac (genus *Muntiacus*) of Asia at 60 cm (2 ft) high, have only small spike-like antlers but they make up for this by having long canines in the upper jaw hanging down outside the mouth like tusks. They use these for making slashing cuts at an opponent. At the other end of the size scale, the moose (*Alces alces*) of North America, by far the largest living deer, and its counterpart in Eurasia, the elk, both 2-2·2m (6-7ft) at the shoulder, have enormous antlers with flattened surfaces edged by spikes or tines. The largest pairs of moose antlers span 2·1m (6½ft).

The giraffe (*Giraffa camelopardalis*), is the tallest mammal of all time at up to 5·5m (18ft) high. It is also most ungainly-looking, with its long neck, small head, long legs, sloping back and long tufted tail, yet it is graceful in movement. Its 'crazy paving' coat, in chestnut and white, gives it perfect camouflage as it stands among the

acacia trees of the African plains, pulling off leaves with its 45cm (1½ft) tongue in complete disregard of the sharp thorns. Its horns are no more than knobs on the forehead, but they may be from two to five in number. When giraffes fight an enemy, such as a lion imprudent enough to try to kill a calf, they strike at it with their large, broad cloven hoofs. When the males fight between themselves, they slap at each other with their necks. The okapi (*Okapia johnstoni*) a cousin of the giraffe with a shorter neck, lives in the forests of west Africa.

The remaining ruminants also have horns, usually carried by both sexes and consisting of a bony core growing from the skull and encased in horn. They are not shed each year, except in the North American pronghorn antelope (*Antilocapra americana*), the only species of the Antilocapridae and the most speedy of hoofed animals. It is the only antelope with branched horns and it sheds the outer horny sheath each year. Although not as speedy as the cheetah, the fastest land animal, the pronghorn can keep running at 56 kph (34 mph) for several kilometres and can keep up 80 kph (50 mph) or more for some distance.

The bulk of the ruminants are cattle, sheep, goats and antelopes, of the family Bovidae. In terms of numbers of species, size of individuals and abundance, this is a large family. Huge herds of some species roam, or used to roam, the world's grasslands. Bovine animals are found on plains, in forests and up mountains, ranging from tundra to tropical rainforests. Most species live in Africa, with a fair number in Europe

Left: The unique feature of deer is their antlers. These are made of bone and are grown and shed each year. A full set of antlers is a heavy burden and its growth must be a strain on the animal's resources. Why antlers should be grown and shed annually is still a mystery, however.

Opposite: Giraffes are large animals of the African bush. Having such long necks means that they can browse on vegetation at the tops of trees where other animals cannot reach. This helps to ensure that not all the herbivorous animals are competing for the same source of food.

Right: The American bison, sometimes known as the buffalo, used to roam the prairies in millions but it was nearly wiped out. It was given protection just in time, and herds now flourish in reserves.

and Asia, but few in the New World.

There are approximately 110 species of Bovidae, and they can be divided into cattle, sheep, goats and antelopes; however, some unfamiliar species fit awkwardly into this scheme and 'antelope' means little more than 'bovid other than cattle, sheep and goats.

The cattle are basically forest dwellers and their coats often have patterns of spots or vertical stripes to give good camouflage. Moreover, when they are disturbed, they freeze in mid-stride, before slipping quietly away. Wild cattle include the yak (*Poephagus grunniens*), gaur (*Bibos gaurus*) and banteng (*Bibos banteng*), the Indian buffalo (*Bubalus bubalis*) and anoa (*Anoa depressicornis*), all of Asia, the bison (*Bison bison*) of the American plains and its European counterpart, the wisent (*B. bonasus*). All these species are threatened with extinction. Domestic cattle are descended from the now extinct aurochs and were first domesticated over 6000 years ago. The African or Cape buffalo (*Syncerus caffer*) is one of the most feared animals because it has a tendency to charge without warning, propelling its one-tonne body at any animal it considers a threat.

The sheep and goats are animals of open country. They are not usually aggressive – even in wild colonies – and run off immediately on disturbance. Unlike cattle, they have horns placed forward on the head. These horns are usually ringed. Wild sheep and goats are becoming rare, although millions live in captivity.

Domestic sheep come from the mouflon (*Ovis mouflon*) of Corsica and Sardinia. Wild goats include the bighorn and Dall's sheep of America, the argali and urial of Asia, and are also found in the Middle East. Close relatives are the ibex (*Capra pyrenaica*) and chamois (*Rubricapra rubricapra*) of Europe, the takin (*Budorcas taxicolor*) and tahr (genus *Hemitragus*) of Asia, and the Rocky Mountain goat (*Oreamnos americanus*) of North America. The musk ox (*Ovibos moschatus*) of the Arctic is best known for its habit of gathering in protective huddles, facing outwards, when attacked by wolves.

The main home of the antelope is Africa. When Europeans first saw them, they swarmed over the continent in untold millions. Antelopes range in size from the hare-sized dik-diks (genera *Madoqua* and *Rhynchotragus*) to the massive eland (*Taurotragus oryx*), the size of a farmyard bull. The gazelles are graceful antelopes; Thomson's gazelle (*Gazella cuvieri*) is still common, but the springbok (*Antidorcas marsupialis*) has become rare except in the Kalahari. All these animals are able to exist together without eating the land bare, because different antelopes eat different plants, or different parts of plants. Dik-diks push their slender snouts into thick foliage to select the most nutritious parts and long-necked gerenuks (*Lithocranius walleri*) reach higher branches. The need for water also helps to spread the antelopes away from each other. Wildebeest or gnu (*Connochaetes gnu*), need water every day, and huge herds still migrate over the plains when drought forces them to seek well-watered places. Waterbuck (*Kobus ellipsiprymnus*) and lechwe (*Kobus lechwe*) live in damp places, while sitatunga (*Limnotragus spekei*) have broad feet for walking in swamps. Gemsbok (*Oryx gazella*) and Grant's gazelle (*Gazella granti*) can go for days without drinking and live on the driest grasslands, while Arabian oryx (*Oryx leucoryx*) and addax (*Addax nasomaculatus*) live in deserts and are as well-adapted for life there as the camel. The klipspringer (*Oreotragus oreotragus*) lives on cliffs, leaping with incredible agility on the tips of its tiny hooves.

The duikers (genera *Cephalophus* and *Sylvicapra*) are African antelopes, most of which live in woodland. Their wedge-shaped bodies are well suited for forcing a way through the undergrowth. The name is Afrikaans for 'diver', which aptly describes the way that they slip out of sight.

Above: The springbok is a gazelle which was once abundant in South Africa but is now found mainly in the Kalahari Desert. It is named after its habit of leaping 3m (10ft) into the air on stiff legs when alarmed.

Left: The waterbuck is a large antelope which is common in many parts of east and south Africa. It lives in dry savannah country but stays near rivers, hiding in the dense bankside vegetation at night and coming out to feed by day.

Outside Africa, antelopes can be found from Arabia to Mongolia. The blackbuck (*Antilope cervicapra*) once numbered millions on the plains of India. They were hunted with cheetahs by the Maharajahs and were an important prey for tigers, but they have now become rare. In the Central Asian steppes the bulbous-nosed saiga (*Saiga tatarica*) was once hunted for its horns, but its numbers are now increasing.

Index

Numbers in italics refer to
illustrations